Insight Philadelphia

Insight Philadelphia

Historical Essays Illustrated

KENNETH FINKEL

RUTGERS UNIVERSITY PRESS
NEW BRUNSWICK, CAMDEN, AND NEWARK,
NEW JERSEY, AND LONDON

Library of Congress Cataloging-in-Publication Data

Names: Finkel, Kenneth, author.
Title: Insight Philadelphia : historical essays illustrated / by Kenneth Finkel.
Description: New Brunswick : Rutgers University Press, 2018. | Includes index.
Identifiers: LCCN 2017035056 | ISBN 9780813597447 (cloth : alk. paper) |
    ISBN 9780813597430 (pbk. : alk. paper) | ISBN 9780813597454 (epub) |
    ISBN 9780813597478 (PDF) | ISBN 9780813597461 (mobi)
Subjects: LCSH: Philadelphia (Pa.)—History. | Philadelphia (Pa.)—Description and
    travel.
Classification: LCC F158.3 .F56 2018 | DDC 974.8/11—dc23
LC record available at https://lccn.loc.gov/2017035056

A British Cataloging-in-Publication record for this book is available from the British
Library.

Unless otherwise indicated, all images are from *Philly*History.org.

www.rutgersuniversitypress.org

Manufactured in the United States of America

To Margaret, Kirk, Ben, and Mack

Contents

Preface

"It is at least as possible for Philadelphians to feel the presence of Penn and Franklin as for an Englishman to see the ghosts of Alfred or Becket," wrote British essayist G. K. Chesterton a century ago. "The dead are alive" in Philadelphia, he noted, more than any other American city he visited.

Chesterton got it partly right. He recognized that Philadelphia's ghosts were not kings and archbishops. What he didn't get was that the spirits of Penn and Franklin were only the beginning. Philadelphia has a plethora of ghosts, and most are regular folk. They inhabit where we live and work. Their traces can be seen around every corner, heard echoing up every street and alley.

It's a fragile situation, though, this connection with the past. Unless these traces and echoes and their accompanying ephemeral clues are captured and shared in some sensible form, they are sure to fade away. Much has already been lost. And so, in a perennial game of brinksmanship, we rely on bits of fleeting truth, evidence to help reconstruct connections with people, places, and narratives. By identifying what's suspended in that fragile zone between memory and oblivion, known and unknown, we establish a sense of ownership of spirits, stories, and sites. Just as Chesterton put it, in Philadelphia, the past is more than knowing. We *feel* the past.

These essays are meant to be revealing, rewarding, and sometimes simply joyful for the remembering. They start with research in museums, in libraries, in archives, and on the streets. Awakened more with each small discovery, we sense the pulse of the past and know we are gaining a deeper sense of where we are, who we are, and what we have before us. And through the essays, I've engaged in the essential, affirming process whereby Philadelphia's unique and persistent sense of past and place is captured and refreshed.

Books and blogs are not required reading for citizenship in Philadelphia, though they probably ought to be. It takes a shelf—and then some—to raise a city's consciousness. Earning a place on those real and virtual shelves is a goal worth aiming for. It is a noble mission, this searching for and sharing the soul of the city, whatever the outcome. If this book manages to occupy a place anywhere near that collection, it will be in excellent company.

These ninety-five essays started out as blog posts written from 2011 to 2017 for *Philly*History.com, an online database created by Azavea to provide access to and interpretation of photographs in the archives of the City of Philadelphia. From the start, I assumed that uncharted, compelling stories just waiting to be researched and written were embedded in the archive's more than 130,000 online images (and in the millions of additional unscanned images in the archives and other collections). What I found was not always the history I thought I knew. What makes the research trail most interesting is that one can never quite predict what vistas and revelations will be encountered along the way.

That was the plan. Reveal the stories one by one, month after month. Resist worn-out master narratives that are likely to overwhelm still fragile, emerging metanarratives. Let the appeal of the images and the leads from the feathery trails of research light the way. Take advantage of the fact that we live in a time when information that once took weeks or days to uncover now takes hours or minutes. Be guided by a deep belief in research. Reweave tales that sometimes augment but other times contradict what we think while informing, enlightening, and entertaining. Most of all, help the stories unfold on their own terms.

This book introduces some lesser-known sides of the past as well as some new rediscoveries. It tells the tale of the destruction of one of the earliest ancient Greek statues to arrive on American shores and how early gas stations were designed to resemble classical temples. Readers will be introduced to the nation's first general strike, instigated by the city's "coal heavers," and they'll learn about the populist raids on coal cars during an extended cold snap. They'll hear how the police enthusiastically took to using tear gas and about an instance of racial profiling in 1918 that led to a stationhouse murder. There's mayoral censorship of musical and theatrical performances, anti-Semitism in Chestnut Hill, and the burning of Hitler in effigy. There are the tragic deaths of teenage girls employed in a textile mill without a fire escape on Randolph Street and the death of a three-year-old from fish tainted in Society Hill. Readers will encounter the evangelical reformer of Hell's Half Acre at Locust and Warnock Streets and the "tooth fairy project" that revealed toxic levels of lead in the children of North Philadelphia and Kensington. And they'll learn about the first impression made by seventeen-year-old Josephine Baker on stage at the original Forrest Theatre. These stories are not insignificant and should not be mistaken for trivia or nostalgia. They are meant to unlock layers of meaning, demonstrating through stories that *place matters*. This realization is a common phenomenon in Philadelphia history.

In this small town of a big city that's 330 years old and then some, one quickly learns something counterintuitive about the past when it's considered this way. The number of stories does not diminish as they are told and shared. Rather, there's an ever-expanding and even more promising supply. History is most fertile when viewed as a form of currency whose value increases with engagement. As of this writing, with more than two hundred blog posts published, the list of ideas for future essays has grown longer than ever.

Insight Philadelphia

Figure 1.1. Construction of the sesquicentennial bell, center of Broad Street, south of Oregon Avenue, 1926

CHAPTER 1

Defining the City

FINDING PHILADELPHIA'S "WOW FACTOR"

History tells us we left our sense of self at the bottom of Broad Street.

Consider the new spine of light masts stretching up North Broad, two and a half miles from Wood Street to Glenwood Avenue. These forty-one, 55-foot metallic stalks are meant to restore North Broad Street's long-absent "wow factor," according to the folks at the Avenue of the Arts. But history suggests a better way.

Go back to Broad Street and Oregon Avenue in 1926. That was the real deal: a monumental, iconic claim for Philadelphia as the nation's "cradle of liberty." Right in the center of Broad Street, on what is now Marconi Plaza, sesquicentennial designers installed a giant sculpture. Never before or since has the city seen something so bold, so apt—so much fun. Visible for miles, the giant sesquicentennial bell seemed to be in a kind of conversation with the thirty-eight-foot statue of William Penn on City Hall. "Make no mistake," these two sculptures seemed to be saying, "you're in Philadelphia, and there's a message to share. We're saying it here on our most prominent street, and we're making it come alive—with light."

Long before the invention of the electric bulb, light had been the city's best metaphor. In part, Philadelphia was created around the central Quaker belief of an "inner light," that divine spark in everyone that was so essential to the ideas of equality and community. Later came the notions of enlightenment and liberty, traits worthy of a new, independent nation based on freedom.

How were people to bring these metaphors to life on the street? Cue the electric light. For more than a century, Broad Street, the founding city's longest, widest public avenue, has been a light laboratory, a stage for meaningful illumination. At the end of the Spanish American War in 1898, lights adorned the temporary arch at Broad and Walnut. Lights were draped from City Hall to celebrate Philadelphia's 225th birthday in 1908. Powerful spotlights permanently illuminated City Hall's tower in 1916. And as recently as 2005, wild laser light play continued at City Hall. But nothing topped Broad Street's convergence of form, meaning, and light more than the gargantuan, sheet metal blowup of the Liberty Bell switched on in 1926 for the nation's 150th birthday.

Unfortunately, no one knows the name of the creative genius who proposed this eighty-foot sculpture covered with twenty-six thousand, 15-watt light bulbs. We do know that D. W. Atwater of the Westinghouse Lamp Company designed the illumination. Activated on May 31, 1926, the sesquicentennial bell predated pop art by a long shot: Andy Warhol and Claes Oldenburg weren't even born until the late 1920s. Warhol painted his Campbell's soup cans thirty-six years later; Oldenburg installed his giant clothespin fifty years later. "I am for art that is flipped on and off with a switch," wrote Oldenburg in his very avant-garde pop art manifesto in 1961. "I am for the blinking arts, lighting up the night."

Philadelphians in the 1920s were way ahead of the curve. They knew how, where, and with what to light up Broad Street. They were in touch with Philadelphia's "wow factor."

———

Sources: Kevin Bretz, *Philadelphia's Paradox: The Sesquicentennial Exposition of 1926 in History and Memory* (Philadelphia: La Salle University,

2014), academia.edu; Getty Images, "Constructing Bell"; Claes Oldenburg, "I Am for an Art: Claes Oldenburg on His 1961 'Ode to Possibilities,'" *Sightlines, Walker Art Center*, https://walkerart.org/magazine/claes-oldenburg-i-am-for-an-art-1961; Inga Saffron, "Changing Skyline: After $14 Million on Light Masts, North Broad Remains in the Dark Ages," *Philadelphia Inquirer*, October 16, 2015.

Figure 1.2. Independence Hall Tower interior, clock room, photographed by Wenzel J. Hess, May 13, 1929

All these years when we *thought* we were celebrating a shrine to eighteenth-century independence, we were inadvertently confirming something quite different: the nineteenth-century obsession with time. And it has taken a toll on how we understand the past.

After a recent restoration, the giant clock in the bell tower at Independence Hall tells time again, but it won't tell us very much about the eighteenth century. Visitors assume this tower and its clock date back to the tower of the 1750s and believe that both were present at the signing of the Declaration of Independence in the 1770s—but they weren't. The original tower at Independence Hall had *no* clock. Time was, literally, pushed off to the side, as seen in an engraving from 1778. The State House's *original* bell tower provided a soundtrack for life in the eighteenth-century city, one measured not in terms of hours but by civic events: ascensions of royalty, meetings of legislature, protests portending revolution. The one thing the eighteenth-century bell tower *didn't* tell—and wasn't intended to—was time. Back then, the mundane act of telling time was simply not valued enough to be included in the most prominent, symbolic steeple in the city.

That original tower was important, but it was also rotten. By the time of the British surrender, upper wooden sections had to be pulled down for fear of their collapse. And for nearly fifty years, no tower rose above the rooftops at Fifth and Chestnut. When William Strickland proposed a design for a "restored" steeple in 1828, his idea only vaguely resembled the long-lost original. According to historian Charlene Mires, a lawyer with a nearby office complained about Strickland's initial design, "No man will be able to look at that building with its new steeple and be able to persuade himself that it represents the ancient State House."

Strickland hadn't set out to actually *re-create* the original steeple. At the level where four dignified windows once looked out, he placed four glaring, backlit faces of a giant clock *to look at*. In this new, rising commercial-industrial Philadelphia, Strickland's steeple reminded the citizenry of their freedom but conflated that message with something new: Philadelphians specifically and Americans in general were falling under the spell of time. And it was changing their lives.

George G. Foster, a journalist from New York, visited the steeple in the midcentury: "Clink-clank! what have we here! We go through this little door and stand in the center of the Illuminated Clock! . . . The wheels are as broad as mill-stones and the weights are attached to cables strong enough to fasten a steamboat to the wharf. . . . The pendulum, of the size of a steamer's walking-beam, moves slowly to and fro, once in two seconds, clink clank! Morning and noon and night, Summer and Winter, up here alone in its mysterious and silent realm of wheels and springs and machinery, ever sits the brooding Spirit of the Clock."

By the middle of the nineteenth century, the "spirit of independence" had begun to join with (and possibly succumb to) this "spirit of time." As Foster observed it, "That which stamps itself most legibly and universally upon the [Philadelphia] character, the manners, the faces, the very costume, of its inhabitants, is the business of buying and selling, turning everything to the best possible account, and seizing hold of everything instantly by the utility handle. . . . The very clock on the State-House steeple appears to be calculating how much it can make by striking."

Foster exaggerated, of course. But other Philadelphians were not using time in their calculations in the name of progress and profit. As Philadelphia barreled forward to its destiny as a manufacturing center, time became increasingly monitored and manipulated. The city that proudly counted down its first century of independence in years would soon count minutes as a measure of production. Among the city's most noted innovators was the Quaker engineer Frederick Winslow Taylor, who made efficiency a science. In Taylor's famous time-motion studies, he broke factory jobs into component parts, used a stopwatch to measure workers' motions again and again, and studied them in order to systematically enhance productivity and profit.

When Strickland designed the tower of Independence Hall in 1828, he had no clue how profoundly the industrial mind-set would come to transform the city and the nation. Strickland couldn't have known that "Taylorization," as it came to be called, would define an American way of life. He might have been naïve about the significance of a giant, four-faced clock in the steeple atop what was then and is now the nation's most revered shrine, but we, with the benefit of hindsight and history, have *no* excuse.

The clock in the tower at Independence Hall is a feature of the eighteenth century by proximity only. Will future restorations acknowledge that fact? Time will tell.

———

Sources: Charlene Mires, *Independence Hall in American Memory* (Philadelphia: University of Pennsylvania Press, 2002); George Rogers Taylor, "'Philadelphia in Slices' by George G. Foster," *The Pennsylvania Magazine of History and Biography* 93, no. 1 (January 1969): 23–72; "Obituary, F. W. Taylor, Expert in Efficiency, Dies," *New York Times*, March 22, 1915.

Figure 1.3. City Hall, decorated for visit of Admiral Tōgō, 1911

"With Secret Service men and city detectives following in a motor car and mounted policemen galloping ahead and behind, the Japanese commander was whirled around the west side of City Hall and South on Broad street. Those who caught a fleeting look at his immobile face gave him a noisy welcome. From the windows of the Bellevue-Stratford fluttered the flags of the United States," Japan's flag, and the admiral's own, which the resourceful hotel staff had finished stitching together only minutes before.

Admiral Heihachirō Tōgō had arrived.

Down in the bowels of the Bellevue-Stratford, "the pantryman of the culinary department" had readied his creation: a three-and-a-half-foot model of Tōgō's famous battleship, the *Mikasa*. The model looked exactly right, down to "the number of guns pointing from turrets," the chocolate sailors manning the small-fire guns, and the surrounding waves of "billowy green bonbons." Tōgō's eyes "twinkled when he saw the midget ship." He "gravely drew himself to attention and saluted."

Philadelphians fell all over themselves in August 1911, celebrating their forty-eight hours with Admiral Tōgō. The samurai, who had studied naval warfare under British tutelage, had put all his finely honed skills to work against the Chinese and the Russians. Only five years before, Tōgō had won the Battle of Tsushima, which was known as "the most decisive sea battle in history."

Now this "Conqueror of Russia's Fleet," who had represented the Japanese government at the June coronation of King George V in England, was headed back home—but not before an American grand tour. Tōgō sailed from Liverpool to the United States on the *Lusitania*. He visited President Taft at the White House and laid a wreath at Washington's tomb at Mount Vernon. From there, he would continue to the Naval Academy in Annapolis to witness drills by Army cadets at West Point and would dine at Oyster Bay with former president Theodore Roosevelt, who had presided over the negotiations between the Japanese and the Russians that resulted in the Portsmouth Treaty. For that, Roosevelt had earned the Nobel Peace Prize in 1906.

In a whirlwind tour of Philadelphia, Tōgō visited Independence Hall. He stood before the Liberty Bell and took a long, deep bow before the portrait of George Washington. Tōgō toured the Philadelphia Navy Yard and inspected a new style of "fighting mast" on the battleship *Minnesota*. He plied the Delaware in a tugboat and visited the yards of Camden's New York Shipbuilding Corporation, which honored Tōgō with large cannon that boomed a nineteen-gun salute. Back on Broad Street, Tōgō visited Baldwin Locomotive Works, which he noted was "well known in our faraway country." He marveled at the Mint and met the mayor. But August heat crimped Tōgō's stamina, and he passed on a scheduled visit to William Cramp and Sons Shipbuilding Company, where the *Kasagi*, his battleship and original flagship in the Japanese-Russian War, had first taken to water.

On his final evening in Philadelphia, having dined casually in his fourth-floor suite at the Bellevue-Stratford, Tōgō requested a "motor ride" to escape the city's stifling humidity. His driver navigated into the cool recesses of Fairmount Park, presumably allowing a glimpse of the ancient Japanese Temple Gate, recently purchased, installed, and landscaped at the expense of two Baldwin executives.

In all his comings and goings, Tōgō hardly had a chance to examine the two large electric signs mounted in his honor over the north and south portals of City Hall. But in the quiet of this dark, steamy August night, Tōgō's car returned down Broad Street. He read aloud the words on the big, electric sign: "Welcome to Togo." Then he "instructed the chauffeur to stop and for a few minutes he studied the design carefully. The blending in lights of the American and Japanese flags pleased him, but he was greatly mystified at the significance of the blue and yellow flag which neither he, his aide, his secretary or the Secret Service agent recognized." A nearby policeman informed him that it was the insignia of Philadelphia.

The Admiral "seemed amused" and delighted at this "real, official municipal welcome," the likes of which he had never seen before—and probably wouldn't again.

———

Sources: Jonathan Clements, *Admiral Tōgō: Nelson of the East* (London: Haus, 2010); Gale Group, Inc., "Heihachiro Togo Facts," *Encyclopedia of World Biography*, 2010, http://biography.yourdictionary.com/heihachiro -togo#XtmeMOJlfTLV4GW1.99; "Togo Here Next Month," *New York Times*, July 16, 1911; and the newspaper collection at the Special Collections Research Center, Paley Library, Temple University, Philadelphia, Pa., including "Admiral Togo, Japan's Hero, Arrives Here. Conqueror of Russia's Fleet Is Given Great Ovation," August 10, 1911, and "Togo Leaves City after Day Spent Seeing Its Sights," August 11, 1911, both in the *Philadelphia Inquirer.*

When Americans Feared the Crack in the Liberty Bell

A crack in the Liberty Bell? No news there. But the discovery of a new crack that threatened to cross through the word *Liberty* on the Liberty Bell? *That* story resonated throughout the land.

About a century ago, Philadelphia's itinerant icon of patriotism sprouted a seventeen-inch hairline crack extending clear across the bell's crown. Metallurgist Alexander Outerbridge suggested it was *so* severe that vibrations from Chestnut Street traffic might "carry the crack around the bell and break it in two." Philadelphians, who had long considered the bell an easy-come, easy-go ambassador for freedom, cried out for a no-travel rule.

The hairline crack may have already been there when the bell made its debut in New Orleans at the World Industrial and Cotton Exposition in 1885. Or it might have appeared during the train ride to Chicago for the Columbian Exposition in 1893 or when the bell made its way to Atlanta in 1895, Charleston in 1902, Boston in 1903, and Saint Louis for the Louisiana Purchase Exposition in 1904. *Something* like caution prevailed in 1905, when the city turned down the bell's proposed trip over the Rocky Mountains to Portland for the Lewis and Clark Exposition in 1905—the year Outerbridge inspected the bell.

Discovery of a new crack resulted in something like fear—for a while, anyway. Even when newspaper headlines warned, "Liberty Bell's Crack Longer," the idea of one last cross-country hurrah before permanent retirement in Philadelphia rang true in the national imagination. Between 1909, when the new crack was discovered, and 1915, when San Francisco opened its Panama-Pacific Exposition, the bell stood silently at the center of a battle of expertise, politics, and patriotism.

The *Washington Post* presented an emotional case for travel in a November 1912 article headlined, "500,000 Want Liberty Bell: California School Children Sign Petition Asking Relic for Exposition." San Franciscans ushered their petition, a two-mile-long scroll, out of town with military honors. And when the petition arrived in Philadelphia, local officials balked in the national limelight. "Trip of Liberty Bell Hot Issue," declared the *Boston Globe*, "Showing at San Francisco Would Do No Harm, Mayor Thinks." In fact, Rudolph Blankenburg, Philadelphia's newly inaugurated reform mayor, claimed that "he could see no particular danger in sending the historic relic on another journey . . . the display of patriotism aroused by the bell . . . more than overbalanced any danger that might be incurred." A few weeks later, he approved the cross-country swan song, which stood out, Gary Nash writes, like "the grand crescendo of the Liberty Bell's seven road trips." San Franciscans agreed.

Of course, the possibility of "Liberty" falling apart on their watch instilled in the city fathers a special kind of fear: Would the Founding Fathers return to haunt them? So they took a few precautions. First, they would hold onto the bell through July 4, 1915, telephonically transmitting its sound (as loudly as a wooden mallet might manage to ring it) during the opening ceremonies in San Francisco. Second, before it crossed the country, they had a six-pronged "steel spider" installed inside the bell, hoping it might keep things together. As luck or fate would have it, the bell survived in one piece.

But we know the truth in this tale: liberty is *never* certain and nearly *always* threatened—sometimes even by those charged with its protection.

———

Sources: Gary B. Nash, *The Liberty Bell* (New Haven: Yale University Press, 2010); Gary B. Nash, "Liberty Bell," *Encyclopedia of Greater Philadelphia* (Camden: Rutgers, 2010); "Liberty Bell Clapper Gone; Replaced by Steel Support," *Evening Public Ledger*, May 4, 1915; "Liberty Bell Timeline," Independence Hall Association, USHistory.org.

Figure 1.4. Looking west on McKean Street from Front Street, July 20, 1901

The proudest moment for the Philadelphia row house was in Chicago, of all places. Organizers put up a two-story "workingman's house" at the Columbian Exposition, reported Talcott Williams in 1893. "There's nothing more wonderful in all that marvelous Exposition," he stated, "than this proof that the laws, the habits, and the business of a city of one million people can be so arranged that even the day labor earning only $8 or $10 a week can own the roof over his head and call no man landlord."

Williams proudly noted that Philadelphia's eighty thousand row houses built in the previous six decades had dramatically refashioned the city. "Philadelphia is not a city of palaces for the few, but a city of homes for the many—which is better," he wrote. "It may not be magnificent, but it is comfortable."

Seven out of eight Philadelphia families lived in "separate houses." By comparison, in New York, "only one family in six lives in a separate house."

More than a matter of a family enjoying the "daily blessings" of "its own bath-tub, its own yard, its own staircase, and its own door step," Williams claimed this invention was nothing less than "one of the world's great industrial miracles." He considered the modest Philadelphia row house a declaration of independence in brick and mortar—a moral, populist victory that earned for the city domestic and civic superiority. Philadelphia's expanses of two-story row houses, wrote John H. Gallagher in an oft-cited 1893 passage, "typify a higher civilization, as well as a truer idea of American home life, and are better, purer, sweeter than any tenement house systems that ever existed."

But for all the praise, there was a definite downside. Williams even admitted that "street after street of small, two-story brick houses looks rather mean and dingy," also noting that cobblestone pavements were bound to appear "rough and dirty." But he concluded, it's "better to have bath-rooms by the ten thousand in small homes, than to have brilliant fountains playing in beautiful squares." Even advocates like city-planning pioneer Andrew Wright Crawford couldn't deny the "monotonous architectural effect" caused by endless miles of row houses. According to Crawford, real estate developers were to blame: "In order to build the greatest number of houses on a street, they want it straight and rectangular. They don't care for the persons who are to live in these houses afterwards, and still less do they care for the good of the city as a whole."

"This idea has been carried out with unremitting perseverance," claimed Crawford. All natural undulations had been leveled, "throwing [a] severe mantle of unlovliness" over the city's many neighborhoods. "It is too late for Philadelphia to profit much by the broader intelligence of the present time," he admitted, "but it is possible that other cities and towns may learn something from her misfortune." It wasn't as if Philadelphians hadn't been warned early—and often.

Visiting from industrial London in the 1840s, Charles Dickens described Philadelphia as "a handsome city, but distractingly regular. After walking about it for an hour or two, I felt that I would have given the world for a crooked street." In the 1830s, Thomas Hamilton noted that "the traveler is at first delighted with this Quaker paradise" but "every street that presents itself seems an exact copy of those which he has left behind." Hamilton's patience eventually wore thin, and he felt "an unusual tendency to relaxation about the region of the mouth, which alternately terminates in a silent but prolonged yawn." He continued, "Philadelphia is mediocrity personified in brick and mortar. It is a city laid down by square and rule, a sort of habitable problem,—a mathematical infringement on the rights of individual eccentricity,—a rigid and prosaic despotism of right angles and parallelograms." And as early as 1790, none other than Thomas Jefferson advised that those contemplating designs for the nation's next and permanent capital avoid Philadelphia's "disgusting monotony"—a complaint Jefferson believed was shared by "all persons."

A century and a half later, when novelist Jack Dunphy set his tale of the unpleasant life and desperate death of John Fury in working-class South Philadelphia, he employed the city's endless rows with their familiar, expressive, and depressing power. Walking home after yet another hard day on the job as a coal-wagon driver,

> Fury crossed Washington Avenue and walked down Nineteenth Street past Mifflin Street and Snyder Avenue until he came to a narrow side street. The street crushed between bigger streets was a poor affair, similar in width, to an alley. Its houses smothered close together, jammed two stories high, and with small wooden porches hung on their fronts, looked like stony red-faced criminals serving a life sentence. Stuck together and dependent one upon the other, they seemed to live in constant fear that someday and somehow one would be pardoned and leave and so jeopardize the rest of them. They stood then, these square red bricked houses, and there were many of them in Philadelphia, tortured

row upon row of them, doing penitence and allowing life with its worn semblance of freedom to crowd within them.

No coincidence that "Philadelphia noir" grew popular in the twentieth century—it had been percolating for some time.

———

Sources: Andrew Wright Crawford, "The Street the Basic Factor in the City Plan," *Charities and the Commons* 19, no. 18 (February 1, 1908): 1493–1502; Charles Dickens, *American Notes for General Circulation* (New York: Harper and Brothers, 1842); John H. Gallagher, "Real Estate Holdings and Valuations," in *The City of Philadelphia as It Appears in the Year 1894*, ed. Frank H. Taylor (Philadelphia: Geo. S. Harris and Sons, 1893), 82–84; Thomas Hamilton, *Men and Manners in America* (Philadelphia: Carey, Lea and Blanchard, 1833); Thomas Jefferson, "I. Jefferson's Draft of Agenda for the Seat of Government, [29 August 1790]," *Founders Online*, National Archives, last modified February 1, 2018, http://founders.archives.gov/ documents/Jefferson/01-17-02-0136-0002, originally published in Julian P. Boyd, ed., *The Papers of Thomas Jefferson*, vol. 17 (Princeton: Princeton University Press, 1965), 460–461; Adam Levine, "The Grid versus Nature," in *Nature's Entrepot: Philadelphia's Urban Sphere and Its Environmental Thresholds* (Pittsburgh: University of Pittsburgh Press, 2012), 139–159; J. Rodman Paul and Andrew Wright Crawford, *Special Report on the City Plan by the City Parks Association of Philadelphia* (Philadelphia: City Parks Association of Philadelphia, 1902); Talcott Williams, "Philadelphia: A City of Homes," *St. Nicholas: An Illustrated Magazine for Young Folks* 20, no. 1 (March 1893): 324–336.

Figure 1.5. Garbage wagon, photographed by Wenzel J. Hess, January 26, 1938

The "Philadelphia Gothic" genre enjoyed a major breakthrough in the 1840s thanks to riots, crippling poverty, racial and religious discrimination, and of course, the lurid literature of Edgar Allan Poe and George Lippard. But the genre's debut goes back to the 1790s, when Charles Brockden Brown mongered his own brand of Philly-based fear. Philly Noir has always been with us.

What other literary stopping points are there along our gritty, smoke-veiled alleys?

Enter John T. McIntyre, the Northern Liberties native who left school at eleven and graduated "into the streets." For a time, McIntyre hauled "buckets of cow's blood from an abattoir . . . to a tannery" and did "pretty much nothing" until the age of twenty in 1891, when he began a balky writing career for newspapers and theater. His first stab at fiction, *The Ragged Edge: A Tale of Ward Life and Politics*, appeared in 1902 and begins, "Weary horses dragged ponderous trucks homeward, the drivers drooped upon their high seats and thought of cans of beer; a red sun threw shafts of light along the cross-town streets and between the rows of black warehouses."

"McIntyre's analytic eye examines the neighborhood drama to its minutest detail," writes Ron Ebest, "the campaign, the clubs, the bars, the weddings, the wakes—complete with keening mourners—the schools, the churches, the houses and streets down to their dustiest brick." McIntyre proved a master of gritty, urban detail:

> They turned into a quiet street leading toward the river. A cellar door opened, and a broad barb of light shot across the sidewalk; from the midst of this rose a pallid, spectral form, and stood looking calmly into the night. But it was only a baker, clad in his spotless working dress, popping out of his overheated basement for a breath of air. A great stack, towering skyward, and vomiting a blazing shower of sparks into the night, showed that they were nearing the mill. The huge, low, shed-like buildings lifted their corrugated walls, like the beginnings of greater structures; a knot of men were gathered about the wide doorway; they had limp, damp towels twisted about their necks and all smoked short pipes. Rows of puddlers, naked to the waist, their bodies glistening with perspiration, stood before the furnaces "balling" the molten metal; from time to time one would drench himself with water, and once more face the Cyclopean eye glaring so angrily upon him.

Beyond rich descriptions of the city, Ebest praises McIntyre's "uncanny ability to replicate speech. So skillfully does he render Irish dialect, Irish-American pidgin, urban slang, and Yiddish-inflected English that complex conversations between multiple speakers can be read and followed without such guidelines as 'he said' or 'she said.'" The "sound of their voices" renders McIntyre's people recognizable, if not familiar.

> A red-faced, bare-armed woman opened a door in Murphy's court and
> threw a pan of garbage into the gutter. Her next door neighbour was
> walking up and down the narrow strip of sidewalk, hushing the cry of
> a weazened baby.
>
> "Is Jamsie not well, Mrs. Burns?" inquired the red-faced woman.
>
> "Sorry the bit, Mrs. Nolan; he's as cross as two sticks. It's walk up an'
> down the floor wid him I've been doin' all the God's blessed night. Scure
> till the wink av slape I've had since I opened me two eyes at half after
> foive yisterday mornin'."
>
> "Poor sowl! Yez shud git him a rubber ring till cut his teeth on; it's an
> illigant t'ing for childer', I'm towld."

"I am an incurable Philadelphian," McIntyre liked to say. "I know it. I know the people. I've lived with them and they are part of me."

The *Chicago Daily Tribune* agreed. "Mr. McIntyre's people are the teamsters, the saloonkeepers, the corner grocer, the secondhand dealer, the undertaker, the sewer builders, the contractors and their gangs, and the families of all these people." McIntyre writes "in the language of the tenement house district," and his conversations are rich in "the racy and picturesque vernacular of the race-track, the saloon, and the political club." Here is another florid example:

> The saloon was the only all-night establishment in the neighbourhood.
> It glittered with clusters of electric lamps and broad, gilt-framed mirrors; a marble-topped bar backed by pyramids of glasses and bottles
> stood upon one side.
>
> They talked in a desultory way for some time, consuming much beer
> and many plates of sandwiches. Dawn stretched a grey hand through
> the window and dimmed the clusters of lights; and when they ranged

along the bar for the last drink, the streets were filling with people hurrying toward their work.

Ragged didn't make waves in literary circles. It would be another thirty-four years before McIntyre received major recognition, this time for *Steps Going Down*, his Depression-fueled novel also embedded in Philadelphia. "It is the world of the rooming houses that exist handy to the burlesque theatres," wrote Robert Van Gelder in the *New York Times*, "a world removed from the established order and largely inhabited by persons who at some time in their lives have developed the habit of trying to live by their wits, but have imperfectly mastered the procedure." Van Gelder continued, "The houses are drearily furnished, poorly lighted, damp and cold in Winter, hot and noisy in Summer; the rooms are painted in dirty, sickish green; the air heavy with the odors of slatternly living. . . . The men play pool, drink beer, find cocaine handy if they can get it and brood a great deal over lost opportunities." He praised the way McIntyre captured the "the sharp-edged talk of the wise guys."

Percy Hutchinson, also in the *New York Times*, singled out McIntyre's ear for American dialogue. His characters didn't "speak so much as volley forth words and phrases as a machine gun spits bullets," Hutchinson wrote, suggesting that "a foreigner knowing this book could be excused for concluding that American speech is a continuum of explosive sentences, and conversation a marathon contest in repartee."

Could this have been a novel ripe for Hollywood? According to one of McIntyre's obituaries in 1951, Hollywood lacked "the nerve to turn a John McIntyre book into celluloid. They were 'too true to life.'"

———

Sources: Ron Ebest, "Uncanny Realist: John T. McIntyre and Steps Going Down (1936)," *New Hibernia Review* 8, no. 3 (2004): 86–99; Robert Van Gelder, "Books of the Times," *New York Times*, September 3, 1936;

Percy Hutchinson, "Mr. McIntyre's Story of the American Underworld: *Steps Going Down* by John T. McIntyre," *New York Times*, September 6, 1936; John T. McIntyre, *The Ragged Edge: A Tale of Ward Life and Politics* (New York: McClure, Phillips and Co., 1902); Kevin Plunkett, "Noir Town: The Hard Life of John McIntyre, the Legendary Philly Novelist Nobody's Heard Of," *Philadelphia City Paper*, March 16–22, 2006; "Good First Novel," *Chicago Daily Tribune*, October 4, 1902; "John T. McIntyre," *Book News: A Monthly Survey of General Literature* 21, no. 243, November 1902 (Philadelphia: John Wanamaker, 1903); "John T. M'Intyre, Novelist, 79, Dies," *New York Times*, May 22, 1951.

Figure 1.6. Thirteenth Street, north of Buttonwood Street, photographed by John McWhorter, March 24, 1959

How could David Goodis *not* have known John T. McIntyre and envied his accomplishments as a writer?

McIntyre's novel, *Steps Going Down*, published by Farrar and Rinehart in 1936, landed a top award in the All Nation's Prize Novel Competition. Studying journalism at Temple University, Goodis was shooting for a writing career. If Goodis wasn't contributing to the *Owl*, Temple's student magazine, he was working on his own novel, published in 1939, shortly after his twenty-third birthday. In *Retreat from Oblivion*, Goodis crafted an international intrigue of love and war drenched in alcohol. The publication would propel his writing career from Philadelphia to Greenwich Village and the Upper West Side in New York, then on to Hollywood.

However, Goodis never completely left Philadelphia. In Hollywood, he survived by couch surfing; when in Philly, he'd return to his childhood bedroom in East Oak Lane. And within a few years, Goodis came home for good. What brought him back? Goodis didn't exactly take to California culture. Sure, Hollywood adapted his second novel, *Dark Passage*, for a film starring Humphrey Bogart and Lauren Bacall, but producers ditched his original ending. Meanwhile, at home, Goodis's new wife, Elaine, filed for divorce. Goodis wrote a revenge novel called *Behold This Woman* (1947) that was set—where else?—in Philadelphia. "The book is raw," his website, davidgoodis.com, declares. "Goodis' pain is raw. His scars are unhealed. The novel oozes with resentment. Clara [his Elaine character] teases men. She manipulates men. She exploits men." Goodis had found his footing, even if he didn't entirely know it at the time: writing Philadelphia noir.

After wrapping up obligations out west, he returned to Philadelphia full-time in 1950 and made the seamier side of his native city the subject of a dozen novels, finding inspiration in Philadelphia's own distinctive noirscape: skid row, the waterfront, working-class neighborhoods, and dark, frigid, wind-blown streets. Goodis put out as many as ten thousand words per day and took gritty to new levels of literary despair.

Cassidy's Girl, published by Gold Medal in 1951 (the year of McIntyre's death), turned out to be Goodis's proof of concept. This sodden tale of sympathetic losers living and drinking on the Delaware waterfront sold a million copies, partly due to scenes like this:

> On the river side of Dock Street the big ships rocked gently on the black water like monstrous hens, fat and complacent in their roosts. Their lights twinkled and threw blobs of yellow on the cobbled street bordering the piers. Across Dock Street the stalls of the fish market were shuttered and dark, except for cracks of light from within, where purveyors of Delaware shad and Barnegat crab and clam and Ocean City flounder were preparing their merchandise for the early-morning trade. As Cassidy passed the fish market, a shutter opened and a mess of fish guts

came sailing out, aimed at a large rubbish can. The fish guts missed and landed against Cassidy's leg.

Cassidy moved toward the opened shutter and glowered at the fat, sweaty face above a white apron.

"You," Cassidy said. "You look where you're throwin' things."

"Aw, shut up," the fish merchant said. He started to close the shutter. Cassidy grabbed the shutter and held it open. "Who you tellin' to shut up?"

Another face appeared within the stall. Cassidy saw the two faces as a double-headed monstrosity. The two faces looked at each other and the fat face said, "It ain't nothin'. Just that liquored-up bum, that Cassidy."

In the next few years, Goodis produced *Street of the Lost* and *Of Tender Sin*, *Moon in the Gutter* and *The Burglar*, the last adapted for a 1957 film. Dan Duryea and Jane Mansfield feature in scenes like this one:

He turned his back on her, moved to the cashier's stand. He paid his check, left the restaurant and stood on the corner waiting for a cab. The night air had a thick softness and the smell of stale smoke from factories that had been busy in the day, and the smell of cheap whiskey and dead cigarettes and Philadelphia springtime. Then something else came into it and he breathed it in, and he knew the color of this perfume was tan.

She stood behind him. "Usually I don't gamble like this." He faced her. "Where would you like to go?"

"Maybe someplace for a drink."

"I don't feel like a drink."

"Tell me," she said. "Are you hard to get along with?"

"No."

"You think we can get along?"

"No."

Goodis's *Down There*, published in 1956, begins with a classic scene of relentless desolation:

There were no street lamps, no lights at all. It was a narrow street in the Port Richmond section of Philadelphia. From the nearby Delaware a cold wind came lancing in, telling all alley cats they'd better find a heated cellar. The later November gusts rattled against midnight-darkened windows, and stabbed at the eyes of the fallen man in the street.

The man was kneeling near the curb, breathing hard and spitting blood and wondering seriously if his skull was fractured. He'd been running blindly, his head down, so of course he hadn't seen the telephone pole. He'd crashed into it face first, bound away and hit the cobblestones and wanted to call it a night.

But you can't do that, he told himself. You gotta get up and keep running.

Filmmaker François Truffaut picked up *Down There* and produced *Tirez sur le Pianiste* (*Shoot the Piano Player*) in 1960. The setting shifted from Philadelphia to Paris—from Port Richmond to an equivalent French district. Truffaut captured the feel—the existential texture—just right. That's what mattered most to readers and audiences not familiar with the authentic desperation of Goodis's Philadelphia.

———

Sources: David Goodis, *Cassidy's Girl* (NightHawk Books, 2015), Kindle, originally published by Vintage Books in 1951; David Goodis, Shoot the Piano Player (New York: Vintage Books, 1990), originally published as *Down There* (*New York:* Fawcett Publications, 1956); "David Goodis," Internet Movie Database (IMDb), http://www.imdb.com/name/nm0328959/; Robert Polito, ed., *David Goodis: Five Noir Novels of the 1940s and 50s* (New York: Library of America, 2012); Geoff Mayer and Brian McDonnell, *Encyclopedia of Film Noir* (ABC-CLIO, 2007), 31–33; Dennis Miller, "Dark Journeys: The Best of Noir Fiction," *Huffpost* (blog), *Huffington Post*, December 11, 2014, http://www.huffingtonpost.com/dennis-miller/dark-journeys-the-best-of_b_6310606.html.

Of all the things that happened at Philadelphia's Convention Hall Auditorium—appearances by Pope John Paul II, Martin Luther King, and Nelson Mandela; performances by the Beatles, the Rolling Stones, and the Grateful Dead; boxing matches featuring Rocky Marciano, Sugar Ray Robinson, Sonny Liston, and Joe Frazier (his pro debut); Atlantic Ten Conference and Big Five basketball games; and concerts on the hall's monster M. P. Moller pipe organ—what is the most memorable, the most worthy of being considered a *great* moment in history?

The Convention Hall Auditorium also hosted four national political conventions. In 1936, Democrats nominated Franklin D. Roosevelt for a second term there; in 1940, Republicans nominated Wendell Willkie. No earthshaking memories in either instance. Then in 1948, both major parties returned. Thomas Dewey left as the candidate for the GOP, and the Democrats confirmed their choice of Harry Truman after what was described as "a huge floor fight."

Bingo.

What took place when the Democrats met is worth remembering—big time. The incumbent Truman hoped to sail to his first nomination unruffled. But in working out the party platform, issues that would come to define the second half of the twentieth century surfaced, and drama unfolded.

Late into the July Philadelphia night, in a proverbial smoke-filled room, Democrat leaders debated the planks of their platform. And the next day, the thirty-seven-year-old mayor of Minneapolis Hubert Humphrey delivered the speech of a lifetime to a packed, tense hall. It is considered one of the "Top 10 Convention Moments" in American political history.

"Because good conscience, decent morality, demands it—I feel I must rise at this time to support . . . the great issue of civil rights," declared Humphrey. He later told the story of the night leading up to his speech: "All we knew was that we, a group of young liberals, had beaten the leadership of the party and led them closer to where they ought to have been . . . I had taken on our establishment and won. It was a heady feeling."

Some delegates on the convention floor reacted to the speech with significant grumbling. Humphrey addressed their concerns:

> Now let me say this at the outset that this proposal is made for no single region. Our proposal is made for no single class, for no single racial or religious group in mind. All of the regions of this country, all of the states have shared in our precious heritage of American freedom. All the states and all the regions have seen at least some of the infringements of that freedom—all people—get this—all people, white and black, all groups, all racial groups have been the victims at time[s] in this nation of—let me say—vicious discrimination.
>
> We have made progress . . . But we must now focus the direction of that progress towards the . . . realization of a full program of civil rights to all.
>
> Friends, delegates, I do not believe that there can be any compromise on the guarantees of . . . civil rights.

Humphrey's handwritten addition on the typescript of what he wrote and read that day conveys nothing less than raw exuberance. He wrote extra-large phrases and emphasized them with underlining.

> My friends, to those who say that we are rushing this issue of Civil Rights, I say to them we are <u>172 years late.</u> To those who say that this Civil-Rights program is an infringement on <u>States' Rights</u>, I say this: The time has arrived in America for the Democratic Party to get out of the shadow of States' Rights and to walk forthrightly into the bright sunshine of Human Rights. . . . This is the issue of the 20th century.
>
> I ask you for a calm consideration of our historic opportunity. Let us do forget the evil passions and the blindness of the past. . . . we cannot and we must not turn from the path so plainly before us. . . . now is the time to recall those who were left on that path of American freedom. . . .

My good friends, I ask my Party, I ask the Democratic Party, to march down the high road of progressive democracy.

A contingent of Southerners objected. The party's position called for school integration, antidiscrimination in employment, universal access to restrooms, and antilynching laws.

NPR's Ron Elving later retold what happened next: "The Mississippi delegation walked out in its entirety, about half of the Alabama delegation. About three dozen delegates *in toto* walked out of the convention and vowed to nominate their own Dixiecrat candidate for president, Strom Thurmond from South Carolina" with their own Dixiecrat platform. Knowing this, and knowing how many of these issues are still very much with us, it's riveting to hear Humphrey's delivery.

This would be neither the first nor the last time that a major, memorable speech on race and rights was delivered in Philadelphia, a place whose associations with freedom and independence always seem to flavor the rhetorical pepper pot. Humphrey's masterpiece—he never had another quite like it—ranks with Philadelphia's other great oratorical moments on the subject of race, which include presidential candidate Barack Obama's "A More Perfect Union" speech delivered at the National Constitution Center in 2008 and another by Angelina Grimké at the opening of Pennsylvania Hall in 1838. As Grimké spoke, Pennsylvania Hall was under siege by a mob opposing her convention's antislavery position. And a few days later, they'd burn the building to the ground.

The 1948 the drama looked different, but the confrontation about civil rights as human rights remains eerily similar.

———

Sources: Ron Elving and Steve Inskeep, "In 1948, Democrats Weathered Civil Rights Divide," *Morning Edition*, NPR, August 27, 2008; Hubert H. Humphrey, "Address of Mayor Hubert H. Humphrey to Democratic National Convention, July 14, 1948," speech text files, Hubert H. Humphrey

Papers, Minnesota Historical Society, http://www2.mnhs.org/library/ findaids/00442.xml; Gerhard Peters and John T. Woolley, "Platform of the States Rights Democratic Party," American Presidency Project, August 14, 1948, http://www.presidency.ucsb.edu/ws/?pid=25851; "Angelina Grimké Weld's Speech at Pennsylvania Hall," *History of Pennsylvania Hall Which Was Destroyed by a Mob on the 17th of May, 1838* (New York: Negro Universities Press, 1969), http://www.pbs.org/wgbh/aia/part4/4h2939t.html; "Top 10 Convention Moments #4 1948 DNC—Hubert Humphrey," Real Clear Politics (website), August 25, 2008.

Figure 1.7. Campaign rally for President Herbert Hoover at Reyburn Plaza, October 31, 1932

Herbert Hoover wasn't in Philadelphia long during his campaign swing for reelection in October 1932, and he didn't have much to say. In fact, Hoover's entire visit lasted only thirty minutes. Still, Philadelphians turned out in a major way for the Republican incumbent—an estimated thirty thousand—"the biggest assemblage massed in the central city district in years," reported the *New York Times*. It was seen as proof positive that "William S. Vare, the . . . still powerful leader of the Philadelphia Republican organization, really had determined . . . to send his machine all the way down for the President."

"It was Mr. Vare's show," wrote the *Times*. "His political henchmen were there in person and had enough support to throng Reyburn and City Hall Plazas and nearby streets." The crowd cheered Vare when he rose to introduce the president. Then boos began to echo across the plazas as Hoover rose to speak and continued throughout his very brief remarks. (Hoover "took no notice" and the boos were later explained away as the work of Communists.)

Hoover looked over the crowd, paused, and then took a few moments praising William Penn, the Liberty Bell, and "the greatness of this city and of this Commonwealth"—anything to avoid acknowledging what was on everyone's mind: the Great Depression had left at least one in four Philadelphians unemployed, and two months earlier, on the same site, police had attacked 1,500 jobless "hunger marchers" in an incident known as the Battle of Reyburn Plaza.

The president turned away from the podium and walked back to Broad Street Station with his entourage to take the train to New York City, where a smaller crowd at Madison Square Garden would hear him deliver a major speech. This was no ordinary campaign, Hoover told the twenty-one thousand in attendance. Americans were in the midst of "a contest between two philosophies of Government." The Democrat opponent, Franklin Delano Roosevelt, was "appealing to the people in their fear and their distress . . . proposing changes and so-called new deals which would," Hoover claimed, "destroy the very foundations of the American system of life."

"We are told that we must have a change, that we must have a new deal." This, Hoover declared, would undo "generations of testing and struggle." The new deal, he stressed, would rock "the principles upon which we have made this Nation." A vote for Roosevelt was risky. "Be safe with Hoover," implored his campaign slogan.

Meanwhile, Roosevelt's own "brain trust" crafted their campaign strategy to avoid "gaffes that might take the public's attention away from Hoover's inadequacies and the nation's troubles." Three years into the Great Depression, Hoover was deeply unpopular even in Philadelphia, where there were 553,435 registered Republicans and 85,236 registered

Democrats. By summer, Roosevelt had developed a strong lead in the polls. But by late October, that lead had shrunk, and Hoover had a narrow chance of winning Pennsylvania—but only if he could dominate in its most populous city.

That's where Vare came in. On Election Day, only 39 percent of the nation's voters got behind Hoover; Roosevelt won by a landslide with 57 percent. His command of electoral votes was even more stunning: 472 to 59. Roosevelt carried forty-two states, earning 206 more electoral votes than the 266 needed to win. But Roosevelt *didn't carry* the Keystone State. Of Hoover's fifty-nine electoral votes, thirty-six were from Pennsylvania, thanks to Philadelphia and the Vare machine.

By the time of Roosevelt's inauguration in early March 1933, more than nine thousand American banks had failed, industrial production had been cut in half, and about thirteen million wage earners were without jobs—more than 280,000 of whom were Philadelphians. What could the freshly minted president possibly say under these conditions? "This is pre-eminently the time to speak the truth, the whole truth, frankly and boldly. Nor need we shrink from honestly facing conditions in our country today," Roosevelt declared. "This great Nation will endure as it has endured, will revive and will prosper. So, first of all, let me assert my firm belief that the only thing we have to fear is fear itself."

Now *that* was a speech worth getting out for.

———

Sources: Lawrence Davies, "Vare Gears Machine to Win Philadelphia," *New York Times*, November 6, 1932; Gerhard Peters and John T. Woolley, "Papers of Herbert Hoover," American Presidency Project (website); Gerhard Peters and John T. Woolley, "Franklin Delano Roosevelt's First Inaugural Address, March 4, 1933," American Presidency Project, http://www.presidency.ucsb.edu/ws/index.php?pid=14473; Roger D. Simon, "Great Depression," *Encyclopedia of Greater Philadelphia* (Camden: Rutgers, n.d.);

Associated Press, "Reds Blamed for Boos at Philadelphia," October 31, 1932; *Encyclopaedia Britannica Online*, s.v. "United States Presidential Election of 1932," https://www.britannica.com/event/United-States-presidential -election-of-1932; William E. Leuchtenburg, "Franklin D. Roosevelt: Campaigns and Elections" Miller Center, University of Virginia, https:// millercenter.org/president/fdroosevelt/campaigns-and-elections.

Figure 1.8. Newsstand at the "Chinese Wall," northeast corner of Seventeenth and Market Streets, photographed by Francis Balionis, July 25, 1952

In the middle of the twentieth century, the *Bulletin* seemed to be everywhere. Blue newsstands with gold lettering had grown familiar at intersections throughout the city. In Philadelphia, nearly everybody could get the *Bulletin*, and many did.

When the paper turned one hundred years old in 1947, circulation stood at the highest its owners would ever see. Peter Binzen described the party for the paper's 1,700 employees at the convention center. Management ordered a six-foot-tall cake and read congratulations (and faint praise) from President Harry Truman ("I have never known it to hit below the belt") and *Time* magazine ("*The Bulletin* may be unspectacular, but it is a good newspaper").

Such remarks mattered little to the *Bulletin*'s approximately 750,000 readers. The city had not outlived the "corrupt and contented" tagline given by Lincoln Steffens in 1903; it had embraced it. For every registered Democrat, there were two registered Republicans, whose politics, wrote John Lukacs, were "a kind of Business-Biblical Americanism of the Old Protectionist Dispensation." For generations, he wrote, "interior life was what counted in Philadelphia."

But things were changing. Soon after 1950, Philadelphia forfeited its rank as the third largest American city to Los Angeles. The city hovered at the brink of a political and civic reform that would tear down all kinds of walls, not least of which was the so-called Chinese Wall that cut the western half of Center City in two.

Riding high, the *Bulletin* sought to secure its position with advertising that played on the soul of what would become known as "the private city." This campaign turned into one of the longest-lived in advertising. For twenty-eight years, Americans, even non-*Bulletin* readers, awaited the next illustration by Richard Decker, placed over the slogan that quickly became famous: "In Philadelphia, nearly everybody reads the *Bulletin*." Decker, the son of Chestnut Street stationers, had a prolific career as a cartoonist for the *New Yorker*. Ben Yagoda describes him as "a virtuoso of the panoramic full-page gag" with a brand of humor that "sprang from the one key element that was unexpected or out of joint." Each of these *Bulletin* advertisements worked from the same premise: while a scene of some drama unfolds, everyone in the crowd—except one excited, skinny, balding fellow—is complacently reading their copy of the newspaper.

Each would be considered a cartoon except for the fact that they were advertisements. That their humor came at the expense of nearly every Philadelphian gave a few cultural critics reason to take offense. According to Nathaniel Burt, the ads spoke to "the Philadelphia lack of curiosity, the inability and unwillingness to observe the unknown, no matter how spectacular." They projected "Philadelphia's enormous self-satisfaction, the delight in the *status quo*; above all, the intense groupiness, the cheerful conformity . . . their complete exclusion of the oddball, the intense, the enthusiastic and the alarmed—no matter how proper his concern." Burt concluded the message about Philadelphia was "nearly everybody reads the *Bulletin* . . . except the peculiar."

Philip Stevick considered Decker's ads "uncompromisingly derogatory," especially in light of the fact that Philadelphia had long been the butt of national jokes as "a sleepy town." When "faced with the unexpected, or the dramatic, or the exciting, or indeed the life threatening, Philadelphians, the ads seem to say, cannot be roused from their daily papers. . . . Experience itself is simply not interesting."

Burt's observations date to the 1960s, when the Philadelphia of W. C. Fields still loomed large in the national imagination. And even in the 1990s, when Stevick considered the campaign, Philadelphia had not yet shaken its historic self-depreciation. Today, in the second decade of the twenty-first century, the city no longer has the *Bulletin*, or any robust newspaper with healthy circulation, but it is a city comfortable in its own skin.

Sometimes it's the artist, not the historian, who first holds a light up to the truth. Philadelphia-born-and-raised singer and dancer Joan McCracken found fame in the original 1943 production of *Oklahoma!* and then in a politically incorrect period piece *Pass That Peace Pipe* from the film *Good News*. Instead of taking umbrage with the *Bulletin* campaign, McCracken, the daughter of a Philadelphia newspaperman, found inspiration in the Decker advertisements for the *Bulletin*. McCracken got Decker's joke and played into it. In her dance piece titled "Paper!," she cast *herself* in the role of the Philadelphia "oddball." On stage in New York, she seemed to be the only one who really got Decker's humor.

———

Sources: Peter Binzen, *Nearly Everybody Read It: Snapshots of the Philadelphia Bulletin* (Philadelphia: Camino Books, 1998); Nathaniel Burt, *The Perennial Philadelphians: The Anatomy of an American Aristocracy* (New York: Little, Brown, 1963); John Lukacs, *Philadelphia, Patricians and Philistines, 1900–1950* (New York: Farrar, Straus and Giroux, 1981); Lisa Jo Sagolla, *The Girl Who Fell Down: A Biography of Joan McCracken* (Boston:

Northeastern University Press, 2003); Philip Stevick, *Imagining Philadelphia: Travelers' Views of the City from 1800 to the Present* (Philadelphia: University of Pennsylvania Press, 1996); Sam Bass Warner, *The Private City: Philadelphia in Three Periods of Its Growth* (Philadelphia: University of Pennsylvania Press, 1969); Edwin Wolf II, "The Origins of Philadelphia's Self-Depreciation, 1820–1920," *The Pennsylvania Magazine of History and Biography* 104, no. 1 (January 1980), 58–73; Ben Yagoda, *About Town: The New Yorker and the World It Made* (Boston: Da Capo Press, 2001).

PHILADELPHIA'S SCARLET STREAK

Even though he despised the color, as long as Frank Rizzo carried a badge, the patrol cars of the Philadelphia police were lipstick red. Rizzo snapped at officers who spoke of them as "red cars," and one can only imagine what he said when he heard them referred to as "rotten tomatoes" or "red devils." As soon as Rizzo rose to the position of police commissioner in 1967, he announced a plan to replace the red with a less strident blue and white. But Mayor James H. J. Tate made it clear: such decisions were above Rizzo's pay grade. Traditional red would reign for five more years.

The color-change order came down on Tuesday, January 4, 1972—Rizzo's first full day as mayor. He barely minded the ribbing that his brother, Joe, the fire commissioner, would finally be able to tell police cars apart from vehicles in *his* department. For the newly inaugurated Rizzo, "Blue Tuesday," as the papers called it, was a red-letter day.

Why, exactly, was red so objectionable?

Philadelphia's scarlet streak dated back to 1929, a time when color, let alone bright colors, were rare on your basic black Henry Ford automobile. And 1929 was anything but an ordinary year for the Philadelphia police. The department was in a tailspin, having been documented as systemically corrupt. "Spreading gangland warfare" and simmering scandal "exploded" into "a spectacular grand jury investigation" in August 1928. The city's annual underground Prohibition-era economy of alcohol and other "amusements" had soared to $40 million. Nearly 1,200 bars remained open. Across the city were 13,000 speakeasies and 300 "bawdy houses." And half of the total proceeds were skimmed off for "protection." Investigators learned that much of that $20 million passed through the hands of police officers and district captains handpicked by ward leaders. The Philadelphia Police Department wasn't part of the solution; it was the city's crime problem.

Mayor Harry Mackey ordered a complete city-wide "clean up" of the department, including redistricting. In the shakeup, 4,500 officers were transferred; at least 85 were dismissed. Precautions assuring visibility and accountability of the reconfigured force were put in place.

When reform-minded leaders instituted the "Red Car System" in 1929, it almost certainly was not an allusion to Nathaniel Hawthorne's classic *The Scarlet Letter*, where red stood out as Hester Prynne's badge of public shame after being found guilty of adultery. But less than a year after revelations of deep, widespread, and systemic corruption, the choice of scarlet for patrol cars stood at the forefront of attempts to increase visibility and accountability. Years later, some might well have considered the color as a vestige, a residual echo, of a precaution aimed at introducing transparency for a disgraced police force. Just possibly, some police could still feel the punitive stridency of red.

Red had long been associated with Philadelphia, usually in a positive way. S. Weir Mitchell titled his Philadelphia-based historical romance *The Red City*. Elizabeth Robbins Pennell waxed on in *Our Philadelphia*, a book-length love letter, about how "peace breathed, exuded from the red brick houses with white marble steps." But there was also a distinct downside to Philadelphia red. Gothic novelist George Lippard considered the infatuation excessive. "The eye is wearied by one unvarying sameness of dull red brick," he noted in *The Quaker City*, observing that "the man who paints a house blue or yellow or pink or white, or any other hue . . . than this monotonous red, is . . . set down by his neighbors, as slightly weak minded or positively crazy."

As police commissioner in 1969, Rizzo ordered 255 new red Ford V8s with air-conditioning, power brakes, power steering, and bucket seats. Pacifico Ford's $911,802 price tag was the lowest of three required bids. This would be among the city's last large orders of red cruisers. A few years later, when the city shifted to blue and white, public reaction was largely positive. "I like it," one woman told a reporter on Market Street. "It doesn't scream at you." But a cabbie worried, "It just didn't stand out like the red."

Absolutely right. After forty-three years, Philadelphia's scarlet streak had come to an end.

———

Sources: John Clancy and Don McDonough, "It's a Blue Tuesday for Police Red Cars," *Philadelphia Inquirer*, January 5, 1972; William A. Lovejoy, "Phila.'s Blue 'Red Cars' Draw Favorable Comment," *Bulletin*, February 17, 1972; William G. Shepherd, "The Price of Liquor," *Colliers*, December 1, 1928, 8; Albert C. Wagner, "Crime and Economic Change in Philadelphia, 1925–1934," *Journal of Criminal Law and Criminology* 27, no. 4 (Winter 1936): 483–490; Russell F. Weigley, *Philadelphia: A 300 Year History* (New York: W. W. Norton, 1982); "Huge Rum Bribes to Police Bared in Philadelphia," *Chicago Daily Tribune*, September 1, 1928; "Graft Findings Hit 85 Philadelphia Police," *Washington Post*, March 14, 1929; "Police Cars to Stay Red," *Bulletin*, May 22, 1968; "City Gets Low Bid of $2530 Apiece for 255 Red Cars," *Bulletin*, November 11, 1969; "Rizzo Gets His Way on Police Cars," *Bulletin*, January 4, 1972.

Figure 1.9. Penrose Avenue Bridge, October 4, 1951

It's a shame no one has anything good to say about the drive from Philadelphia International Airport to Center City. It's a gritty but grand entrance, this ride on PA 291, a.k.a. the Penrose Avenue Bridge or Platt Memorial Bridge to US 76, a.k.a. the Schuylkill Expressway—a ride punctuated by the usual roadwork, billboards, questionable signage, and occasional pothole. Those features are found just about anywhere. What makes this stretch truly special is the rich urban choreography visible from atop the viaduct of concrete pylons rising from the brackish marsh. *That* scene offers complex and meaningful drama.

The Platt Memorial Bridge experience is considered an embarrassing nuisance. Hosts of out-of-town guests apologize for it. Hospitality hates it. The *Inquirer*˙ has called it a "grimy industrial gateway . . . arching over sprawling oil tanks and . . . steaming stacks." Most Philadelphians consider this entrance the worst of the worst, but it may actually be the best. I feel sorry for those who go out of their way to avoid Philadelphia's gritty entrance. They miss the point.

Arriving via the Platt is a genuine aesthetic Philadelphia experience. It's an everyman, everywoman, everyday encounter for the drivers and passengers in the fifty-six thousand vehicles that pass over this 1.7-mile, sixty-two-year-old bridge. Sure, as the *Inquirer* says, it "begins in weeds and ends by a junkyard," but that's the beauty and the irony of it. By traversing the bridge in our cars, we're threading a needle, that fragile zone in time and space between gasoline being refined and cars being crushed. Our reason for passing through breathes life into the scene and gives it a reason for being.

No, it's not beautiful in the traditional sense, but we *need* this stuff. And isn't Philadelphia at its best when it's averse to pretense? We're barreling along; there's sewage treatment on our right, an oil refinery on our left—plumes of smoke, gas flares burning effluent high above the natural no-man's-land below. Yet this scene is nearly entirely man-made, taking place above the loneliest and least welcoming stretch of the meandering Schuylkill, two miles beyond the last bit of honest green at Bartram's Gardens. This is about the automobile and its victory in the twentieth-century city. As drivers, we're offered a commanding straight shot to and from the city. Rising over the crest of the Platt Bridge is among the most dramatic and authentic that Philadelphia ever gets. Why should we allow it to embarrass us? Why would we want to avert our eyes?

Philadelphians opened the bridge in 1951, twenty years after the idea was first proposed and just as the automobile had gained dominance over the nineteenth-century city. With a ribbon cutting and a celebratory dinner hosted by American Automobile Association, the former swing

---

˙ References to the *Inquirer* refer to the *Philadelphia Inquirer*.

bridge from Philadelphia's Iron Age was reduced to fading memory. Sixty years later, in June 2011, the Pennsylvania Department of Transportation (PennDOT) identified this bridge as one of five thousand in the commonwealth that are "structurally deficient" and launched a three-year "rehabilitation project."

There's structural integrity, and then there's experiential integrity. What wakes up both citizen and visitor and puts them in the true Philadelphia frame of mind, what completes the whole Platt Bridge experience, is the car shredder at its base. But SPC Corporation, which operates this Godzilla grinder, this Rockosaurus of rust, is planning to leave town. After abandoning a plan to relocate to Eddystone, Pennsylvania, SPC's parent company, Camden Iron and Metal, announced a plan to move back to the city of its namesake. "Sooner or later," the company claims, "we're going to move."

What a pity. Just as we've grown accustomed to Philadelphia's most apocalyptic and ironic vision, just as we've become fully conscious of this twentieth-century manifestation of unsustainability, we're about to lose its most dramatic expression. As the song goes, "You don't know what you've got till it's gone," and then it says something about a parking lot.

Exactly.

———

Sources: Linda Lloyd, "See Ya, Scrap," *Inquirer,* February 9, 2010; Paul Nussbaum, "Platt Bridge Work Makes Arriving from Airport Even More Dismal," *Inquirer,* August 7, 2012; "Penrose Avenue Bridge," Philadelphia Architects and Buildings, American Architects and Buildings, https://www.philadelphiabuildings.org/pab/app/pj_display.cfm/97042.

Figure 1.10. Rocky statue at the Philadelphia Museum of Art, July 29, 1982

The Rocky statue has been in place for more than a decade now, and it has been four since the film character gave Philadelphia a boost and Sylvester Stallone a brand worth hundreds of millions. But eventually, possibly sooner rather than later, Rocky will have to step aside as a Philadelphia story that has outlived its time.

Born during a recession in a place with an evaporating manufacturing economy, Rocky's day job as bill collector speaks to the lack of opportunity in a city of deteriorating homes and a paucity of jobs. In the 1970s, Philadelphians still believed that they still had a shot at bringing the factories back. It took several decades more for the leadership (by then Ed Rendell in the 1990s) to openly admit that industry as Philadelphia knew it was gone and a constellation of emerging and maturing economies (education, medicine, tourism, and technology) would have to replace it.

Philadelphians have come to their senses and moved on. Except, it seems, when it comes to Rocky. Like Archie Bunker's Queens, Rocky's Philadelphia is now mostly gone, although not entirely. The spirit of the 1970s occasionally finds traction. In 2006, the same year that Rocky returned to the Parkway, Joey Vento posted a sign at his steak joint on Ninth Street: "This is America: when ordering 'Speak English.'" Vento spoke his mind, as Tom Ferrick put it in a recent *Metropolis* column: "And what was in that mind? A heavy dose of macho. One primal scream. Several tablespoons of jingoism. A half-cup of xenophobia. A dash of hate."

When Joey Vento died in 2011, so did a little bit more of *that* Philadelphia, Rocky's Philadelphia. Vento clumsily said what Stallone's Rocky artfully implied. "Outsiders" were changing the hue and cry of the workplace, schools, and streets. Vento, Ferrick pointed out, targeted Philadelphia's Mexican immigrants. Rocky targeted African Americans: first, Apollo Creed, played by Carl Weathers, then James "Clubber" Lang, played by Mr. T. Of course, Rocky's racism was neatly tempered by Hollywood, but it was significant in Rocky's persona as well as the brand's success.

The Rocky story is one of personal victory rather than civic victory. In the 1970s, Rocky couldn't begin to turn around a city still steeped in mid-century noir, but he could, bouncing at the top of the Art Museum's steps at dawn in grey sweats, realize a form of personal success.

Today, Philadelphia offers more. Uncounted thousands visit the Rocky statue every year, admiring themselves with arms raised in souvenir images. There's a connection here with a twentieth-century Philadelphia story that has survived into the twenty-first. But how meaningful is it now? Isn't this statue—whether it's considered a movie prop or a franchise logo or even contested as art—just an artifact of twentieth-century American popular culture, along the lines of Archie Bunker's chair? Visitors to the Smithsonian's National Museum of American History see *that* artifact behind glass in the context of past popular culture.

Someday, the Rocky statue will be framed in a similar narrative. When that day comes, Philadelphia will have something to offer about what the city *is*, not what it *was*. But first, we'll have to get past the idea that Stallone has done more for Philadelphia's image than anyone since Ben Franklin, as Commerce Director Dick Doran put it in the 1980s. We'll still be moved a little (or a lot) by the Rocky story, and the artifact will always be with us. Only, in the future, we'll think of it as on the shelf rather than the pedestal, along with many other compelling stories and symbols of past Philadelphias.

The question is, when Rocky steps aside or is forced aside—and this should happen sooner than later—what will take his place? That we have yet to figure out. But the time is coming for Rocky to become history—and there's nothing wrong with that.

———

Sources: Tom Ferrick, "Joey Vento Está Muerto," *Metropolis*, August 29, 2011, http://www.phlmetropolis.com/2011/08/joey-vento-esta-muerto.php; Michael Gallantz, "Critical Dialogue: Rocky's Racism," *Jump Cut: A Review of Contemporary Media*, no. 18 (August 1978): 33–34; Laura Holzman, "A Question of Stature: Restoring and Ignoring Rocky," *Public Art Dialogue* 4, no. 2 (October 2014): 249–265; Danielle Rice, "The 'Rocky' Dilemma: Museums, Monuments, and Popular Culture in the Postmodern Era," in *Critical Issues in Public Art: Content, Context, and Controversy*, ed. Harriet F. Senie and Sally Webster (New York: HarperCollins, 1992), 228–236.

Figure 1.11. One Liberty Place and the Philadelphia skyline from the south, December 5, 1987

What kind of a city *should* Philadelphia be? Ponderous, historical, and homey, stuck in its quaint ways, admiring its own image in the rear view mirror? Or should Philadelphia throw in its hat and become lively, contemporary, and international, willing to join the *what's what* of world cities?

Developer Willard Rouse didn't think it was a real choice as he put the make-it-or-break-it question to the people of Philadelphia in the spring of 1984. Rouse proposed breaking the city's "gentleman's agreement," that quirky, decades-old pact more ephemeral than legal. Never on the books, it had been kept alive in boardrooms as a ready-made, self-deprecating put-down. Anyone suggesting a project of more than five hundred feet would be brought up short by city planner Edmund N. Bacon with the same line: "It's only a gentleman's agreement. The question is, are you a gentleman?"

There were a lot of places in the city where you couldn't even *see* City Hall Tower or the statue of the founder. "If you stood at Rittenhouse Square right now and looked for William Penn," Rouse pointed out, "you would not find him." According to Benjamin M. Gerber's chronicle of the gentleman's agreement's demise, the *Inquirer* editorial board agreed: "much of the symbolism of Penn's supremacy was already lost amidst 'a stubby tide of undistinguished office buildings already [lapping] just shy of Penn's pantaloons.'"

Inquirer architecture writer Thomas Hine had seen it coming. "The breakthrough might come in a private office building, or as a public monument," he wrote in 1983, "but it seems that sooner or later, the city will rise over William Penn's head." The following April, Rouse presented two projects—a short one and a tall one (he only intended to develop the latter). The debate that ensued became the "Battle of Billy Penn" as Gregory L. Heller tells it in his biography of Bacon. It played out everywhere—in the streets, in the media, and in the public mind—as Philadelphia redefined itself at the end of the century that had begun with the installation of a nearly thirty-seven-foot bronze founder above a humble skyline.

"The way people talked about One Liberty Place when plans for this skyscraper were announced," wrote Paul Goldberger in the *New York Times*, "you would have thought that this was not a new building but some sort of nuclear weapon. One Liberty Place would be the ruination of Philadelphia, cried the project's opponents, the sign that this somewhat genteel city had sold out to real-estate developers and become just like anyplace else." The crier-in-chief, of course, was the retired Bacon, whose energy, style, and way with words fueled the debate. The height limitation "sets Philadelphia apart from all other" cities. And Bacon warned, "Once smashed it is gone forever."

Liberty Place was built, of course.

In 1987, when it opened, some couldn't forget that architect Helmut Jahn had adapted it from a much taller, unbuilt tower proposed for Houston. Some critics couldn't forgive that it looked like a bulked-up version of

New York's Chrysler Building. Hine admitted that Liberty Place "loomed" but appreciated how, amid the "stubble" of existing office buildings, it turned "the uninspiring commercial agglomeration into a complete visual composition." Liberty Place stood "like a mountain among the foothills."

Philadelphia's height limitation had been "an empty gesture, hollow and pretentious," wrote Goldberger in the *Times*. "The urban order that Philadelphians had for so long cherished was a myth . . . it was a fallacy to pretend that City Hall still commanded the skyline . . . William Penn barely stuck his head above his grim surroundings." With Liberty Place, "City Hall . . . is still there, still great, and still at the critical center of the city. The only thing that has been lost is the illusion that William Penn was lording over it all." Goldberger glowed that Liberty Place "transcends the old order, and establishes a new one, at a level of quality good enough to justify throwing away the old."

Liberty Place would "dislodge this historical center which . . . informed our city from the beginning," predicted Bacon. "In our arrogance, we replace it with a floating center up for sale to the highest bidder." In that sense, Liberty Place and the still taller Comcast Center buildings would confirm his worst fears.

What was sacrificed in the end? Sure, the skyline would never be the same. It would never again take on the same kind of meaning. In the debates of the 1980s, Philadelphians were forced to think long and hard about *where* they found substance and *how* they found meaning. "We may be giving up something insubstantial, but not meaningless," observed John Bower, architect of the Gallery.

In the twenty-first century, Philadelphians would search for substance and meaning in places other than the skyline. And maybe that's not such a bad thing.

———

Sources: Benjamin M. Gerber, "'No-Law' Urban Height Restrictions: A Philadelphia Story," *The Urban Lawyer* 38, no. 1 (Winter 2006); Paul

Goldberger, "Giving New Life to Philadelphia's Skyline," *New York Times*, November 15, 1987; Gregory L. Heller, *Ed Bacon: Planning, Politics, and the Building of Modern Philadelphia* (Philadelphia: University of Pennsylvania Press, 2013); Thomas Hine, "Office Buildings of the Future May Eclipse William Penn," *Inquirer*, April 17, 1983; "A Matter of Keeping Philadelphia under His Hat," *Inquirer*, March 4, 1984; "Round and Round on How High to Build," *Inquirer*, April 26, 1984; "Plans for a 2d Skyscraper Give Rise to the Height Issue Again," *Inquirer*, August 10, 1986.

Figure 2.1. Southeast corner, Twenty-Fifth and Kimball Streets, May 11, 1916

CHAPTER 2

The Neighborhoods

"The Quintessential Object of Industrial Philadelphia"

Philadelphia's most effective tool in its industrial transformation during the late nineteenth century wasn't a tool at all, although it could be considered a machine for living. As architectural historian George Thomas once put it, the row house was "the quintessential object of Industrial Philadelphia."

The Philadelphia row house had roots far older than the Industrial Revolution. In 1800, Scottish-born "architect and house-carpenter" Thomas Carstairs took the familiar idea of identical houses in a row and stretched it out for a full city block on Sansom between Seventh and Eighth Streets, turning real estate into revenue and meeting the city's growing appetite for housing. Over the next several decades, as the city filled up its seventeenth-century grid, the row house evolved into an upscale solution for urban living. Architects John Haviland and Thomas U. Walter demonstrated how the repeated form could also become something chic and generous. But as the city's population soared past one million in 1890, the row house was reclaimed for the working class. By the end of the century, Thomas writes, "As far as the eye could see, there were some fifty square miles of row houses and factories, most of which had been built in the previous generation."

The two- and three-story row house had become part the city's successful mix of immigration, employment, real estate, coal, and banking.

Between 1887 and 1893, no fewer than 50,288 row houses were built, enough for a quarter million people. Philadelphians had seen a row house construction boom before—more than 50,000 were built between 1863 and 1876. But now, in the last decades of the nineteenth century, the Philadelphia row house had grown compact, simplified, and adapted to the lives of the working family. With the help of Philadelphia's 450 savings and loan associations, a two-story "workingman's house," as it became known, could be had for about $3,000 and paid off in about a decade.

Sure, other cities—New York, Boston, Brooklyn, and Baltimore—had row houses, but Philadelphia's were more efficient, plentiful, and affordable. The late nineteenth-century Philadelphia row house helped make Philadelphia the "Workshop of the World."

In 1893, the world took notice. The Columbian Exposition in Chicago exhibited a single specimen, a two-story workingmen's house designed by Philadelphia architect E. Allen Wilson. (Other models of American housing on display included an Eskimo house and a logger's cabin.) The Philadelphia exhibit in Chicago was so popular that, legend has it, curious visitors wore out the floorboards.

The Philadelphia model was more than a solution to a housing problem; it became an effective tool for building modern society. "The two-story dwellings of this city are, beyond all question, the best, as a system, not only owing to the single family ideas they represent, but because their cost is within the reach of all who desire to own their own homes," glowed John H. Gallagher, a row house proponent in the early 1890s. "They have done more to elevate and to make a better home life than any other known influence. . . . They are what make Philadelphia a city of homes, and command the attention of visitors from every quarter of the globe."

Between 1890 and 1910, Philadelphia grew from a city of a million to 1.5 million by adding more miles of row houses with ever greater repetition and monotony. Variations of one sort or another added to the grammar and typology of row house forms. Over time, some would be demolished, others would collapse, and still others would have their original brick facades veneered with permastone, a literal interpretation of the romantic idea that—even in a modern industrialized city—home is a castle.

———

Sources: John N. Gallagher, "Real Estate Holdings and Valuations" in *The City of Philadelphia as It Appears in the Year 1894*, ed. Frank Hamilton Taylor (Philadelphia: G. S. Harris and Sons, 1894); James F. O'Gorman, *Drawing toward Building: Philadelphia Architectural Graphics, 1732–1986* (Philadelphia: University of Pennsylvania Press, 1986); George E. Thomas, *William L. Price: Arts and Crafts to Modern Design* (Princeton: Princeton Architectural Press, 2000); William John Murtagh, "The Philadelphia Row House," *Journal of the Society of Architectural Historians* 16, no. 4 (December 1957): 8–13.

Keeping Philadelphia's Neighborhood Names Honest

Want to start an argument? Ask a Philadelphian (any Philadelphian—a new one, a longtime one—it makes no difference) how many neighborhoods there are in the city. Want to turn the heat up even more? Ask them to pin down the borders between one neighborhood and another—especially if it means something to them. These are questions that stir primal urban juices.

It's a centuries-old game of push and pull that culminates in a heady sense of "placeness" that grows over time and defies resolution. It's part of a powerful human, hierarchical, and historical process that's gone on since the start of urban time and continues to this day. And let's hope it's not resolved any time soon. The day Philadelphians happily join hands over neighborhood-identity issues is the day I'll vanish from the city, never to return.

The names and numbers of neighborhoods vary dramatically depending on who you ask. The last edition of the *Bulletin Almanac* published

in 1976 listed 42 neighborhoods. More recently, when the *Metropolis* blog
reported the "Percent of Individuals Living in Poverty," Tom Ferrick used
the acceptable breakdown of 56 city neighborhoods. But the Philadelphia
Office of Housing and Community Development lists 97. *Philly*History
.org uses a robust 155 names, and the Philadelphia Neighborhoods page at
Wikipedia has crept up to nearly 170. When the *Philadelphia Almanac and
Citizen's Manual* published its final edition in 1995, a dogged editorial team
reported 395 neighborhood names, both current and defunct. And since
then, the Philadelphia Department of Records built on that to arrive at a
compilation that tops off at 449.

We should welcome Philadelphia's web of placeness and the ever-
present arguments it spawns as evidence of life and meaning. And in those
arguments, we'll find stories of places left behind (the citizens of Flat Rock
rejected Bridgewater and Udoravia before adopting the more colorful
Manayunk). Some names simply disappeared, as did Rose of Bath, a.k.a.
Bathtown, which was swallowed up by Northern Liberties. Others are
simply lost in the mists of time: Goat Hill, Good Intent, Goosetown, and
Grubtown. But the one thing we know for sure is that each and every one
of these places had its following for a time.

When it comes to Philadelphia neighborhood names, we should welcome the idea that after the city's twentieth-century decline, less can be
more. Our honest embrace of that lesser, as-is Philadelphia is a rare and
admirable thing, which is why we should also accept the heavily patinated,
"nightmarish post-industrial landscape" along the streets north of Center
City known to some as "The Eraserhood."

When the Divine Lorraine Hotel stood in ruins, it was well-positioned
as the iconic northwestern outpost of the rising sense of placeness that
celebrated Philadelphia's misfortune and moodiness. The entire neighborhood was a ready-made set for a short, loving video by Shawn Kil-
roy that recalled the time when David Lynch lived across from the city
morgue at Thirteenth and Wood Streets and studied painting at Pennsylvania Academy of the Fine Arts. Lynch stored up experiences and

impressions in Philadelphia that fueled his 1977 black-and-white surrealist film *Eraserhead*.

Lynch found Philadelphia "horrible, but in a very interesting way. There were places there that had been allowed to decay, where there was so much fear and crime that just for a moment there was an opening to another world. It was fear, but it was so strong, and so magical, like a magnet, that your imagination was always sparking in Philadelphia." He continued, "I just have to think of Philadelphia now, and I get ideas, I hear the wind, and I'm off into the darkness somewhere."

The Eraserhood name is a deft act of preservation—preservation of the spirit that made Philadelphia what it is, for better and for worse. Either way, both ways, it's *our* Philadelphia—but we're richer for coming to terms with the bitter (and compelling) truth, just as it is being erased from memory.

———

Sources: Tom Ferrick, "Percent of Individuals Living in Poverty, 2000 to 2009 [in 56 Neighborhoods]," *Metropolis*, 2010; Kenneth Finkel, ed., *The Philadelphia Almanac and Citizens' Manual* (Philadelphia: Library Company of Philadelphia, 1995): "Philadelphia Neighborhoods and Place Names," Philadelphia Department of Records, City of Philadelphia, http://www.phila.gov/phils/docs/otherinfo/placname.htm; The City of Absurdity: The Mysterious World of David Lynch, David Lynch Quote Collection, s.v. "Philadelphia," http://www.thecityofabsurdity.com/.

Figure 2.2. Southeast corner, Seventh Street and Cecil B. Moore Avenue, August 30, 1904

It didn't make sense.

Several public schools in Kensington and North Philadelphia were performing dramatically below both national and local standards in the mid-1960s. In reading and arithmetic, fourth graders in schools (all in Philadelphia's Fifth District) were, according to Peter Binzen, "a year and two months behind national norms and three months behind the Philadelphia city average." Of all the city's 195 elementary schools, "the one with the lowest fourth-grade reading score was located dead in the middle of District 5," wrote Binzen. "The total performance of children in this school was abysmal."

Was it something in the air? In the water? The street grit? Herbert Needleman, a public health physician at the University of Pennsylvania, had a hunch that all three might be the case. About the same time as Binzen was conducting his research for *Whitetown, U.S.A.*, Needleman set out to measure the lead levels of inner-city children and targeted the Fifth District. Ideally, Needleman would have wanted bone biopsies to obtain the most reliable data, but that wasn't possible. So he adopted a method employed by environmental scientist and peace activist Barry Commoner, who had raised public awareness about cancer-causing strontium-90 from nuclear tests. Commoner had obtained *his* data by analyzing children's teeth. Needleman collected sixty-nine baby teeth in the Fifth District and compared their lead levels to those of a control group from the Eighth District in the northeast section of the city.

"Urban children had nearly five times the concentration observed in their suburban counterparts," read the results of the "tooth fairy project," as it became known. Lead poisoning in the Fifth District, manifested in psychological and neurological symptoms, including permanent developmental delays, was described as "stark and startling." The contrast with data collected in the Eighth District? Cases of lead poisoning in the northeast section of the city were "vanishingly rare."

The "tooth fairy project" became a watershed public health moment. The Fifth District would gain notoriety as Philadelphia's "lead belt," and lead would be considered a severe national public health problem—one not entirely understood and very much out of control.

Continuing his research, Needleman reported on what he found in the Fifth District schools, identified only by their initials. *PT* is Potter-Thomas at Sixth and Indiana, *PLD* is Paul Laurence Dunbar at Twelfth and Columbia (Cecil B. Moore), *JRL* is James R. Ludlow at Sixth and Master, *GC* is George Clymer at Twelfth and Rush, *JE* is James Elverson at Thirteenth and Susquehanna, and *JF* is Joseph Ferguson at Seventh and Norris. In these schools and others, Needleman's team collected and tested "interior dust," "playground dirt," and "gutter dirt." They tested 219 children for lead and confirmed their earlier grim findings.

The children of Philadelphia's "lead belt" were seriously at risk.

Lead-laden industrial Philadelphia had left behind a toxic legacy. The city's "lead belt" had long been home to the Philadelphia Lead Works, Standard White Lead, Color and Putty Works, Western White Lead Co., as well as other nineteenth- and twentieth-century manufacturers upwind from the tested schools. They spewed pollution and tainted the water, soil, and dust. More, the very houses citizens called home had been painted, again and again, with paint containing "pure white lead." Thousands of deteriorating nineteenth-century homes coated with layers of chipping and peeling paint were slowly poisoning their occupants. In an environment *this* compromised, with lead embedded in everything and everywhere, researchers found startling levels in their samples collected inside the schools, from playgrounds, and from the streets. Lead had made its way into the teeth, into the blood, and into the brains of growing, learning children.

They didn't have a chance.

Lead paint would be banned in 1978. But according to a recent *Childhood Lead Surveillance Annual Report*, Philadelphia *still* ranks as Pennsylvania's "top county for children under 7 years of age tested for lead." Experts believe one in ten children in Philadelphia have elevated blood lead levels—maybe even higher—but they don't really know. Today, decades later, the vast majority of urban children are not even tested.

It *still* doesn't make sense.

———

Sources: Laura Benshoff, Eleanor Klibanoff, Marielle Segarra, and Irina Zhorov, "The Legacy of Lead in Pennsylvania Cities," *Keystone Crossroads*, 2016; Peter Binzen, *Whitetown, U.S.A.* (New York: Random House, 1970); Gerald Markowitz and David Rosner, *Lead Wars: The Politics of Science and the Fate of America's Children* (Oakland: University of California Press, 2014); Herbert Needleman et al., "Lead Levels in Deciduous Teeth of Urban and Suburban American Children," *Nature* 235, no. 5333 (January 1972); "Subclinical Lead Exposure in Philadelphia

Schoolchildren—Identification by Dentine Lead Analysis," *New England Journal of Medicine* 290 (1974): 245–248; "Dentine Lead Levels in Asymptomatic Philadelphia School Children: Subclinical Exposure in High and Low Risk Groups," *Environmental Health Perspectives* 7 (May 1974): 27–31; 1976 Bulletin Almanac (Philadelphia: *Evening and Sunday Bulletin*, 1976); "America's 'Lead Wars' Go Beyond Flint, Mich.: 'It's Now Really Everywhere,'" *Fresh Air*, NPR, March 3, 2016; Pennsylvania Department of Health, *Childhood Lead Surveillance Annual Report*, 2014.

Figure 2.3. "Geographical distribution of Negro population, Philadelphia 1932" (City Plans Division, Bureau of Engineering and Surveys)

More than eighty-five thousand mostly rural Southerners arrived in Philadelphia in the 1920s, seeking opportunity. What they encountered was discrimination, segregation, and poverty. The Great Migration, followed by the Great Depression, added a double disadvantage for Philadelphia's

African American population. The city founded on principles of toler-
ance, mercy, and justice had modified its original DNA, and hypersegregation had taken hold.

Between 1920 and 1930, the largest increases in the city's African
American population were seen in only ten out of forty-eight wards. These
ten wards absorbed more than fifty-seven thousand of the newcomers,
more than two-thirds of the citywide increase. North, West, and South
Philadelphia saw the largest rises, as maps created in 1932 by the City Plans
Division in the Bureau of Engineering and Surveys graphically illustrate.
These maps document block-by-block ghettoization and overcrowding in
neighborhoods immediately to the north, south, and west of Center City
and provide a rarely depicted snapshot of life in Philadelphia.

In many of the city's other neighborhoods—the nearer and farther
stretches of the northeast, the northwest beyond Nicetown and Germantown, and deep within South Philadelphia—the African American
population didn't grow at all. And where it did grow, it became more
concentrated. No fewer than eight wards saw declines in African American population, including Center City's historically black seventh ward
(the subject of W. E. B. DuBois's classic *The Philadelphia Negro: A Social
Study*, published in 1899). Between 1920 and 1930, this neighborhood,
which stretched west from Seventh Street between Spruce and South
Streets, saw a once-robust African American population diminish from
12,241 to 8,430.

Philadelphia's demographic narrative in the 1920s—when its African
American population became uneven, isolated, clustered, concentrated,
and centralized—is now summarized by demographers in one word:
hypersegregation. How would that play out in the 1930s and beyond?

Without adequate supports to address assimilation, overcrowding,
and poverty and without mechanisms to guide the transition from rural
to urban life, tens of thousands of new Philadelphians found themselves
on the eve of the Great Depression without survival strategies. And
when the Depression arrived, it hit hypersegregated African American

neighborhoods the hardest. In 1931, unemployment among Philadelphia's African Americans exceeded 40 percent; two years later, it rose to
50 percent.

In the mid-1930s, the collision of place, time, and people would be seen
in another set of powerful graphics: Philadelphia's redlining maps. Taken
with the maps from the Philadelphia's Department of Records, we see an
unfortunate progression of evidence. Neighborhoods identified as having dramatic increases in African American populations in the 1920s and
with concentrations of African American in the early 1930s—hundreds
and hundreds of them—would be systematically designated as occupied
by "colored" and described as "decadent" and in "hazardous" condition.

That was in the depths of the Depression. Recovery would take the rest
of the twentieth century—and then some.

———

Sources: Amy Hiller, "Redlining in Philadelphia," in *Past Time, Past Place:
GIS for History*, ed. Anne Kelly Knowles (Redlands: Esri Press, 2002),
79–92; D. S. Massey and J. Tannen, "A Research Note on Trends in Black
Hypersegregation," *Demography* 52 (2015): 1025.

Figure 2.4. Devil's Pocket, near Taney and Catharine Streets, January 28, 1919

"I have seen a pope, I have seen Julius Erving at the top of his game. I have seen a city administration burn down a neighborhood. I watched Randall Cobb slowly realize he would never become a heavyweight champion, of the world. One night I almost saw myself die."

Pete Dexter was writing his long, gritty good-bye to Philadelphia.

The night Dexter nearly saw himself die was in 1981, after he wrote a *Daily News* column about a botched drug deal that resulted in murder. The deceased's brother, according to Dexter, "bartended in Devil's Pocket, which has got to be the worst neighborhood in the city—maybe anywhere." And he was angry. But Dexter "thought he could talk to him and work it out, so I went down there" with Randall "Tex" Cobb.

Both Dexter *and* Cobb nearly saw themselves die that night.

"It has been our good fortune that Pete Dexter did not die at the hands of those heroes with ballbats and tire irons," Pete Hamill would write. "He has gone on to write some of the most original, and disturbing, novels in American literature."

"In an age when words and storytelling were what counted, not bloviated ranting and raving," claimed Buzz Bissinger, Dexter covered "more ground in 900 words than most writers could cover in 9,000." He continued, "I know the city, and nobody has ever captured it the way Dexter has, shining his light on these punks and drunks and cops and hollowed-out men and women just hoping to grab on for one more day. Wherever there is loneliness in the city—and with the withering of its manufacturing and working-class roots, there's no shortage of loneliness—Dexter seems to find it."

Dexter had the sense to appropriate Devil's Pocket for the setting of the novel about his near-death experience. Doc's, the bar where Dexter and Cobb had their clocks cleaned, was at Twenty-Fourth and Lombard, A place more accurately called (forgive me) the Graduate Hospital area. It was located a good half mile away from Devil's Pocket, which, at Catharine and Taney Streets, is hard by the southwestern wall of the Naval Home.

No other neighborhood name fit Dexter's story as brilliantly as "Devil's Pocket." We can forgive the artistic license. After all, if not for Dexter's storytelling, Devil's Pocket might have faded into the same gentrified oblivion, where other Philadelphia neighborhood names of character have gone. (Who has heard of Texas, Smoky Hollow, Beggarstown, or Rose of Bath these days?)

Devil's Pocket has always had resonance. William Paul Dillingham, who focused on Philadelphia's poor Irish in his 1911 study *Immigrants in Cities*, noted the small triangular court called Asylum Place, "popularly known as 'The Devil's Pocket.'" He wrote of its ten two-story brick houses, "poorly built and in bad repair," overcrowded with a mix of newly arrived and first-generation Irish. Residents of Devil's Pocket got jobs at nearby mills and their water from shared hydrants in small backyards near the "dry" toilets. Just the same as nearby Gibbons Court, drainage at the Devil's Pocket ran along the pavement.

Devil's Pocket would become known as one of those places many Philadelphians heard about, talked about, and avoided. An 1898 bicycle tour urged riders to bypass this "nest of unnameable lawlessness." The bicyclist wouldn't even venture west of Grays Ferry Avenue; he had heard stories and would give Devil's Pocket "a wide berth even in broad daylight."

But there was no wide berth for Pete Dexter, even if he had to fudge the coordinates of Devil's Pocket to help make the most of his Philadelphia story.

———

Sources: Buzz Bissinger, "Philadelphia Stories," *New York Times*, March 4, 2007; Pete Dexter, *God's Pocket* (New York: Random House, 1983); Pete Dexter, *Paper Trails: The Life and Times of Pete Dexter* (New York: Harper-Collins, 2007); William Paul Dillingham, *Immigrants in Cities: A Study of the Population of Selected Districts in New York, Chicago, Philadelphia, Boston, Cleveland, Buffalo, and Milwaukee*, U.S. Immigration Commission, U.S. Government Printing Office, 1911; Steve Volk, "Paper Man," *Philadelphia Weekly*, March 7, 2007; Christopher Wink, "Booze, Grudges and Paranoia: What Makes a Journalist a Journalist," ChristoperWink Blog, July 28, 2007; "Trips Awheel," *Inquirer*, February 6, 1898.

Figure 2.5. Grays Ferry Avenue at South Street and Twenty-Third Street, looking southwest, photographed by Wenzel J. Hess, May 22, 1936

South Street's civic temperature—and Philadelphia's by degree—can be measured by checking in at the triangular intersection at South Street, Twenty-Third Street, and Grays Ferry Avenue. This pizza-slice-shaped piazza continues to change with the times, proving once again that what goes around comes around.

About a century ago, Christopher Morley (who resided nearby on too-quiet Pine Street) enviously noted the "uproarious and naïve humours" a few blocks away. "On South Street," Morley wrote, "the veins of life run close to the surface." By the 1970s, things had settled down, though not necessarily in a good way. "The street lay like a snake sleeping; dull-dusty, gray-black in the dingy darkness," wrote David Bradley. "At the three-way intersection of Twenty-Third Street, Grays Ferry Avenue, and South Street a fountain, erected once-upon-a year by a ladies guild in remembrance of some dear departed altruist, stood cracked and dry, full of dead leaves and cigarette butts and bent beer cans, forgotten by the city and the ladies' guild, functionless, except as a minor memorial to how They Won't Take Care of Nice Things."

Ah, but given time, they will care. If given half a chance.

In 2014, we witnessed a waking up, a coming around to this very "nice thing" along the western end of South Street. Not exactly "uproarious" and hardly "naïve," the movement began three years before with a celebration of the diagonal in a city made up of right angles. And it is more than saving one of the city's rare, vintage horse troughs. The Grays Ferry Triangle effort has been a grassroots project since 2011, one bolstered by arguments that spaces are better, often far better, when reclaimed by and for the community. To demonstrate and consolidate support, there's been an annual Plazapalooza, a spate of social media and a poll showing 98 percent of near-neighbor support for promoting pedestrianism and banning the can on at least *one* tiny but potent stretch of Philly byway.

The following spring, a six-month trial street closure started, and this "underused South of South space" got a "pedestrian-friendly makeover." Would this experiment in participatory urban design be temporary? Would South Street again revert to being a place that "Won't Take Care of Nice Things"? Or has Philadelphia made the turn toward becoming a postpetroleum city whose veins not only "run close to the surface" but pulse with something more organic than gasoline?

———

Sources: David Bradley, *South Street: A Novel* (New York: Viking Press, 1975); Anthony Campisi, "When Streets Give Way to Plazas," PlanPhilly, August 19, 2011; Bill Chenevert, "Grays Ferry Triangle Plaza Takes Shape: An Underused South of South Space Gets a Pedestrian-Friendly

Makeover," *South Philly Review*, June 13, 2014; Christopher Morley, *Travels in Philadelphia* (Philadelphia: David McKay Company, 1920); Philip Walzer, "Go West, South Street Urban Pioneers Have Led the Way to the Other Side of Broad," *Inquirer*, January 6, 1989; "SOSNA Improves, Celebrates Grays Ferry Ave Triangles," PlanPhilly, March 25, 2013.

Figure 2.6. Sewer construction near Seventh and Courtland Streets, detail, September 14, 1903

Rolling Hills? Maybe once upon a time. At the dawn of the twentieth century, when the City of Homes meant row houses as far as the eye could see, Philadelphia *had* to be flat—or as close to flat as humanly possible—if it was to have *any* value on the real estate market. One by one, nature's dips, rises, and rolls were raised up or shaved down as the city grid marched north. Once flattened, Philly invited horse-drawn streetcars on its newly leveled streets, which meant developers were followed by new residents. Mile by mile, the city boomed to more than double its population between the Civil War and 1900.

As midcentury became the turn of the twentieth century, Broad Street forged northward past Ridge Avenue to Monument Cemetery (Temple University today). It then trundled over the bridge at Cohocksink Creek (soon to become Dauphin Street), over Gunners Run (just south of the would-be Allegheny Avenue) and past Hunting Park, where a racecourse-turned-public park sprawled to the east. Now little more than a wide lane, Broad Street approached the largest creek so far—the Wingohocking. And as it flowed eastward to join Frankford Creek, the Wingohocking did what creeks do: it meandered a bit to the north, then south, crossing four times where Courtland Street was supposed to be between Broad and Sixth.

What's to be done when the dips and gullies are actually valleys surrounded by rolling hills? Philly's flatlanders had a ready-made solution. They would run the creeks through giant culverts: massive, man-made, underground masonry aqueducts large enough to allow Mother Nature to carry on unimpeded out of sight and possibly out of mind. Even more convenient, these hidden creek beds could double as the city's backup sewer system on an as-needed basis during occasional floods. Above, on the surface, it's business as usual. Or at least that was the idea. The Wingohocking would be channeled where it used to meander. Over it, anything lower than the "ideal" grade would be covered with a deep layer of fill. Ambitious? To be sure. But doable.

"There have been great changes in the face of [Philadelphia], in its levels and contour, and in the direction and beds of its water-courses," wrote historians Scharf and Westcott in the 1880s. "Some streams have disappeared, some have changed their direction, nearly all have been reduced in volume and depth . . . in the building of a great city." Those changes may have been plentiful, but they were *nothing* like what was about to happen along the Wingohocking. As historian Adam Levine tells it, "In some watersheds, it took many years to completely obliterate the main stream and its tributaries." The conversion of West Philadelphia's Mill Creek to sewer "took more than 25 years, and the city's largest such project, the burying of both branches of Wingohocking Creek, took about 40 years." Raising the eighty-acre Wingohocking Valley up to city-grid grade would require as much as forty feet of fill and a lot of time.

Aside from urban aesthetics and environmental ethics, this massive project had every reason to work—if the contractors had used rock and soil for fill. But in one of Philadelphia's most egregious and purposeful bungles, the fill hauled in by specially designed streetcars was ash and cinder, an estimated five hundred thousand cubic yards of it. In time, the consequences would be as dire as the hauling and dumping project had been efficient. "It took decades for the inadequacy of the ash to be revealed," writes Levine. When the fill washed away, gas lines ruptured and the neighborhood above found itself in the midst of "an epidemic . . . of sagging porches, cracking foundations," and worse—much worse.

The saga of Philadelphia's Logan Triangle had begun.

––––––––

Sources: Peter G. Chirico and Jack B. Epstein, "Plate 2: Map Showing Distribution of Fill in the Frankford and Germantown Quadrangles, Philadelphia and Montgomery Counties, Pennsylvania and Burlington County, New Jersey," *Geographic Information System Analysis of Topographic Change in Philadelphia, Pennsylvania, During the Last Century*, U.S. Geological Survey (website); Harold Cox, "Filling Low Land: A Story of Ash-Dumping in the Wingohocking Creek Watershed," in Harold Cox, *Utility Cars of Philadelphia (1971)*, History of Philadelphia's Watersheds and Sewers, updated December 4, 2009, phillyh2o.org; Frederick Cusick, "U.S. Studies Say Sinking Houses Built on Bad Fill," *Inquirer*, November 2, 2000; Adam Levine, "From Creek to Sewer: A Brief Overview of Topographical Change in Philadelphia," History of Philadelphia's Watersheds and Sewers, updated February 9, 2018, phillyh2o.org; Adam Levine, "The Grid versus Nature," in *Nature's Entrepot* (Pittsburgh: University of Pittsburgh Press, 2012), 139–159; Thomas J. Walsh, "Redevelopment Hopes Sinking for Logan Triangle," PlanPhilly, January 23, 2010.

Figure 2.7. Proposal for Pastorius Circle, Hartwell Lane, and Lincoln Drive in Chestnut Hill, drafted by J. H. Hutchinson, May 16, 1913

Chestnut Hill celebrated its legacy in 2016. The party was on for what Henry Howard Houston and his son-in-law, George Woodward, started in the 1870s. Houston had spent some of his fortune from the Pennsylvania Railroad on tracts of land for a community first envisioned as Wissahickon Heights. Woodward continued the development of Chestnut Hill—*that* name stuck—designing, defining, and carefully expanding decades into the twentieth century. Today, both men are being "revered as pioneers in sustainability and pillars of the community . . . champions for creating, preserving and promoting the well-regarded quality of life in Chestnut Hill."

But is it a legacy worth celebrating? Or does it need to be rediscovered—and recognized for what it *really* was? "The real key to that community's character," wrote Dan Rottenberg in the *Inquirer* back in 1986, "is the rare brand of benevolent feudalism practiced there for more than a century by the Houston-Woodward family. Just as feudal lords protected their tenants from barbarian invaders, so the Houstons and Woodwards protected their tenants from the equally frightening forces of economic and social change."

George Woodward, it turns out, was "something of an eccentric" with particular, if not peculiar, preferences. He disliked cars with internal combustion engines ("loud and smelly") and drove electric models. He didn't care for light from incandescent bulbs, so he read by kerosene lamps. Woodward dressed in golf knickers and woolen stockings. He shared his ideas about life in an autobiography titled *Memoirs of a Mediocre Man*. But when it came to a vision for expanding and populating Chestnut Hill, Woodward had some very specific preferences as to who was less than mediocre.

Woodward picked up a principle while a student at Yale and later shared it in a talk titled "Landlord and Tenant." According to Woodward, "we used to say in a college fraternity that one fool member always reproduced another fool member. Working on the reverse of this principle, one social asset reproduces his kind in a real estate venture." Implementing his vision of community for the many rental homes he built in Chestnut Hill around two private schools, a country club, and an Episcopal Church (St. Martin-in-the-Fields) that his father-in-law dedicated in 1889, Woodward selected tenants carefully. As planned, the well-off rented the high-end homes in his version of *SimCity*. More modest twin houses built by Woodward were *intended* for the working class. But to his mild dismay (and seeming amusement), the "white collars" were attracted to his sturdy worker twins "and rented every house in sight." Ah, well.

Woodward put to work a second lesson learned at Yale, this one from the lectures of social scientist William Graham Sumner. The professor spoke of a new kind of American, "The Forgotten Man," described as "dependable, self-respecting, and quite unexciting." Sumner envisioned his citizen:

> He works, he votes, generally he prays—but he always pays—yes, above all, he pays. He does not want an office; his name never gets into the newspaper except when he gets married or dies. He keeps production going on. He contributes to the strength of parties. He is flattered before election. He is strongly patriotic. He is wanted, whenever, in his little

circle, there is work to be done or counsel to be given. He may grumble some occasionally to his wife and family, but he does not frequent the grocery or talk politics at the tavern. Consequently, he is forgotten. He is a commonplace man. He gives no trouble. He excites no admiration.

Woodward relished his success at having created a community of 180 families where the folks with the lowest incomes turned out to be "exactly the people who pay their bills and seldom complain."

Plus they were all White. And all were Protestant.

Woodward never rented to minorities: Italians, African Americans, or Jews. In 1920, in "Landlord and Tenant," he proudly said so: "I have consistently refused to rent a house to anyone only because he happened to have the price. I have always inquired into antecedents. I have never taken a Jewish family or allowed one to be taken as a subtenant." Other ethnics need not apply either.

This legacy of exclusion in Chestnut Hill became an operating principle that stuck. In 1960, Chestnut Hill–insider Barbara Rex broke free and "used fiction to unmask what she saw as inequities and injustices." Rex described her community as "all-white, privileged, prejudiced, Protestant, aristocratic Philadelphia society, where exclusion was a beast that struck down the weak, unfit, or unwary." In her novel *Vacancy on India Street*, Rex wrote of the deep worry about outsiders moving in:

Connie could not conceive of Joe Setteventi strolling around Flora's yard, the stump of a cigar in his red face, and Mrs. Setteventi waving from the bay window. The Setteventi children were cat lovers, carried cats around in their arms all day. Now the birds would never come back.

"Well, at least they are not Jews," said Connie's friend. "You're just as glad as I am we don't have Jews on India Street! . . . Look what's happened on Franklin Street. They've got Jews over there, three in a row. . . . Nobody lives on Franklin Street anymore."

As for African Americans, according to Rex, "no Negro has ever so much as attempted to violate the special domain" of the neighborhood. "Houses come up for sale in the community, but it simply would not occur to a negro to apply." One of Rex's characters, Clayton Cruikshank, however, "had defiled his sister's memory by daring to sell her house to a Negro." But Cruikshank wasn't playing straight. He "had been seen drunk on India Street on Christmas morning, wearing a woman's hat."

There goes the neighborhood.

Chestnut Hill's legacy? Attractive, well-crafted homes in a leafy, planned community built on Wissahickon schist, cemented with bigotry, and engineered for consistency, complacency, and comfort. But definitely *not* for everybody.

Recognizing and remembering makes all the sense in the world. But why a celebration?

———

Sources: David R. Contosta, *A Philadelphia Family: The Houstons and Woodwards of Chestnut Hill* (Philadelphia: University of Pennsylvania Press, 1992) and "George Woodward, Philadelphia Progressive," *The Pennsylvania Magazine of History and Biography* 111, no. 3 (July 1987), 341–370; Jennifer Lin, "Barbara Rex, 97, Editor, Author and Social Critic," *Inquirer*, January 2, 2002; Dan Rottenberg, "Woodward of Chestnut Hill the Last of Philadelphia's Feudal Lords," *Inquirer*, April 30, 1986; Pete Mazzaccaro, "Weeklong Event Marks Woodward Family's Contributions to the Hill," *Chestnut Hill Local*, May 18, 2016; Barbara Rex, *Vacancy on India Street: A Novel* (New York: Norton, 1967); William Graham Sumner, *The Forgotten Man and Other Essays* (New Haven: Yale University Press, 1918), http:// oll.libertyfund.org/titles/sumner-the-forgotten-man-and-other-essays -corrected-edition; George Woodward, MD, "Landlord and Tenant," *The Survey*, September 1920–March 1921; George Woodward, MD, *Memoirs of a Mediocre Man* (Philadelphia: Harris and Partridge, 1935).

Figure 2.8. Le Bon Bon Club (formerly the Top Hat Cafe), looking east on Locust Street from Thirteenth, October 30, 1959

The Top Hat Cafe opened at 1235 Locust Street in the early 1950s and almost immediately slid off the rails. Outside the bar, on March 1, 1952, Nicholas Virgilio "was slapping around a 16-year old girl . . . when a sailor grabbed his hand to stop him." Virgilio, twenty-three, known as the "lothario of the taprooms" and "Nicky the Blade," "swung around, grabbed a switchblade from his pocket and plunged it into Glenn Long, 19, a sailor stationed at the Navy Yard." It would be the first of several murders by Virgilio, the most notorious of which would be the 1978 bar room execution of an ex-judge in Atlantic City.

The new captain of the police station at Twelfth and Pine, Frank L. Rizzo, knew a bad thing when he saw it. Rizzo targeted the Top Hat for his very first raid. The mayor-to-be showed up at the stationhouse at three thirty in the morning on Friday, May 30. He and three other officers walked two blocks north to the Top Hat. "Within minutes, Rizzo and his team had arrested the bartender, two waitresses, the owner, [and] nine patrons," one of whom scuffled with Rizzo, ripping the captain's new suit. For Rizzo, that raid would be the first of hundreds on the Locust Strip.

Le Bon Bon Club replaced the Top Hat in the midfifties, showing off new neon signage but otherwise the same: strippers mixing with patrons, after-hours service, underage drinking, B-girls soliciting drinks, and other nefarious services. The naked city, literally and figuratively, in all its gritty glory.

A decade later, Rizzo testified in Washington before the Senate Rackets Subcommittee about Philadelphia's "'exotic' dancers-turned-B-girls" of the Locust Strip. "These obscene and indecent shows will simply not be tolerated," he told the press. "They must clean up and run respectable places of business or get out . . . This is the beginning. We're going to keep after them until they clean up."

And Rizzo's sustained campaign seemed to make a difference—for a while, anyway. "For the time being, the personality of Locust St. is being suppressed," wrote Joseph Daughen in the *Bulletin*. "The awesome image of Rizzo's Raiders has apparently thrown fear into the hearts of the stripperie operators, and the come hither hostesses are now thither." But as Jeff Goldblum, playing Dr. Ian Malcolm, a chaos theory expert in *Jurassic Park* put it, "Life, uh . . . finds a way." And where there is life—or lurid life, anyway—journalists will write about it.

Nine years later, the Locust Strip was "a collage of schlock on a one night stand," wrote Fred Hamilton in the *Bulletin*. "The present Locust St. bust-out joint [is] somewhere between the cult of the 33 RPM record and the era of Day-Glo paint," he stated. "It has all the glamour of post nasal drip." He continued his description of the area, writing, "The Strip is not blaring music and flashing neon. It is a handful of broken-down joints . . .

It is busty girls and scratchy records played full volume and all the flat black painted walls you'll ever want to see. The strip is a cliché."

A year later, Sandy Grady noted yet another crackdown on B-girls: "Last week District Attorney Arlen Specter buried The Strip under a ton of padlocks." Nine bars in all were closed, including the Bag of Nails at 1231 Locust, the HMS Pinafore at 1233 Locust, and the Revolution at 1219 Locust. "The Strip looks like the inside of Grant's tomb," wrote Grady.

He found an enraged cabbie: "Look Mac, if you're from out of town hunting action forget it! Locust Street is dead. Go over to Jersey. Listen Mac, this is the fourth biggest town in the country and it's a graveyard," the cabbie fumed. "The do-gooders killed this town."

The cabbie wasn't the only one upset. "Every city has its strip," complained "a girl in a see-through blouse" to *Bulletin* reporter L. Stuart Ditzen. "'Yeah,' agreed a timid looking man in a brown suit who said he was a patron of the padlock bars. 'Every city has its strip.'"

The Why Not Lounge at 1305 Locust Street claimed to be the final holdout. In May 1974, the Why Not went away too. The Pennsylvania Liquor Control Board had ended an era—or so they thought.

Three years later, the *Bulletin*'s D. I. Strunk went in search of the Locust Strip and found it alive, if not very well. He visited the PGA Bunny Club, Salsa, Footlights Lounge, and Bag of Nails. He encountered "girls . . . dressed in pasties and tiny bikinis." He saw them "dance and gyrate against mirrors . . . so smeared that a ton of Windex couldn't clean them."

Strunk saw the "potpourri of racial and social and economic classes who come to drink and look . . . men with knit caps, sailors, businessman, customers, clerks, lawyers" who were all coming "to sit and drink and watch together under the same roof." "I come down here to think and forget about other things," said one regular, a lawyer named Tom. "Everybody has their eyes on somebody else's fancy," philosophized Jerome, a patron standing in the shadows outside All in the Family Lounge.

Life finds a way, indeed.

———

Sources: "Two Girls, 16, Testify They Got Liquor in Cafe," *Philadelphia Inquirer,* March 31, 1952; "Fiery Hearing Climaxes Raid on Cafe by Rizzo," *Philadelphia Inquirer,* May 31, 1952; "Rizzo Vows Midcity Cleanup, Nabs 13 in Raids on 3 Clubs," *Philadelphia Daily News,* July 25, 1961; Joseph Daughen, "Center-City Booze Bistros Have Lost Their A-Peal," *Bulletin,* June 14, 1962; Fred Hamilton, "Locust Street Strip: A Collage of Schlock and Lots of Hard Sell," *Bulletin,* August 13, 1971; L. Stuart Ditzen, "Dancers and Barmaids Are Glum as 9 'Strip' Bars Close," *Bulletin,* June 10, 1972; Sandy Grady, "That Crackdown on B-Girls Ends All Our Worries," *Bulletin,* June 13, 1972; Joseph D. McCaffrey, "Era is Ending as Bars Close on Locust St.," *Bulletin,* May 15, 1974; D. I. Strunk, "They Try to Keep Locust Lushland Sedately Sinful," *Bulletin,* October 16, 1977; S. A. Paolantonio, *Frank Rizzo: The Last Big Man in Big City America* (Philadelphia: Camino Books, 1993); Kitty Caparella, "'The Blade' Is Cut Down: Killer Nicholas Virgilio Dies in Prison," *Philadelphia Daily News,* March 18, 1995.

Figure 2.9. "Honeymoon Couple" near Second and Pine Streets, Society Hill, June 17, 1968

When it comes to talking about urban change, words serve their purpose until they are considered inadequate, wrong, or simply out of style. *Slum* and *urban renewal*, for instance, have both enjoyed periods of popularity. Usage of these terms peaked in the second half of the 1960s but then faded. Could it be that we're beginning to see a similar downturn for *gentrification*?

Sociologist Ruth Glass coined *gentrification* in 1964. "Once this process of 'gentrification' starts," Glass wrote of a downtrodden district in London, "it goes on rapidly until all or most of the working class occupiers are displaced and the whole social character of the district is changed." The word focuses on the shifting "social character" of communities—poor neighborhoods becoming upscale destinations.

A year before Glass introduced the term, Nathaniel Burt wryly noted in *Philadelphia Gentleman*, "Remodeling old houses is . . . one of Old Philadelphia's favorite indoor sports, and to be able to remodel and consciously serve the cause of civic revival all at once has gone to the heads of the upper classes like champagne." Burt understood that the "Renaissance of Society Hill [was] just one piece of a gigantic jigsaw puzzle" with the potential "to transform the city completely." But a one-word shorthand for that complex puzzle? Not for Burt.

City planner Edmund Bacon preferred *renewal* in his 1962 film *Form, Design and the City*. But according to Denise Scott Brown, Bacon put too much emphasis on retailing and on "a certain kind of 'center city living' as expressed by Society Hill . . . its coffee bars, tree lined streets, cobbled squares." Such amenities appealed more to "sophisticated intellectuals and professionals" than to anyone else. Anyway, Scott Brown concluded, they are "only part of the story."

The popular press and the public soon became enamored with the idea of gentrification. In October 1977, the *Inquirer* introduced the word on page one for the first time: "Gentrification is an imposing word for a process familiar to all Philadelphians," wrote Richard Ben Cramer, "especially to those who lived 20 years ago in Society Hill, or 10 years ago near the art museum or more recently in Queen Village . . . A neighborhood close to Center City, filled with poorer residents, mostly renters, is suddenly 'discovered' by middle-class people who rush in to buy and renovate the houses in the area. The run-down neighborhood suddenly becomes attractive. Higher-priced shops and restaurants open. The sidewalks, gardens, curbs, even the streets themselves are better tended. And the poor? Well, the poor go elsewhere."

The year following Cramer's story, *gentrification* appeared five times in the *Inquirer* and the *Daily News*. In 1979 and 1980, it was used twenty-five times. Between 1981 and 1990, *gentrification* had become a staple of urban discourse, appearing more than five hundred times. "[Just] as Ruth Glass intended," noted social scientists, *gentrification* "simply yet very powerfully" captured a sense of the "class inequalities and injustices" that existed—even if some preferred the term for the wrong reasons. It implied the existence of a privileged "gentry," bored by their suburban experiment and willing to return to a city with less foliage but a richer quality of life. Popular opinion in some quarters assumed, or hoped, that gentrification would significantly transform the entire city.

The term gained credibility and legitimacy as an accepted shorthand for the cycle of disinvestment, decline, reinvestment, and revival. Public and planners came to believe that gentrification's cycles were desirable and sustainable—a viable model for urban change.

As evidence, advocates presented the soaring values of Society Hill real estate, which rose nearly 250 percent during the 1960s alone. Discussions quickly turned to speculation regarding the location that would become "the next Society Hill." Queen Village? Fairmount? Northern Liberties? But those were three nearby neighborhoods in a city with scores more, most of which lacked proximity to Center City.

Critics saw gentrification as "pompous and irrelevant," an antivernacular "Trojan horse for postindustrial sustainability." Neil Smith's close look at data on the newcomers to Society Hill in the 1960s revealed that the vast majority were not the suburban "gentry" being reurbanized but rather folks from other city neighborhoods. Only 14 percent came from suburbia. Smith concluded that "the so-called urban renaissance has been stimulated more by economic than cultural forces." When it came to making a "decision to rehabilitate an inner-city structure, one consumer preference tends to stand out above the others—the preference for profit."

How had this flawed shorthand made its way into the heart of the urban lexicon? Perhaps the original heady promise of a dual upgrade in class and investment was the result of "too many glasses of chardonnay . . .

shared between researcher and gentrifier," suggested researchers in "Walking Backwards to the Future."

More and more, discussions of gentrification suggest counterintuitive, even contradictory findings that it is *not* the defining experience in Philadelphia or most other American cities. One recent Pew study found that only 15 of Philadelphia's 372 residential census tracts gentrified from 2000 to 2014, and those tracts tended to be contiguous to or near Center City. Meanwhile, in the same years, "more than 10 times that many census tracts—164 in all—experienced statistically significant drops in median household income."

In other words, after more than half a century, "gentrification" may finally be fading as an accurate, reliable, go-to description for urban change. Instead, we should be examining a more complicated array of influences. And in reality, that process is averse to any kind of shorthand.

———

Sources: Denise Scott Brown, "Review of Form, Design, and the City," *Journal of the American Institute of Planners* 28, no. 4 (1962); Richard Ben Cramer, "Back to the City, London Style," *Philadelphia Inquirer*, October 9, 1977; Dylan Gottlieb, "Gentrification," *Encyclopedia of Greater Philadelphia* (Camden: Rutgers, 2014); Tim Butler and Chris Hamnett, "Walking Backwards to the Future: Waking Up to Class and Gentrification in London," *Urban Policy and Research* 27, no. 3 (2009); Susan Mayhew, *A Dictionary of Geography*, 5th ed. (Oxford: Oxford University Press, 2015); Pew Charitable Trusts, *Philadelphia's Changing Neighborhoods—Gentrification and Other Shifts since 2000*, Pew report, May 2016; Neil Smith, "Gentrification," *Encyclopedia of Housing*, ed. Willem van Vliet (Thousand Oaks: Sage, 1998), 198–199; Neil Smith, "Toward a Theory of Gentrification: A Back to the City Movement by Capital, Not People," in *The Gentrification Debates: A Reader*, ed. Japonica Brown-Saracino (Abingdon-on-Thames: Routledge, 2013).

Figure 3.1. Demolition of the Bank of Pennsylvania in 1867, looking
west from Second Street, north of Walnut Street (Library Company of
Philadelphia)

CHAPTER 3

Architecture and Urban Design

PHILADELPHIA AS ATHENS OF AMERICA: MORE THAN SKIN DEEP

Philadelphia's façade of choice used to be one bedecked with columns—and the more the better. Greek and Roman orders ruled from the late eighteenth century clear through much of the nineteenth century. Whether you had a bank, a church, a town hall, a school, or an asylum, classical features sent the preferred message as visitors passed your portal. Want to convey a sense of wealth? Go Greek. Need to speak the language of civic importance or educational authority? Say it with a stack of stone cylinders. Folks were even willing to forgive their pre-Christian origins and pray behind pagan porticoes.

Benjamin Henry Latrobe gets the credit for giving Quaker Philadelphia permission to lose the red brick and cloak almost everything in white marble. And he practiced what he preached in 1811, when he orated that "the days of Greece may be revived in the woods of America and Philadelphia become the Athens of the Western World." Latrobe's own Philadelphia commissions—the Pump House in Center Square and the Bank of Pennsylvania—were, literally and figuratively, classics.

None of Latrobe's major works survive in Philadelphia, although you can see his marble magic in other places. Latrobe went on to Washington, DC; Baltimore; and Richmond before succumbing to yellow fever while on the job in New Orleans in 1820. Where Latrobe left off, his students (and then *their* students) picked up and carried on. There's William Strickland's Merchant's Exchange, Second Bank, U.S. Naval Home, and U.S. Mint. There's Thomas U. Walter's Founder's Hall at Girard College, Mercantile Library on Fifth Street, Jefferson Medical College on Tenth Street, and the First Independent Presbyterian Church on Broad Street.

Philadelphia as the Athens of America was always more than skin deep. The very idea that Philadelphia would inherit Greek arts and ideals goes back to the very beginning when Penn named his city in Greek. That Philadelphia would become the New World's center for democracy, arts, and learning might have been pushed aside for a few busy decades, but it was never entirely forgotten.

In the early 1730s, founders of the Library Company of Philadelphia described Philadelphia as "the future of Athens in America." A few years before that, poet George Webb, called "the first major prophet of the America of Athenaeums, civic temples, and 'new Romans,'" wrote a poem that concludes with a few evocative lines:

> Stretch'd on the Bank of Delaware's rapid Stream
>
> Stands Philadelphia, not unknown to Fame:
>
> Here the tall Vessels safe at Anchor ride,
>
> And Europe's Wealth flows in with every Tide:
>
> . . .
>
> Who (if the wishing Muse inspir'd does sing)
>
> Shall Liberal Arts to such Perfection bring,
>
> Europe shall mourn her ancient Fame declin'd,
>
> And Philadelphia be the Athens of Mankind.

Webb had plenty of company believing in this big idea for small Philadelphia.

No, Latrobe didn't *invent* the idea of Philadelphia as the rightful heir to ancient greatness. He only reminded Philadelphians what they had long known—and urged them to put the Greek out where everyone might actually see it.

———

Sources: David S. Shields, "The Wits and Poets of Pennsylvania: New Light on the Rise of Belles Lettres in Provincial Pennsylvania, 1720–1740," *Pennsylvania Magazine of History and Biography* 109, no. 2 (April 1985); *Benjamin Latrobe: America's First Architect,* directed by Michael Epstein (Washington, DC: Kunhardt, McGee Productions and WETA, 2010), DVD; *"At the Instance of Benjamin Franklin": A Brief History of the Library Company of Philadelphia, 1731–1976,* rev. ed. (1976; repr., Philadelphia: Library Company of Philadelphia, 1995).

Figure 3.2. The Merchants Exchange Building, Walnut and Dock Streets, William Strickland (architect), built 1832–1834 and photographed ca. 1865 (The Library Company of Philadelphia)

By the 1830s, you'd have thought folks might have grown a bit tired of seeing every architect translating everything into Greek. And they might have been, had it not been for William Strickland's way of combining the very old and the very new. The most creative of the homegrown generation of architects and engineers, he didn't shy away from moving the game up a few notches. Strickland pulled out his copy of Stuart's *Antiquities of Athens*, a book that had been around for seventy years and had long been used as a source for architects like Benjamin Henry Latrobe, John Haviland, and Strickland himself.

But the stakes were higher now. Strickland faced the challenge of making architectural sense on a very prominent and oddly shaped building lot bordered by Dock, Walnut, and Third Streets. He found himself working in the shadow of his mentor's masterpiece, Latrobe's Bank of Pennsylvania. This site demanded a commanding solution—and an innovative one. Squeezing a rectangular Greek temple onto a triangular building lot just wouldn't do. Strickland needed to find a bolder design solution and a very carefully considered one. He positioned on the narrow end of this wedge of land a raised, semicircular portico, making the eastern façade look like a grand entrance on a civic square. (In reality, this was the grand, rounded-off *back* of the building. Strickland made Third Street the user-friendly entrance.)

Here in Philadelphia, a few blocks from the city's riverfront, facing the morning sun (the same sun that illuminated ancient Athens), stood Strickland's own masterpiece. Unlike his other Greek Revival buildings, this was no replica ripped from the pages of *Antiquities of Athens*. Here was a 3-D billboard of Greek features to serve "modern" Philadelphia.

For the cupola, which pulled the entire project together, Strickland found inspiration in Stuart's illustration of a 334 BC monument still very much standing on the streets of Athens. The Choragic Monument of Lysicrates was a self-congratulatory, twenty-one-foot pedestal for a choral prize won at a performing arts competition, part of the same festival that produced the great dramas of Aeschylus, Sophocles, and Euripides. Stuart and William Henry Playfair had designed literal replicas in Staffordshire and Edinburgh. Here in Philadelphia, Strickland took great liberties with the design and achieved very American results.

He moved the "monument" from street level to the roof. He blew it up to double the size of the original, making a giant forty-foot-tall, fourteen-foot-diameter skyline-defining structure like no one had ever seen. And instead of interpreting the Choragic Monument of Lysicrates in stone for the ages, Strickland designed it in wood. (It was susceptible to the elements and would have to be replaced about every sixty years.) Now far from Europe, this pop-art-scaled, archeologically correct, and ephemeral monument would echo the past. But even more important, here above Philadelphia's 1830s cityscape, this landmark would live very much in the moment.

The Merchants Exchange—and, in particular, the tower at its eastern end—would also become an essential element in a new, high-tech information network. Long before 1837 when Samuel F. B. Morse patented his telegraph (and way before anyone dreamed of the internet) Europeans and Americans had "optical telegraphs" capable of quickly transmitting coded messages over great distances. As early as 1807, the U.S. Congress had debated and eventually voted in favor of funding a 1,200-mile-long chain of optical telegraph towers connecting New York and New Orleans—a project that eventually fell by the wayside. But it wasn't all that farfetched. More than a decade earlier, Claude Chappe's invention, the "semaphore visual telegraph," came to life in France as a 143-mile connection between Paris and Lille and would grow into a network of more than five hundred towers across Europe, extending 3,000 miles. In 1799, when Napoleon Bonaparte came to power, he envisioned crossing the English Channel with the technology.

So when American architect William Thornton envisioned connecting North and South America in 1800, the possibility wasn't implausible. Before long, American businessmen in Boston and New York had their own optical telegraph networks. And by the time the construction of the Merchants Exchange was underway, an optical telegraph in Boston was already tracking shipping and commerce and guiding investments on a real-time basis. "Time and distance are annihilated" became the popular proclamation, a mantra of the 1830s.

No surprise then that the Merchant Exchange's cupola high above Dock and Walnut Streets played not single or double but *triple* duty: it served as a perch for clerks with telescopes identifying ships making their way to and from the Port of Philadelphia, as an optical telegraph sending and receiving messages that flashed to and from New York across the plains of New Jersey, and—most lasting and resonant of all—as a literal symbol declaring that the city had, at long last, had come into its own as the modern-day version of ancient Athens.

———

Sources: Richard R. John, *Network Nation: Inventing American Telecommunications* (Cambridge: Harvard University Press, 2010); Domenic Vitiello and George E. Thomas, *The Philadelphia Stock Exchange and the City It Made* (Philadelphia: University of Pennsylvania Press, 2010); *Encyclopaedia Britannica Online*, s.v. "Choragic Monument"; Philadelphia Historical Commission, Merchant's Exchange, files, Philadelphia City Hall.

Figure 3.3. Walnut Lane Bridge, June 10, 1910

Sauntering deep in the recesses of Fairmount Park a century ago, Christopher Morley and his know-everything guide were just about "to sentimentalize upon the beauty of nature and how it shames the crass work of man" when they came upon "perhaps the loveliest thing along the Wissahickon—the Walnut Lane Bridge."

Leaping high in the air from the very domes of the trees, curving in a sheer smooth superb span that catches the last western light on its concrete flanks, it flashes across the darkened valley as nobly as an old Roman viaduct of southern France. It is a thrilling thing, and I scrambled up the bank to note down the names of the artists who planned it. The tablet is dated 1906, and bears the names of George S. Webster, chief engineer; Henry H. Quimby, assistant engineer; Reilly & Riddle, contractors. Many poets have written versus both good and bad about the Wissahickon, but Messrs. Reilly & Riddle have spanned it with the poem that will long endure.

As chief engineer of the Department of Public Works and Bureau of Surveys, Webster "had long argued that a high-level bridge between Rox-borough and Germantown would eliminate a hilly five- or six-mile detour into the Wissahickon Creek valley." He considered proposing "a steel via-duct with a wooden floor" but thought better of it. Webster envisioned a bridge more appropriate for the "natural park scenery of rocky and wooded slopes."

In 1905, the city council granted Webster his wish, authorizing construc-tion of an elegant arched bridge and allocating funds to unite the two neigh-borhoods "at the narrowest point of the ravine, along the line of Walnut Lane." The project began July 5, 1906, and lasted two dramatic years.

When complete, Walnut Lane would be the largest concrete bridge in the world, inspired "structurally and aesthetically" by the recently opened Pont Adolphe over the Pétrusse River in Luxembourg.

Forty thousand tons of concrete never looked so much like a line of poetry. Giant arches stretched across the ravine, providing a path more than 145 feet above "the most picturesque portion of the Park." It seemed as if the bridge was "literally springing from out the foliage of the tree tops."

Reilly and Riddle poured concrete arches atop a gigantic, nine-hundred-ton falsework of steel and lumber that "for the sake of economy" was used twice, once for each rib. In a demonstration of skill, faith, and engineer-ing finesse, four temporary concrete piers in the stream bed supported the falsework and provided a glide path for shifting it from under the first finished rib to where the second one would rise. To move the falsework, thirty men operated a massive ball-bearing jack at pier level, nudging the falsework thirty-four feet, inch by inch. The operation took three days. At the conclusion of the job, Reilly and Riddle demolished the piers with dynamite, returning the creek bed to its natural state.

"It is the greatest bridge of its kind in the world," glowed Mayor John Reyburn at the dedication, before school children from Roxborough, Manayunk, and Germantown sang in symbolic unison. "It was conceived and executed by our own men," he boasted and suggested that fact alone made it worth the price. Never mind that its status as the largest concrete arch in the world was quickly surpassed by the new Detroit–Rocky River Bridge in Cleveland and the Grafton Bridge in Auckland, New Zealand. In a city of makers, Philadelphia had made more than a new bridge; it had created "one of the wonders of the world."

Whatever became of all that construction debris, in particular the nine-hundred tons of lumber used to build the temporary falsework? On March 29, 1908, an advertisement in the *Inquirer* put out the word: three hundred thousand feet of new pine lumber, "all sizes and lengths to 30 feet long," was available at the bargain rate of fourteen dollars per thousand feet: "Come to the bridge, take your pick, haul it away." The advertisement didn't bother to specify which end of the bridge, Germantown or Roxborough. But that detail no longer mattered much. East and west were nearly one and the same.

———

Sources: Christopher Morley, "Up the Wissahickon," *Travels in Philadelphia* (Philadelphia: David McKay, 1920); J. A. Stewart, "The New Bridge over the Wissahickon at Philadelphia," *Scientific American*, November 30, 1907; George S. Webster and Henry H. Quimby, "Walnut Lane Bridge, Philadelphia," *Transactions of the American Society of Civil Engineers* 65 (1909); "Mammoth Arch to Span Wissahickon," *Inquirer*, March 20, 1906; "New Walnut Lane Bridge Is Dedicated to City's Use," *Inquirer*, December 17, 1908; "Walnut Lane Bridge," Pennsylvania Historic Bridges Recording Project-II, Historic American Engineering Record, PA-504 (website).

Figure 3.4. Firehouse #2, southwest corner, Warnock and Berks Streets, March 23, 1931

A building boom of 1889 had more structures going up in Philadelphia than during any other year in the entire history of the city. On the streets, that translated to the city pushing outward in every possible direction. On the books, that meant seventy new factories, sixty-five additional shops and foundries, sixty-five stores, thirty warehouses, five freight stations, three market houses, and as many hospitals. The spires of eighteen new churches reached heavenward, punctuating more than eleven miles of new row houses. In North Philadelphia alone, just west of Broad Street, more than 1,800 homes extended the city's grid dynamically, if somewhat monotonously, to the north. Five hundred and eighty new houses pushed the city to the south. And in West Philadelphia, developers obtained building permits for 1,500 additional residences.

Everyone expected 1890 to be an "even more prosperous" year. After all, open land near Twenty-Ninth and Susquehanna that had been selling for $1,000 per acre now fetched up to $30,000 per acre. "Everything points to success," claimed one optimistic developer. "If we build 10,000 houses a year we are only supplying the demand of our growing population."

The thing was, the city's own participation in this phenomenal growth was seriously stunted. Only one solitary fire station and three patrol houses were built in 1889, and politicians scrambled to close the gap. Dancing in their heads were visions of something new rather than the same old firehouses and police stations; those had been outgrown in so many ways. Here was the chance to fix the problem while also crafting new, updated symbols for the expanding metropolis. And who could disagree with more and better services from more and better municipal facilities?

Something about firehouses made them ripe for architectural expression. Could it have been firefighting's historic culture of rowdyism channeling into architectural design? Or, as Rebecca Zurier suggested in *The American Firehouse*, maybe there was "no prevailing 'proper' style for a fire station, [so] architects tried nearly all of them." In firehouses, Zurier wrote, architects executed designs "considered too outlandish for another type of building." She continued, "No one ever complained about a fire station being undignified."

Philadelphia historian John Maass agreed. In the mid-twentieth century, "municipal officials generally want[ed] inconspicuous fire stations lest they be accused of wasting taxpayers' money." But in the 1890s, "political bosses used to glory in building the showiest firehouses." Purposeful extravagance resulted in "a wondrous variety of architectural styles," wrote Maass, from "Greek Revival, Italianate, Second Empire, Richardsonian Romanesque [to] French Chateauesque, Castellated, Half-timbered Tudor, Prairie Style, Spanish Colonial, Pueblo Adobe, Art Deco, Ugly & Ordinary Venturian." The American firehouse had become, and would remain, a genre all its own.

In 1891, the election of Mayor Edwin S. Stuart allowed him to extend the construction campaign citywide. As the Bureau of City Property looked ahead, they allocated more than half of their next yearly budget for "new stations and new engine houses." To help carry out Stuart's vision in style, he brought in architect James H. Windrim as director of public works. But Windrim already had too much work from other clients and turned his partner and son, John T. Windrim, loose on the city streets. Over the next several years, Windrim the younger expanded the city's footprint in a string of gemlike fire stations. By the 1910s, the list had grown long—long enough to be called Philadelphia's Fin-de-Siècle Firehouse Boom.

More than a century later, some firehouses have been lost to time, and a few others remain in various stages of threat and preservation. Here is a partial list of firehouses designed by, or attributed to, Windrim. The last four are extant:

> 1892—Engine Company #42, Front and Westmoreland Streets
> 1893—Engine Company #2, Berks and Warnock Streets
> 1894—Engine Company #43, Twenty-First Street near Market Street
> 1894—Engine Company # 45, Twenty-Sixth and York Streets
> 1894—Engine Company #46, Reed and Water Streets
> 1894—Engine Company #37, West Highland Avenue and Shawnee Street
> 1895—Engine Company # 16, Belmont Avenue near Wyalusing Avenue
> 1895—Engine Company #29, North Fourth Street near West Girard Avenue

———

Sources: "The Boom in Building: More Structures Erected in 1889 than during Any Previous Year," *Inquirer*, November 9, 1889; "A Model Station House: Opening of the New Seventeenth District Fire, Police and Patrol Station," *Inquirer*, May 13, 1890; "A New Style of Station Houses (Front and Westmoreland)," *Inquirer*, September 29, 1892; "A New Police and Fire Station (Chestnut Hill)," *Inquirer*, October 4, 1894; "A New Engine House: Fourth Street above Girard Avenue," *Inquirer*, February 28, 1895; "New Fire Station: It Will Be Opened for Use in a Few Days," *Inquirer*, March 7, 1895; "New Fire House: West Philadelphia Boys Will Occupy It To-Morrow," *Inquirer*, June 21, 1896; Rebecca Zurier, *The American Firehouse: An Architectural and Social History* (New York: Abbeville Press, 1982); John Maass, "Review of The American Firehouse: An Architectural and Social History by Rebecca Zurier," *Journal of the Society of Architectural Historians* 42, no. 2 (May 1983).

Figure 3.5. Engine Company #45, northeast corner, Twenty-Sixth and York Streets, 1908

As director of public works, Windrim had an advantage getting commissions, but there was far more work, and a larger appetite for design diversity, than any one architect could handle. Projects went out to bid, and many architects and contractors responded. What resulted, Philadelphia's Fin-de-Siècle Firehouse Boom, put as many as fifty firehouses on the streets between 1890 and the 1910, a prodigious display of design finesse. Have we ever heard of such a demonstration in municipal architecture?

In the mid-twentieth century, Columbus, Indiana, commissioned more than sixty municipal buildings "by a veritable who's who of modern masters," including I. M. Pei, Eero and Eliel Saarinen, Cesar Pelli, Richard Meier, Harry Weese, and Philadelphia's Robert Venturi (who, in 1967, created Fire Station No. 4).

Philadelphia's names were not *that* big, but the design frenzy at the turn of the twentieth century occurred at the very interesting intersection of public demand and indigenous talent. Where Columbus lured "starchitects" from far and wide and funded their arrival with philanthropy, Philadelphia's homegrown creative burst took place in its own space, in its own time, and on its own terms.

Unfortunately, much of this fine work has gotten lost in the shuffle over the last century. In truth, we barely even know the extent that once was. A few private efforts at compilation hope to fill the yawning information gap (see Mike Legeros's online list of "Historic and Former Philadelphia Firehouses"). It is impossible to just dip a toe in the complicated architectural history of Philly firefighting. It's a steep, slippery, and largely silent slope. But what one encounters makes the ride well worth the price of admission.

Edward P. Hazlehurst and William Samuel Huckel Jr. started a long and prolific partnership in the early 1880s, generating 326 projects of all kinds. Their combination police station and firehouse stood at the northwest corner of Seventh and Carpenter Streets until it was demolished in 1962.

Joseph M. Huston generated impressive projects, including the Pennsylvania State Capitol, a job that proved a show stopper—literally. A scandal involving a conspiracy to defraud the commonwealth led to conviction and a residency for the architect at Eastern State Penitentiary. Before all that, in 1899 and 1900, he designed several firehouses—none of which survive. Huston's stationhouse for the Sixth Police District at Eleventh and Winter Streets, a lovely little Georgian Revival number, has also disappeared.

Not to be confused with the modernist architect Philip Johnson, Phillip H. Johnson was famous for landing, through skill and connectedness, a lifetime contract with the city health department that earned his office more than $2 million over three decades. Johnson's projects included the Philadelphia General Hospital, Philadelphia Hospital for Contagious Diseases and buildings at the Philadelphia Hospital for Mental Diseases (a.k.a. Byberry). He also designed City Hall Annex. Johnson cut his teeth on several firehouse projects including those located at 1016–1018 South Street, Fiftieth and Baltimore Avenue, 1529–1539 Parrish Street, and 2936–2938 Ridge Avenue. All these survive except the last, which was demolished in 1994.

Charles E. Oelschlager's projects included churches, theatres (moving picture and vaudeville), and early gas stations. His 1899 firehouse at Thirty-First and Grays Ferry Road didn't survive to present day, however his three-bay firehouse at 1900 Cambria Street east of Broad remains in use. Behind its terra-cotta, redbrick façade and beneath its green, slate-covered mansard roof were nine horse stalls, sleeping quarters for the crew, four sliding poles, and all the latest appliances, including electric bells and buzzers.

W. Bleddyn Powell's projects included the completion of City Hall. His less grandiose commissions were a combined firehouse/patrol station at Fourth and Snyder, now gone, and a police station at Nineteenth and Oxford that later served as the first Opportunities Industrialization Center.

E. V. Seeler is known for sixty-five projects, including Curtis Publishing Company on Washington Square, the nearby Penn Mutual Life Insurance Building, and the Philadelphia Bulletin Building on Filbert Street, formerly northeast of City Hall. *His* breakthrough took place with the First Baptist Church in 1901, which appeared at the corner of Seventeenth and Sansom Streets, not far from the still-extant firehouse at 1528–1530 Sansom completed two years earlier.

Anyone who has the opportunity should take a Fin-de-Siècle Firehouse Boom tour, at least of those specimens that survive.

_____

Sources: Mike Legeros, Historic and Former Philadelphia Firehouses, updated August 7, 2013, https://legeros.com/history/philadelphia/; Susan Stamberg, "Columbus, Ind.: A Midwestern Mecca of Architecture," NPR, July 31, 2012; The Philadelphia Architects and Buildings Project (PAB), The Athenaeum of Philadelphia, https://www.americanbuildings.org/pab/; and sources listed at the end of the previous essay.

Figure 3.6. Benjamin Franklin Parkway, photographed by D. Alonzo Biggard, May 5, 1936

The Renaissance masters understood cities and imagined inventing new and improved examples. They knew important cities must have wide streets. "Broad Streets are more lightsome," declared Andrea Palladio in 1570. "[When] one side of such a Street is . . . less eclipsed by the opposite Side, the Beauty of Churches and Palaces must needs be seen to the Greater advantage in large than narrow Streets, whence the mind is more agreeably entertained and the city more adorned." William Penn borrowed both idea and name for his own Broad Street.

The masters knew that cities thrive when wide streets host a variety of public activities. Leone Battista Alberti advised that "public ways, which may not improperly be called High Streets" should be "designed for some certain Purpose, especially a public one; as for instance those which lead to some Temple or the Course for the Races; or to a Place for Justice."

In the 1680s, Penn envisioned "our intended Metropolis" to boast something that became the view up Broad Street in the 1890s: a bright, welcoming urban center. He also borrowed both the idea and name for his High Street, which was later renamed Market Street. For the city's first two centuries, Market (then Broad) evolved as the city's public armature, accommodating the public institutions that made the city. From market stall to City Hall, all kinds of civic buildings found their places along Philadelphia's vibrant public avenues: churches, clubs, theaters, opera houses, hotels, hospitals, horticultural halls, even opulent mansions and iconic eateries. If a place was meant to contribute to Philadelphia's public life, it could find a home along the city's civic boulevards.

Here was the city that would "never be burnt, and always be wholesome," Penn declared. He had seemingly avoided re-creating the London left behind. *That* city, with its wooden "rickety, slapdash buildings [leaning] against one another like drunks clutching each other for support" had been poised for disaster, according to Edward Dolnick. London's four-day fire of September 1666 left one hundred thousand of its citizens homeless, stunned amid smoldering ruins. Penn took note, and the vision he and his surveyor, Thomas Holme, had in the 1680s would gradually come together—two centuries later.

Would things change in the twentieth century? As Philadelphians became enamored of the automobile and an ironically accompanying movement called "City Beautiful," Philadelphia outgrew its original public avenues. A mile-long, multilane landscaped boulevard lined with civic buildings bisected the city's northwest quadrant and connected City Hall to Fairmount Park. Same idea; different century.

The Parkway became the twentieth-century version of the Renaissance vision for a "lightsome public way," one that would serve motorized Philadelphia. Along it, all types of institutions would be gathered to enhance and enrich public purpose. Anchored by City Hall at the center of the original Penn grid, planners envisioned Parkway with schools, hospitals, libraries, museums, cathedrals, courthouses, administrative headquarters for schools and agencies, and even a convention hall. If it served the public, it belonged on the new Parkway.

Until now. In recent years, noncultural civic institutions along the Parkway have become interlopers, placeholders of real estate for a rising experience economy. At the start of the twenty-first century, we're witnessing a tilt away from the Renaissance and City Beautiful principles that shaped the city in favor of a newer, more simplistic notion aimed at tourism: "The Museum Mile."

One of the earliest public uses of the phrase was in 2002, as the Barnes Foundation explored relocating to the Parkway. "If the move happens," proclaimed Rebecca W. Rimel, president of Pew Charitable Trusts, "Philadelphia will have a 'magic museum mile.'" Philadelphia leaders began using the phrase with greater and greater frequency, focusing on cultural assets, old and new: the Philadelphia Museum of Art's annex in the Fidelity Mutual Building, the Rodin Museum, the Franklin Institute, the Academy of Natural Sciences, and the would-be Calder Museum. And at Logan Square, the cultural footprint included an expanded Free Library of Philadelphia, Moore College of Art, and the latest installment in this constellation of culture, the Barnes Foundation, which replaced the Youth Study Center. The Barnes opened in the spring of 2012.

The "Museum Mile" was an ambitious idea that reflected a two-dimensional vision, considering that museums alone, no how well-stocked or well-appointed, do not a great city make. "No one spends two hours in a museum, then goes down the street to spend two hours in another," urbanist Witold Rybczynski told the *Inquirer* in 2012. "I don't think it's a great idea to have three museums lined up in a row or three stadiums next to each other—there's no synergy in that." The Renaissance masters understood that in their time. So did Penn and Holmes in the seventeenth century. The question is, What do *we* understand in the twenty-first century?

———

Sources: Patricia Horn and Patrick Kerkstra, "Barnes Wants to Move Art Collection to Phila.," *Inquirer*, September 25, 2002; Kenneth Finkel, "Public Architecture and the Emergence of Public Avenues in Philadelphia, 1800–1920" (master's thesis, Temple University, 1978); Carrie Rickey, "A 'Museum Mile' Is Adding Luster to the Parkway," *Inquirer*, May 6, 2012.

Figure 3.7. Parkway model, looking east, in the mayor's reception room, City
Hall, 1911

Imagine John Reyburn's dismay when he was told the massive Parkway project was headed—*literally*—in the wrong direction. Demolition of the first of 1,300 buildings had been under way for two months when Reyburn, Philadelphia's brand new mayor in April 1907, learned that the swath being cut through the northwest quadrant of Center City was off course.

In a meeting with streetcar magnate P. A. B. Widener only days after his inauguration, Reyburn became convinced of the city's mistake. One of the nation's richest and most voracious art collectors, Widener had been trying for more than a decade to get Philadelphians interested in his vision for a new art museum. Why should the Parkway, which started out at foot of the monumental City Hall, come to an unceremonious end in the park when it could terminate with a glorious new museum set high on Fairmount?

Reyburn agreed with Widener and immediately took it upon himself to adjust the Parkway's course. "[Correct] the present line of the Parkway," he wrote in his first annual address, telling the project managers to continue "the removal of buildings on the new line. . . . I want this improvement to be the magnificent work that it ought to be." The Parkway, he insisted, "is an opportunity that no other City in the United States can boast."

But moving the Parkway's axis would add $2 million to an already complicated and expensive project. Could Reyburn convince the city council, business leaders, and the public that they had already gotten off on the wrong foot and needed more money and time?

First, there was compromise. The Parkway's axis *would* be angled to the south of its former line, but planners would *also* artificially extend the rocky Fairmount itself to the north. Second, there was a rethinking of the far end of the Parkway by the city's design establishment. Architect Charles L. Borie embraced the idea of siting the Philadelphia Museum of Art on Fairmount and went even further. He envisioned a grand plaza surrounded by a cluster of institutions for art and art education. As Borie's partner Clarence Zantzinger put it, "The opportunity is . . . unique in any city in the world." The Parkway was now turning into something more than an ambitious boulevard connecting park and city. It was evolving into a sophisticated civic and cultural solution for the new century.

Reyburn continued to build support by appointing a group of bankers and businessmen to serve alongside city officials on a new Comprehensive Plans Committee. Their work was timed to conclude right before a national conference on city planning convened in Philadelphia. In fact, Philadelphia's commitment to urban design had made the city the location of choice for the Third Annual City Planning Conference in May 1911. Frederick Law Olmstead Jr., who headed up the conference the year before, said as much. In terms of city planning, Olmstead flattered Reyburn, "your city is the farthest advanced in the country."

In City Hall, Reyburn proudly hosted two hundred professionals who came from all over the United States. But what was he doing to build support among the taxpaying, voting citizens of Philadelphia? Journalist and planning theorist Charles Mulford Robinson, the man who popularized the phrase "City Beautiful," happily noted that Reyburn's tactic aimed at building *public* support. The conference, wrote Robinson, "was more than its title suggests or promised." The mayor used it as an excuse to mount the "first municipal planning exhibition in America." And the Parkway would be a main focus.

For this exhibition, the Department of Public Works presented new drawings of the reenvisioned Parkway, and they built a thirty-foot model that resided for a full month in the mayor's reception room. The public showed up in droves; twenty thousand reportedly came the first day. They filed past displays lining the corridors of City Hall to see the model, the exhibition's pièce de résistance.

So what did Philadelphia taxpayers, those who would foot the bill for this largely expanded and hugely expensive project, conclude? The idea of the Parkway, which had first been proposed forty long years before as a modest *way* to the park, now looked like something to be proud of, a public avenue to that would come to redefine Philadelphia.

———

Sources: David Brownlee, *Building the City Beautiful: The Benjamin Franklin Parkway and the Philadelphia Museum of Art* (Philadelphia: Philadelphia Museum of Art, 1989); Kenneth Finkel, "Public Architecture and the Emergence of Public Avenues in Philadelphia, 1800–1920" (master's thesis, Temple University, 1978); Charles Mulford Robinson, "City Plans and Planners," *The Survey* 26 (April–September 1911): 397–400; "City Planners Open Sessions Here Tomorrow," *Inquirer*, May 14, 1911.

Round One: The Battle for Gasadelphia

"The ideal filling station has never been built," scoffed a big oil executive in 1922. "I don't think it ever will be built. But we are trying to get it." This was quite an admission for a man whose company, Standard Oil of Indiana, operated 1,400 stations of its own. The *idea* of the gas station had been around for nearly a decade, but the *form* was still very much evolving. By 1920, 15,000 had cropped up across America; by 1929, more than 120,000 would litter the landscape. Other than dispensing gasoline to a burgeoning number of vehicle owners, no two oil companies could agree what a gas station ought to look like. And with money to be made, there was no time for consensus. So in the name of the bottom line, city streets, boulevards, and highways became a living laboratory of asphalt, brick, tin—and flashing electric signage.

The experiments that ultimately gave us the American Gas Station took many forms: sheds and shacks, pyramids and pagodas, cottages and castles, wigwams and windmills. Some even led to extravagant structures modeled on mosques and temples. Design diversity would be the right way to go, admitted an oil executive, "I would not want them all alike. But I would demand of them a family resemblance—a Hapsburg chin, so to speak." Selling gasoline wouldn't be about gasoline, so much as consistency, service, and branding. The oil exec may not have known exactly what he wanted his stations to look like, but he *did* know he wanted them all "recognizable at a distance."

When did the question of what a gas station might look like first get answered? The year was 1913 when William M. Burton patented his process for the "Manufacture of Gasolene," acknowledging a "great and growing demand." The same year, Henry Ford dropped the price of his Model T to $550 and sold more than 308,000 cars. And that's the year Gulf Refining Company opened the first of its purpose-built, drive-in gas stations in Pittsburgh.

Fuel-hungry drivers could finally abandon the pharmacy's ad hoc pail and funnel. Now they could drive past the lines at the tank wagon's garden hose or the curbside pumps standing like afterthoughts outside grocery and hardware stores. In 1913, for the first time, motorists could pull up to paved stations devoted exclusively to servicing the nation's new fleets of cars. Gulf's first station, an octagonal brick kiosk with a cantilevered pagoda-style roof bore the words "Good Gulf Gasoline" spelled out in lights.

Shortly after the model proved itself in Pittsburgh, Gulf built another in Philadelphia, at Thirty-Third and Chestnut Streets. On a good day, attendants pumped 3,000 gallons from ten, 550-gallon underground tanks. "The liberal patronage of our West Philadelphia Service Station . . . and the number of requests from the North Broad Street District have prompted us to build another service station," read the advertisement in the *Philadelphia Evening Bulletin*. The new station at Broad Street and Hunting Park Avenue opened April 17, 1916. "Courteous attendants will supply you—cheerfully pump your tires or fill your radiator . . . free of charge." Need a road map? They were free too. Gulf had found its solution for design and for service—and would stick with this formula for the next decade and a half.

How did the competition respond? How could Atlantic outdo Gulf in a "new marketing offensive?" The Philadelphia and Pittsburgh-based

Atlantic Refining Company formed a committee to brainstorm. They toured stations throughout the state and beyond and decided that this challenge needed the talent of an architect. Joseph F. Kuntz of the Pittsburgh-based W. G. Wilkens and Company got the commission. Gas stations were about to be ramped up to a new level of design—the likes of which had never been seen before or since. The battle for Gasadelphia was about to take off.

————

Sources: Marc W. Melaina, "Turn of the Century Refueling: A Review of Innovations in Early Gasoline Refueling Methods and Analogies for Hydrogen," *Energy Policy* 35, no. 10 (October 2007); John A. Jakle and Keith A. Sculle, *The Gas Station in America* (Baltimore: Johns Hopkins University Press, 1994); Keith A. Sculle, "Atlantic Refining Company's Monumental Service Stations in Philadelphia, 1917–1919," *Journal of American and Comparative Cultures* 23, no. 2 (June 2000); Keith A. Sculle, "Pittsburgh's Monuments to Motoring History: Atlantic's Fabulous Stations," *Western Pennsylvania History*, Fall 2000; "Try to Build a Trade Mark: Family Resemblance in Filling Station Construction Vital," *Petroleum Age* 9 (January 1, 1922).

Figure 3.8. Atlantic Refining Company Gas Station, southeast corner of Broad Street and Roosevelt Boulevard, November 28, 1924

Forget all you know about modern gas stations: the self-service pumps, the lifts, the bays, stretches of oil-stained concrete, bright signage, and bad coffee. A century ago, the widespread sale of gasoline was inevitable, but the solution as to how and where was not yet understood. With a minimum of flair and imagination, Gulf Refining Company quickly arrived at a method to meet the logistical challenge of filling tanks and succeeded in selling lots of fuel.

Atlantic Refining Company would take a different approach. By the 1910s, expressions of stability, permanence, and civic responsibility (a.k.a. City-Beautiful Classicism) worked their design magic on behalf of railroads, power plants, and movie theaters. Why not also put it to work for the oil industry? Atlantic Refining Company executives knew full well that theirs was often a dirty business. They had known it back in the 1860s when the company first stored and spilled oil, and using chromolithography, spun a positive corporate image on the banks of the Schuylkill River.

Now in the new century, the automobile was the big new thing. It seemed it might be as big as the railroad had been in the last century. The automobile would take over and transform the city, for better or worse. If ever there was a need to deploy the full persuasive powers of architecture, this was that time. Why *wouldn't* rich oil refining companies go on a charm offensive, building gas stations that looked like palaces?

Responding to Gulf's success, and wanting to go their own way, the Atlantic Refining Company's marketing task force turned to the ideas of Charles Mulford Robinson. In his book *Modern Civic Art: Or, The City Made Beautiful*, Robinson considered the boulevards and bridges built to accommodate the automobile and wrote, "It is the triumph of modern civic art, to transform these necessary girdles and girders of the structure of the city into ways of pleasure and beauty. Here the whirr of the electric car, there the rush of swiftly passing motor cars—these are elements of the scene that may count not less distinctly in the total power to please than does the verdure." Millions of cars and the infrastructure for them might be as inspiring as parkland? How would *that* work?

Atlantic seized the spirit of the times and brought in an architect to leverage all this new positive thought for the automobile. Between 1917 and 1922, Joseph F. Kuntz of the Pittsburgh architecture firm W. G. Wilkens had designed a handful of gas palaces in Pittsburgh and no less than sixteen more for Philadelphia. These polychromatic, terracotta temples appeared like beacons on the boulevards. They flattered and pandered to the rising breed of urban drivers. Atlantic set out to appeal to these new "automobilists, who find considerable pleasure touring over . . . smooth and well-kept roadways and bridges." While Gulf staffed its very utilitarian stations with men, Atlantic populated their gasoline temples with women outfitted in dark-blue woolen uniforms, riding breeches, and black leather accessories. And with seventeen pumps, Atlantic advertised, "there will be absolutely no waiting" for service.

The product was essentially the same as Gulf's, but the *experience* was very different. Atlantic became known and widely admired for its "Greek temple effects." Architect Kuntz developed a unique design for each new location, which he refined in drawings and tested in miniature plaster models. Knowing that customers would need gasoline day and night and aware of concern about the possibility of electric lights igniting fumes from fuel, Kuntz concealed electrical lights to outline the buildings and their colonnades. By 1922, sixteen busy Philadelphia intersections had Kuntz' gas temples, including Fortieth and Walnut, Cobbs Creek Parkway, Walnut and Fifty-Fifth, and Broad and Lycoming, just a few blocks south of the first success at Broad and the Boulevard.

What would Gulf do to keep its customers loyal and happy? They did the only thing a modern gas station *could* do: they kept their prices competitive and offered road maps and oil changes—for free.

———

Sources: John A. Jakle, "The American Gas Station, 1920 to 1970," *Journal of American Culture* 1, no. 3 (September 1978); Nelson P. Lewis, "The Automobile and the City Plan," *Proceedings of the Eighth National Conference on City Planning, Cleveland June 5–7, 1916,* New York, 1916; Bruce A. Lohof, "The Service Station in America: The Evolution of a Vernacular Form," *Industrial Archeology* 11 (1974); William B. Rhoads, "Roadside Colonial: Early American Design for the Automobile Age, 1900–1940," *Winterthur Portfolio* 21, no. 2/3 (Summer–Autumn 1986); Charles Mulford Robinson, *Modern Civic Art: Or, the City Made Beautiful* (New York: G. P. Putnam's Sons, 1903); Keith A. Sculle, "Pittsburgh's Monuments to Motoring History: Atlantic's Fabulous Stations." *Western Pennsylvania History,* Fall 2000; K. H. Lansing, "Gasoline Selling a Fine Art," *Petroleum Age* 9, no. 3 (1922).

Figure 3.9. Construction of the PSFS Building, southwest corner, Twelfth and Market Streets, August 14, 1931

No matter that New York's Empire State Building, which opened in 1931, was more than two-and-a-half times taller than Philadelphia's PSFS Building. The Quaker City's skyscraper was many times more modern. Philadelphia had "gone Gershwin" with an architecture "slick and sheer and shining . . . alive to the tempo of the day." The effect was refreshing compared with "the frumpy, bastioned City Hall" a few blocks to the west. PSFS embraced modernism not for its own sake but for the solutions it offered that were, above all, functional. As urban planner Frederick Gutheim later gushed, "When functionalism in the United States was raw, red and steamy new it found few more devoted followers than Howe and Lescaze."

The sleek, streamlined bank and a twenty-seven-story slab of glass-walled offices by architects George Howe and William Lescaze turned out to be "the biggest and proudest thing in Philadelphia." Known for its commanding role in the skyline with four, twenty-seven-foot letters in red neon, PSFS provided an even more innovative achievement closer to the ground. There, its architects solved the difficult question of how a skyscraper might relate to, and make the most of, a busy urban intersection.

That design challenge fascinated bank president James M. Willcox, who wasn't interested in style per se but was committed to where and how to most effectively, practically, and aesthetically design and build. Willcox balked at Howe's traditional-looking first proposal in 1926 and instead had him create a temporary street-level bank to test customer demand. Meanwhile, Willcox commissioned Howe to design a set of neighborhood branches that started looking historical and wound up as modern. Then in 1928, Howe left his longtime firm of Mellor, Meigs, and Howe and *really* embraced modernism.

For the Twelfth and Market Street site, diagonally across from the Reading Terminal, Willcox had an ambitious list of demands. He wanted a bank, commercial space, hundreds of thousands of square feet of office space, and at first, he even demanded five stories of above-ground parking. By late 1929, when Howe and his new partner, the young, progressive Swiss architect William Lescaze, got to work on the revived project, the biggest question was how to acceptably address Willcox's complex program for the street level. He said he distrusted "ultra-Modern." What he wanted, Willcox later explained, was "ultra-Practical." It was the architect's job to prove that modern and practical could be one and the same.

If some savvy Gatsby type were to whisper a single word to guide the project to a smart, elegant, and ultrapractical solution, that word would have been *steel*. Even though Howe was not used to or comfortable with the material, the PSFS commission obliged Howe "to face the problem of steel construction." And steel's possibilities "startled" Howe. He wasn't used to such "novelty," such "frank interpretation of modern functions," and soon realized he was now free to get at "the underlying principles governing architectural design." With drawings envisioning something complex, elegant, and modern, Lescaze showed the way to a building the likes of which no one in America had ever seen. According to architectural historian William Jordy, Lescaze's street level promised a building "bathed in a mysterious luminescence . . . weightless as it rises effortlessly in the night above its scrubby competition."

The weight of the office tower would be supported by rows of steel columns. And a steel truss would bridge the giant banking floor with a sixty-three-foot span. Howe and Lescaze delineated their second-story banking hall with a sweeping band of windows, leaving "the ground floor free for . . . the kind of shopping traffic from which the bank drew its clientele." Above, three more floors of bank offices served as a transition from the base to a boldly cantilevered, twenty-seven-story office tower. Then came the great, skyline-defining neon sign.

Before Howe started the project, he and his partners used architecture to help clients avoid, if not totally escape, urban reality. "The critical weakness of the romantic architect," Lewis Mumford criticized Howe in 1925, "is that he is employed in creating an environment into which people may escape from a sordid workaday world." By the end of the decade, with the encouragement of an enlightened patron and the vision of a creative partner, Howe managed to complete his own aesthetic conversion. In the PSFS Building, Howe and Lescaze addressed a new purpose for architecture: "to remake the workaday world so that people will not wish to escape from it."

The PSFS Building turned out to be "much more than a superb marriage of function and technological innovation," wrote Robert A. M. Stern. "It is a superbly crafted object, refined in its every detail . . . that rarest of phenomena of our time, a working monument." And its style wasn't one more in a long line of styles; the PSFS showed the way to live *in* the world and ways to make the most of it. This achievement might have been called many things, but in 1931, they called it modernism.

———

Sources: Frederick Gutheim "The Philadelphia Saving Fund Society Building: A Re-appraisal," *Architectural Record,* October 1949, 88–95; Howe et al., "The PSFS Building: Philadelphia, Pennsylvania, 1929–1932," *Perspecta* 25 (1989): 79–141; William H. Jordy, "PSFS: Its Development and Its Significance in Modern Architecture," *Journal of the Society of Architectural Historians* 21, no. 2 (May 1962); William Harvey Jordy, *"Symbolic Essence" and Other Writings on Modern Architecture and American Culture* (New Haven: Yale University Press, 2005); Lewis Mumford, "The Architecture of Escape," *The New Republic* 43, no. 558 (August 12, 1925): 321–322; Robert A. M. Stern, "PSFS: Beaux-Arts Theory and Rational Expressionism," *Journal of the Society of Architectural Historians* 21, no. 2 (May 1962); Robert A. M. Stern, *George Howe: Toward a Modern Architecture* (New Haven: Yale University Press, 1975); "A New Shelter for Savings," *Architectural Forum,* December 1932.

Figure 3.10. Reading Terminal Headhouse, detail, northeast corner, Twelfth and Market Streets, ca. 1950 (Library Company of Philadelphia)

Just as Howe and Lescaze were getting to work on their PSFS Building in the late 1920s, Harry Sylk was starting up his drug store chain. Before long, the two would play out their similarities and differences—International Style versus pre-Populuxe—on the street at one of Philadelphia's most dynamic intersections.

The intersection of Twelfth and Market Streets had been Philly's hot corner since the 1890s, when the Reading Railroad installed its masonry cliff of a headhouse in front of a giant iron train shed. People animated the sidewalk. Archival images of Twelfth and Market confirm: this intersection was the heart, and possibly the soul, of Center City. Problem was, the blank, anonymous corner niche of rusticated headhouse didn't add all that much visually. For a long time, the corner demanded little attention, only the decision to walk straight, right, or left.

Until PSFS. Howe and Lescaze's monumental curve of granite, steel, and glass made the Reading Terminal Headhouse seem vintage by comparison—so nineteenth century, so out of date. Could the power of PSFS possibly inspire its diagonally opposite corner to move into the twentieth century? It could. And in true twentieth-century fashion, the swagger and shamelessness of American retail took up the challenge.

In the late 1920s, brothers Harry, Albert, and William Sylk started a "cut rate" store on Ridge Avenue and built a retail empire. The Sun Ray chain eventually grew to more than 150 stores in Pennsylvania, Delaware, New Jersey, and Maryland. The Sylks were promoters as much as retailers. In 1947, when flying saucers were spotted in Roswell, New Mexico, Sun Ray promoted its new store in Patterson, New Jersey, by dropping discs from an airplane and offering free ice cream to anyone who brought one in. At Easter, Sun Ray gave its customers free chicks. The Sylks didn't just advertise on the radio; they bought two stations, WPEN, AM and FM.

Store location remained their first priority. "Wherever there was a Woolworth's store," Harry Sylk told the *Inquirer*, "we tried to open a store right next to them." Signs became Sun Ray's other top priority. The Sylks likely stood on the sidewalk across from the commanding curve of PSFS, appreciating Howe and Lescaze's commitment to retail at street level. This was similar to their language, only the Sylks spoke it with an earthier accent. *Their* corner, the Sylks figured, could be updated with modern lines and materials. Where PSFS purred, they would brag and holler. "Sun Ray; Super Kiosk," proclaimed their first sign as it curved around the corner. Over time, and abiding by the time-tested principle that there's no such thing as redundancy when it comes to promotion, the words *Super Kiosk* were replaced with *Sun Ray Drug Co*. Neon lit it all.

A powerful display? Sure, especially at night. And cluttered. And disappointingly unanimated. Why use neon halfway? asked Max Sarnoff, the Sylk's sign man extraordinaire. While on the West Coast, Sarnoff had seen the light move: "I wanted to put show biz in the sign business." Back from

Hollywood via Miami Beach, Sarnoff later told *Sign Builder Illustrated* how proud he was of his giant, animated, neon mortar and pestles for Sun Ray. But nothing Sarnoff did combined lights and action like his giant Sun Ray sign, with neon bands chasing around the corner of Twelfth and Market—a bit of Las Vegas in the Quaker City.

———

Sources: Denise-Marie Santiago, "A. Sylk, 85; Drug-Chain Executive," *Inquirer*, December 23, 1990; "Andy Wallace, Harry S. Sylk, 90; Established Chain of Sun Ray Drugs," *Inquirer*, November 30, 1993.

Figure 3.11. From City Hall Tower, looking northwest, photographed by
Charles L. Howell, April 10, 1929

In order to succeed in its grand City Beautiful ambitions, the Parkway
had to overcome a handful of awkward design moments. The first, at
the base of City Hall, the boulevard got off on the wrong foot. Instead
of elegance and clarity, Broad Street Station's tower pokes and juts into
what should have been an open vista. A second awkwardness appeared at
Logan Square, where the Parkway sliced through at an off-center diagonal. The Parkway's third clumsy challenge was at the rocky base of Fairmount itself.

Jacques Gréber brilliantly addressed two of the awkward moments. At
Fairmount, he employed a giant set of steps to extend the Parkway's axis to
the entrance of the museum. At Logan Square, Gréber introduced a large

off-center traffic circle disguised as a Beaux-Arts fountain, creating an illusion of centrality. The remaining design challenge, at the base of City Hall, was at the point of the greatest demands and conflicting responsibilities. As early as 1911, a proposed plaza design for the start of the Parkway became loaded up with a host of additional functions and new buildings: a new headquarters for the Free Library, the Franklin Institute, a massive courthouse, and even a convention hall. Fortunately, most of these projects would later migrate to Logan Circle. But by 1920, the expanse at the start of the Parkway still felt and looked unfinished, a jumble of cars, towers, and pedestrians.

Enter Edmund N. Bacon, who spent some of his early years wondering what this awkward space could become. Bacon worked on the problem for his thesis in architecture at Cornell in 1932. His plans for a giant circular terminus for the Parkway would simmer for another three decades.

Later, as head of the Planning Commission, Bacon worked with Vincent Kling to advance a version of his idea. In the spring of 1962, even the aged Gréber gave Bacon's idea a thumbs-up. The soon-to-be-named JFK Plaza would feature a giant ninety-foot-wide fountain, large and symmetrical enough, on this little square, to strongly punctuate this terminus of the Parkway.

Aspirations for this overburdened space called for something more than a giant geyser in a pool. A design competition turned up nothing winnable, not even Robert Venturi's proposed seemingly NASA-inspired fountain that would have provided much-needed scale and wit. As Venturi explained his solution in *Complexity and Contradiction in Architecture*, "The form is big and bold so that it will read against its background of big buildings and amorphous space and also from the relatively long distance up the Parkway. Its plastic shape, curving silhouette, and plain surface also contrast boldly with the intricate patterns of the buildings around.... This fountain is big and little in scale, sculptural and architectural in structure, analogous and contrasting in its context, directional and nondirectional, curvilinear and angular in its form, it was designed from the inside out and the outside in." Venturi recognized what the site demanded: a hyper-legible feature, a bold solution.

This brings us to the most recent redesign for JFK Plaza, a.k.a. LOVE Park. Hargreaves Associates and Kieran Timberlake accommodated competing demands for the space, which continues to try to be many things for many interests at the expense of being big and bold. The fountain will survive in shrunken form; the now-beloved circular visitor center is offered new life; a greensward quietly dominates as it might on a college quad. A century later, we find ourselves rediscovering the plaza's original awkward complexity.

LOVE Park is again bereft of boldness, or as Bacon would put it, a powerful "design idea." Unless LOVE alone is enough to carry the day. Maybe, just maybe, the relatively small (but big-hearted and extraordinarily popular) LOVE statue can save the park? "Let us try what love will do," declared William Penn long ago. "Force may subdue but love gains." Penn was writing about his policy of peace with Native Americans. More than 330 years later, we'd like to believe that the power of love might solve all kinds of problems, maybe even our most demanding design challenges.

Maybe, by some miracle, love *is* all we need at LOVE Park.

———

Sources: Ashley Hahn, "Designers Show Saucer Some LOVE," PlanPhilly/WHYY, April 30, 2015; Gregory L. Heller, *Ed Bacon: Planning, Politics, and the Building of Modern Philadelphia* (Philadelphia: University of Pennsylvania Press, 2013); Inga Saffron, "Waiting for a Design to Love," *Inquirer*, April 10, 2015; Inga Saffron, "A Bold Vision for LOVE Park," *Inquirer*, May 1, 2015.

Figure 4.1. Statue of Demeter, entrance of the Pennsylvania Academy of the Fine Arts at Broad and Cherry Streets, photographed by Madill, May 19, 1925

CHAPTER 4

Preservation and Stewardship

WHEN PHILADELPHIA'S EARTH MOTHER BIT THE DUST

Broad Street once had its very own Greek deity, a two-millennia-old statue of Demeter (Roman, Ceres), the goddess of agriculture, Zeus's consort, and Persephone's mother. Her statue had previously presided for decades under a spreading hawthorn tree in the courtyard of the Pennsylvania Academy of the Fine Arts then at Tenth and Chestnut Streets. In the 1870s, architects Frank Furness and George Hewitt had a eureka moment as they composed the new building's polychromatic façade in redbrick, brownstone, sandstone, and granite. Furness and Hewitt completed their composition by installing the Greek original in the niche over the entrance, proving there was still some juice left to the claim that Philadelphia was the "Athens of America."

How did Philadelphia get its Greek goddess? As Columbia University archeologist William B. Dinsmoor told it, Commodore Daniel Todd Patterson took advantage of his authority, his wealth, and his presence in the Mediterranean in the 1820s. Patterson's ship, the USS *Constitution*, embarked on a military mission that doubled as a treasure hunt. First, he and his crew visited the ruins of Carthage and made off with some large mosaics. Second, at the catacombs of Melos and Aegina, they managed to purchase collections of glass and terracotta. From Sunium, they took pieces of the temple. And while near Athens in 1827, the *Constitution* anchored close enough to Megara to find the prize of the entire expedition: statues of Demeter and her daughter Persephone.

A small group of "emaciated" Greeks led Patterson and his crew three miles inland to the buried statues. And while the Commodore didn't know exactly what they were, he knew they were ancient and authentic. Justifying his purchase as an act of charity to feed Greek families, Patterson bought the less "mutilated" of the two statues and assigned twenty-five of his men the job of getting his treasure back to the *Constitution*. Patterson also did his best to acquire a missing part. "I was unable to procure the Head 'tho I offered a high price," apologized Patterson in the letter of July 16, 1828, presenting the statue to the academy.

More than a century later, while conducting research for his 1943 article "Early American Studies of Mediterranean Archaeology," Dinsmoor homed in on Patterson's exploits and concluded that this haul was indeed remarkable. Not only was the figure sculpted by the same expert hand as the Persephone Patterson had left behind, but Dinsmoor concluded that Philadelphia's Demeter was "the largest piece of ancient sculpture brought to this country before the Civil War." Dinsmoor also realized his scholarly efforts were too little, too late.

In the summer of 1937, fearing that the now-cracked goddess might fall and kill passersby, academy officials priced out its removal. As the discussions went on and the estimates came in, the idea of removal gave way to outright destruction. Sculptor Louis Milione claimed he could "demolish the figure for the sum of $250"—one quarter of the estimate of bringing Demeter to earth in one piece. Budget-conscious academy officials quickly accepted Milione's bid and, as the *Philadelphia Inquirer* soon reported, the statue was "knocked apart with maul and sledge and pneumatic drill and ignominiously hauled off."

"The fate of the Demeter is somewhat embarrassing to consider," wrote Dinsmoor during the depths of World War II, "in view of the fact that the events occurred only recently and in our own enlightened environment, rather than in Nazi terrorized Europe." Philadelphia's Greek tragedy also played out as an American irony. In the 1940s, sculptor Charles Rudy recycled two chunks of Demeter's debris and created *Pekin Drake* and *Two Hearts That Beat as One*. Today, both are in the academy's collection.

———

Sources: William B. Dinsmoor, "Early American Studies of Mediterranean Archaeology," in "The Early History of Science and Learning in America," special issue, *Proceedings of the American Philosophical Society* 87, no. 1 (July 14, 1943): 70–104, http://www.jstor.org/stable/985002; William B. Dinsmoor, letter, registrar files, Department of Fine Arts and Archeology, Pennsylvania Academy of the Fine Arts, Columbia University, June 8, 1943; Helen Weston Henderson, *The Pennsylvania Academy of the Fine Arts and Other Collections* (Boston: L. C. Page and Company, 1911); Daniel F. Patterson, letter to John Vaughn, registrar files, Pennsylvania Academy of the Fine Arts, Columbia University, July 16, 1828; *Catalogue of the Thirty-Fifth Annual Exhibition of the Pennsylvania Academy of the Fine Arts* (Philadelphia: Pennsylvania Academy of the Fine Arts, 1858); "Charles Rudy Sculpture," *Pennsylvania Academy of the Fine Arts Exhibition Checklist*, November 6–December 12, 1948.

Figure 4.2. John R. Hathaway removing first brick in demolition for the park-way, 422 North Twenty-Second Street, February 22, 1907 (The Parkway Group)

Inspired by a grandiose vision of civic progress, in the fall of 1907, the city of Philadelphia gave notice to more than seven hundred property owners whose homes stood in the way of the City Beautiful. The idea of a grand boulevard connecting City Hall and Fairmount Park had been talked about for more than thirty years. Now the Parkway was a work in progress with a timeline. In January, contractor Howard E. Ruch signed a contract with the city to demolish everything from Callowhill to Ham-ilton Streets. He had ninety-five days to complete the job, even though the majority of the residents were still occupying their homes.

John R. Hathaway, director of public works, decided if eggs were going to break, he might as well make an omelet. Hathaway cast displacement and demolition as historic "improvement" and commandeered George Washington's birthday to choreograph a ceremony around the start of the demolition campaign.

The first house to come down would be one of the few emptied row houses. On February 22, officials dressed for the occasion gathered at Ruch's nearby office and then, just before noon, held a procession to 422 North Twenty-Second Street, the first residence marked for demolition. An account of the event described how "the party . . . entered the house and one by one [climbed] up a rickety ladder . . . onto the roof. There, just as the clock struck 12, the Director raised his silver pick and began loosening a brick on the chimney. . . . Several hundred persons on the street below gave a cheer as the first brick was pecked out and held aloft." At a luncheon following the ceremony, city councilman John W. Ford presented Hathaway with the silver pick in a custom-made, satin-lined case. Accepting it, Hathaway proclaimed, "I regard this as an era in Philadelphia's history, and I shall cherish this souvenir to my dying day."

A contrasting scenario was playing out around the corner at 2223 Hamilton Street. John Kelley and his wife were attempting to keep the bricks of their home in place. While Hathaway and his "Parkway Group" conducted their ceremonial street theater, Kelley, who had previously believed "there was a chance of his home escaping demolition," learned all hope was lost. Already ill and grieving "over the fact that the house which he and his family occupied was to be dismantled," Kelley soon received a final notice to vacate. Within days, he died. "Grieved to Death over Loss of Home," read the newspaper headline.

———

Sources: "Working on Parkway Property: Owners Are Notified to Vacate," Inquirer, October 23, 1906; "Contract Awarded for Parkway Work," Inquirer, January 1, 1907; "Gold Pick for Parkway: Hathaway to Remove First Brick Tomorrow Noon," Inquirer, February 21, 1907; "Parkway Started by Razing of First Building," Inquirer, February 23, 1907; "Parkway Progress Opposed by Tenants," Inquirer, March 1, 1907; "Grieved to Death over Loss of Home," Inquirer, March 3, 1907.

Figure 4.3. Japanese pagoda, Fairmount Park, ca. 1910

The 1904 St. Louis Louisiana Purchase Exposition was a gigantic affair: nearly twice the size of Chicago's Columbian Exposition in 1893 and quadruple that of Philadelphia's Centennial Exhibition in 1876. For Japan, the increasing scale of America's world's fairs turned out to be the perfect platform to demonstrate its expanded ambitions on the world stage. The Japanese occupied seven acres in St. Louis, more than any other nation besides the United States.

Japan had emerged as the Far East's imperial nation and its colonial power—"the protector of Chinese territory," according to historian Carol Christ. (Just a few months before the fair opened, Japan had attacked Russia on Chinese soil and was on its way to a decisive victory, the first time an Asian country would defeat a European power.)

Japan also expressed its dominance in the creative realm. As the self-proclaimed heir of Asian culture and the "sole guardians of the art inheritance," Japan positioned itself as keeper of the "museum of Asiatic civilization." When Russia backed out of its commitment to exhibit in St. Louis, Japan the imperial power and cultural ambassador stepped in with purpose and commandeered the vacated Russian space.

Japan's exhibition buildings were "built entirely by native carpenters" in styles perfected hundreds of years earlier, declared one guidebook. Set in landscapes with gardens, hills, waterfalls, lakes, and bridges and accented with imported, centuries-old "beautifully trained dwarf trees . . . drooping wisteria . . . peony, scented lily and blushing maple," it all added up to a "harmonized . . . artistic" whole. For visitors from around the world, Japan curated a one-of-a-kind experience that sent a powerful message: Asian power had arrived.

There was more. By the fair's main entrance, millions were lured onto the Pike, a mile-long, carnival-like collection of attractions open late into the evening. The Pike offered up contortionists, dancing girls, and a "zoological paradise" complete with an elephant water slide. Visitors went "deep-sea" diving, scaled miniature replicas of the Tyrolean Alps, rode burros along constructed cliff dwellings, and toured "Blarney Castle."

Especially popular were rides inspired by the biblical version of creation and another ride built on a "hereafter" theme. The Pike also staged military reenactments: the Boer War, the Spanish-American War, and the Russo-Japanese War, even though it was still in progress.

No concession on the Pike stood out more than Japan's. Entering through a massive, 150-foot gateway—a "replica of the famous portal in Nekko, Japan"—visitors strolled "a Street of Tokyo," brought alive by eighty actors in traditional costume. Everything was new, though constructed to appear ancient and venerable, except for one artifact that didn't need to feign authenticity, a 45-foot-tall temple gate that, for the previous three centuries, had graced the Hitachi Provence about 120 miles northeast of Tokyo.

What would become of such a treasure when the crowds returned home? John H. Converse and Samuel Vauclain, Philadelphians who had made their fortunes at Baldwin Locomotive Works, imagined the "Nio-Mon, or, Temple Gate" as a picturesque addition to Fairmount Park. They bought it and paid for its transportation, reconstruction, and landscaping—complete with tons of boulders worn smooth in the nearby Darby Creek. With additional help from John T. Morris, Converse and Vauclain transformed the grove between Memorial Hall and Horticultural Hall into a picturesque and peaceful destination.

But peaceful in a big city park is sometimes also vulnerable. From the start, the City and the Fairmount Park Art Association (where Converse and Morris served on the board) took protective measures. Artifacts exhibited inside the temple gate's second-story chamber were transferred to Memorial Hall and later to the Philadelphia Museum of Art. (One survives in the Asian art gallery.) But without fences or a guard, Philadelphia's new treasure became an easy target.

Architect Albert Kelsey had seen it coming: "I deplore the possibility of this beautiful temple becoming merely another scattered unit in a poorly planned park that has not, in many instances, been laid out to heighten the effect of the many valuable works of art it possesses." Morris called for the installation of "wire guards" to prevent "acts of barbaric young

American(s), who take pleasure in stoning these fine specimens of Japanese wood carvings." "If the building is not protected it will soon go to decay," Morris fretted. "If visitors are permitted to do as they want in the interior it will soon be a disgrace." Cycles of vandalism and repair continued from the installation in 1906 to the 1930s, when the temple gate got a facelift as part of the Works Progress Administration. But to no avail. Within a few more years, Park Commissioner John B. Kelly was ready to throw up his hands. Kelly suggested the gate might just have to be "torn down."

On the eve of the temple gate's golden anniversary in Philadelphia in May 1955, the city installed scaffolding to carry out another cosmetic overhaul. But before the project got under way, the temple gate burned to the ground. The culprit, according to the Philadelphia Fire Department, wasn't vandalism, but the "carelessly discarded cigarette" from the repair crew.

Who mourned the temple gate? Who had time to? The fire made way for Shofuso, another cultural treasure from Japan, which found its way to Fairmount Park two years later.

———

Sources: Carol Christ, "The Sole Guardians of the Art Inheritance of Asia: Japan and China at the 1904 St. Louis World's Fair," *Positions: East Asia Cultures Critique* 8, no. 3 (2000): 675–709; Lee Gaskins, "At the Fair: The 1904 St. Louis World's Fair," The Pike, 1908, http://atthefair.homestead.com/Pike.html; Hajime Hoshi, *Handbook of Japan and Japanese Exhibits at World's Fair* (research paper, St. Louis, 1904); Christeen Taniguch, "Historical Narrative of Shofuso," Shofuso.com; Hsuan Tsen, "Spectacles of Authenticity: The Emergence of Transnational Entertainments in Japan and America, 1880–1906" (PhD diss., Stanford University, 2011); "1904: The World's Fair," Missouri Historical Society, http://mohistory.org/exhibitsLegacy/Fair/WF/HTML/Overview/; "Nio-Mon, or Temple Gate," *Bulletin of the Pennsylvania Museum* 4, no. 13 (January 1906): 12; Shofuso Japanese House and Garden, nomination for designation as a historic site, Philadelphia Historical Commission, 2012.

Figure 4.4. Cannonball House across from Fort Mifflin, September 3, 1976

Peter Cock couldn't have picked a more out of the way location for his farmhouse. In the 1680s—and forever after, actually—*nobody* coveted the swampy rise that broke the horizon near the Schuylkill as it meandered to the Delaware. Why would they? With so much rich, drier land in every direction and with William Penn's ambitious "green Country Town" drawing folks six miles upstream, these brackish bogs were, literally, a Swedish settler's backwater. But the site proved good for farming and provided well enough for the next owner to expand the farmhouse. That brick house stood quiet and alone for the better part of the eighteenth century.

Then all hell broke loose on the lower Schuylkill.

With the American Revolution in high gear and the British occupation of Philadelphia under way, control of the city's port meant that the British would need to take the American-controlled fort downriver at Mud Island, just below the mouth of the Schuylkill. At Fort Mifflin, as the installation would become known, several hundred American troops were garrisoned. And for weeks, they foiled British attempts to reach the city by river. A siege lasting through the fall of 1777 would be the largest bombardment of the Revolutionary War. Six British ships bristling with 209 cannons would overwhelm the American's ten. Over five days, with an estimated ten thousand cannonballs flying, the fens of the Schuylkill were neither quiet nor safe any longer.

At the start of the final siege, on November 11, a cannonball entered the rear wall of the old farmhouse and exited the front wall. From that day forward, the old Swedish farmhouse would carry a new name: the Cannonball House. For the next 219 years, the Cannonball House, a survivor that would come to be considered the oldest house in Philadelphia, would be treated with veneration, deference, and respect. Artists would sketch it, antiquarians would photograph it, and the Historic American Buildings Survey would document it.

By the start of the twentieth century, as the city's population expanded and its farmland shrunk, the now city-owned Cannonball House served as a "model farm" until the demand for sewage treatment overwhelmed the need for demonstrative agriculture. And the Cannonball House quietly accommodated as the Southwest Treatment Plant enveloped it. When operations started in December 1954, one hundred million gallons of sludge passed through each and every day.

As the bicentennials of the battle of Fort Mifflin and the birth of the nation approached, Philadelphia's oldest house became its newest problem. The 1950s sewage plant nearby needed more space. "I wish the British had done a better job," Water Commissioner Carmen Guarino joked to a reporter.

In 1974, the Philadelphia Historical Commission decided that the Cannonball House wasn't important enough to be listed on the National Register but was *too* important to be demolished. The commission urged that it be moved to a new site across from the entrance to Fort Mifflin. And in 1975, the main section of the Cannonball House was lifted from its foundations and wheeled slowly down the road. The Environmental

Protection Agency, expecting locals to take on the restoration job, picked up the $168,000 moving tab. For next twenty-one years, the Cannonball House remained in preservation purgatory, a house without a home. And Fort Mifflin had a historic headache on its would-be parking lot.

In this uprooted state—deteriorated and on temporary cribbing—the orphaned Cannonball House was unable to charm its way onto even the preservation-inclined agenda of *Inquirer*'s architecture critic Thomas Hine, who wrote in December 1981 that the "Cannon Ball Farm House has little claim to our minds and hearts . . . it requires some bravery to choose to forget it."

A forgetting would take place, though without any bravery. One day, in November 1996, what the British didn't do, what sewage engineers wouldn't do, the city, in violation of its own requirements, *did* do. It demolished the Cannonball House. Raw sewage got treated, historic preservation got mistreated, and Fort Mifflin got its parking lot.

———

Sources: Ron Avery, "Farewell to Farmhouse Cannonball House Taken down by City," *Philadelphia Daily News*, November 21, 1996; Ron Avery, "Neglect of Historical Building May Cost City," *Philadelphia Daily News*, December 18, 1997; Tom Hine, "Cannon Ball Farm House: Bite the Bullet and Let It Go," *Inquirer*, February 15, 1981; Historic American Building Survey (HABS), Cannonball Farm, Philadelphia, Pa. (Philadelphia: PA-134, 1937–1940); Sarah L. Ruhland, "The Fragility of Significance: The Rise and Fall of the Cannon Ball House" (master's thesis, University of Delaware, Spring 2007).

Figure 4.5. Manufacturers' Club, northwest corner, Broad and Walnut Streets, December 28, 1916

Going back a century or so, a well-dressed edifice would carry itself with a proud bearing. Such buildings lined public avenues instilling character through style and substance. At the Manufacturers' Club, for instance, a grand entrance framed by pairs of freestanding columns finished in the Corinthian classical order welcomed (or intimidated) visitors. Rising above, entablatures and colonnades gave way to corbels, pediments, tasteful arches, and courses of dentils—all in Green River limestone. Bas-relief carvings of winged creatures and heraldry marked the corners. Stretching skyward, the towering eyeful culminated with an architectural "ta-da" at its uppermost heights. Before the admirer's gaze was finally relinquished skyward, a final, rooftop finesse—a bold cornice—captivated the eye.

More than shade or protection from the elements, such overhangs provided a powerful visual terminus and stature. Projecting over the sidewalks, cornices reached outwards as declarations of potency, demonstrations of consequence that transformed buildings into destinations and pedestrians into spectators. And here, at the heart of Center City at Broad and Walnut, the group proclaiming its grand arrival was the city's newest nouveau riche: the manufacturers.

Throughout the second half of the nineteenth century, Philadelphians had come to expect architectural statements along the rooftops of South Broad Street. La Pierre House and the Academy of Music claimed a more modest skyline in the 1850s. Horticultural Hall and the Art Club updated it in the 1890s. Philadelphia's earliest skyscrapers on Broad Street offered their own kind of "visual liveliness." Architectural historian David Brownlee observed that the "chateau-esque pinnacles of the Bellevue Hotel, the boldly massed modern classicism of the Fidelity (now Wells Fargo) Building, the strong cornices of the two Land Title towers, and the art deco belfry of the PNB (built as the Lincoln Liberty) Building rise together with City Hall's tower to create one of the world's most distinctive and animated skylines." What's missing today, writes Brownlee, is the biggest, boldest, roofline of them all. The Manufacturers' Club "suffered a bad haircut" when it's "giant Florentine shadow caster, proportionately one of the biggest cornices in the city, was removed."

The Manufactures' Club's earlier, five-story Queen Anne–style building by Edward P. Hazlehurst and William Samuel Huckel Jr. opened at 1409 Walnut in the 1880s. Membership quickly expanded beyond the city's textile manufacturers to include *any* industry. By 1912, 1,800 members strong, the club had acquired the site of the Hotel Bellevue after it merged with the Stratford. One architectural competition later, the club signed on architects Edward P. Simon and David B. Bassett and builders A. D. Irwin and A. O. Leighton, and the construction of the ten-story steel frame clubhouse was under way.

Simon and Bassett designed in the Italian Renaissance style, and a rendering was exhibited in 1912 at the Eighteenth Annual Architectural Exhibition held by the Philadelphia chapter of the American Institute of Architects and the T-Square Club. They included a paneled mahogany lobby, a lounge and café above a basement billiard room, and a rustic tiled grille. On the second floor, members found the library and rooms for card playing. An auditorium for 1,200 took up much of the third floor. Then there were three floors of guest rooms, an elaborate banquet hall overlooking Broad Street, and an airy dining room topping it all off. "One of the handsomest and best equipped clubhouses in the world," praised one architectural journal. A welcome contrast to "the familiar bleak 'skyscraper,'" wrote another. "A tall building of truly artistic conception . . . one of the most impressive sights of South Broad Street."

Simon partnered with Bassett from 1908 to 1919 and produced another great cornice in 1917 atop the historically designated Pomerantz Building at 1525 Chestnut Street. *Hidden City* called this cantilevered cornice "audacious." Its historical nomination described it as a "radical," extending "more than seven feet out from the plane of the façade" and causing it to "almost . . . float above the sidewalk." Instead of harkening back to classical times, this feature endowed its building with something more ironic. Simon and Bassett "used the daring projection of the cantilevered cornice as a reminder that the building's structure is modern." This also applied to the spreading cornice at the Manufacturers' Club. But onlookers wouldn't know that from the street. Not any longer.

How did this most expressive and defining attribute disappear? Cornices were considered dangerous. Almost immediately after the club opened, Philadelphians read of an Italian earthquake that knocked cornices off buildings in Rome. Closer to home, cornices and ornamental coping were known to fall off Philadelphia's own City Hall. "Danger in Cornices," read one headline. To reassure a worried public, city officials removed five tons from the upper reaches of City Hall. It was only a matter of time before the Manufacturers' Club at Broad and Walnut would get a similar shearing.

———

Sources: David Brownlee, "Looking Up on Broad Street," *Eyes on the Street,* PlanPhilly, November 2, 2011; Jon Vimr, "A Preservation at A. Pomerantz," *Hidden City Daily,* June 13, 2013; A. Pomerantz and Co., nomination for historic designation, Philadelphia Historical Commission, 2013; The Manufacturers' Club, Philadelphia Historical Commission files, visited December 8, 2015; "Architectural Criticism, The Manufacturers Club, Philadelphia," *Architecture: The Professional Architectural Monthly* 29–30 (1914), 97; "Philadelphia Exhibit," *The American Contractor* 35 (May 2, 1914): 122–123; "Avezzano Destroyed," *Inquirer,* January 14, 1915; "Danger in Cornices: City Hall Stripped of Tone of Coping to Prevent Accident," *Inquirer,* Jan. 29, 1919.

Figure 4.6. Horticultural Hall, Broad and Manning Streets, ca. 1896

Philadelphia's decades-long "reign of architectural terror" had finally come to an end. The powerful influence of Frank Furness, whose "violent mind" generated a "degree of depravity not to be measured in words," had played out. In its place, critic Ralph Adams Cram saw the rise of refinement and "delicate sensibility" from a new posse of architects: Wilson Eyre, Cope and Stewardson, and Frank Miles Day.

"These four," claimed Cram in the *Architectural Record*, "became one voice crying in the wilderness, a voice proclaiming artistic salvation through the doctrine of good taste." Day had signaled the start of a revolt in the late 1880s with his Art Club at Broad and Chancellor Streets. But this "unmistakable work of a young man just back from Europe" came across as a bit too earnest. "Variety and picturesqueness were sought at any cost," wrote Cram. While the building stood as a welcome "manifestation of delicacy and sweetness, of fine instincts and subtle sympathies," the result was disappointing. "Calmness, reserve, simplicity are lost," concluded Cram. The Art Club was "weak . . . in mass, composition and scale"—not quite the architectural breath of fresh air he had hoped for.

But it was a start, "a solid foundation" on which to build. With the Art Club, Day marked "the entrance of a new influence in a devastated field." And as Day "found himself," he'd come to realize that "salvation is not by fine line alone." As Cram saw it, architectural salvation arrived at last in the mid-1890s in the form of "two important structures" by Day. First was the American Baptist Publication Society at 1420–1422 Chestnut Street, an "elaborate, ambitious, magnificent" creation featuring "all kinds of splendor, an efflorescence of balustrades, dormers, pinnacles and diaper work" on the tower. Then there was the "bold yet delicate" architectural gem of a building in Horticultural Hall at 250 South Broad Street.

"A fine example of Italian Renaissance architecture," complimented Asa M. Steele in *Harper's Weekly*. Its "arched entrances and windows" contrast "with simple expanses of wall of golden-yellow Pompeian brick . . . surmounted by a roof of Spanish tiles," and its façade resonates with "vitality and richness," showing off "ornate bronze gates, windows of emerald glass, and touches of brilliant gold, pink and green upon medallions, balcony grills, and deep overhanging eaves."

Inside and out, the hall "breathes the atmosphere of blossoms, orchards, and woodlands," wrote Steele. "The grand staircase of pink and white marble rises from the vestibule into a bower of green marble columns, and green and gold galleries surmounted by a bronze-gold-dome topped with opalescent glass. . . . The entire main floor can be thrown open from end to end, giving the whole the appearance of an idealized sylvan vista."

Day and his brother (Henry Kent Day joined the firm in 1893) had produced a successful, mature design, a "strong and simple composition, with a just disposition of voids and solids," Steele declared. "Nothing appears that does not justify itself by its inherent beauty . . . and as a result one has the same impulse to sit down before it with sketchbook and pencil that manifests itself in Italy."

"Horticultural Hall," wrote Cram, is "about the best thing Mr. Day has done . . . In detail it is just as delicate and lovely as the earlier work, but this detail is more carefully used, and disposed with far greater craft." Although the Days hadn't done many buildings, "their influence has been profound and far-reaching." And most importantly, they "stood unflinchingly for good taste and for intrinsic beauty . . . they treated their art with respect." Maybe most of all, according to Cram, "they never forgot that an architect must be first of all a gentleman, and they held faithfully to the gentleman's creed 'Noblesse oblige.'" The Days, Cram declared, have "turned back the tide . . . that was overwhelming Philadelphia, and they set up their standard as a rallying point for all men loyal to good taste, to seriousness of purpose, to faithfulness in the small things of architecture as in the great."

But the twentieth century had another thing in store. As it turned out, greatness was fleeting for the Days' buildings on Broad Street. Horticultural Hall, the last up, was the first to be cut down, in its twenty-first year. Only a few interior elements survive in the building's remake as the Shubert Theatre (now the Merriam Theater). The Art Club hung on into the mid-1970s before it also succumbed: the adjacent Bellevue-Stratford Hotel needed a parking garage.

————

Sources: Ralph Adams Cram, "The Work of Messrs. Frank Miles Day & Brother," *Architectural Record* 15, no. 5 (May 1904): 397–421; Asa M. Steele, "Horticultural Hall, Philadelphia," *Harper's Weekly* 41 (November 20, 1897): 1144; "Magnificent Home for Horticulture: The New Building Is Completed and Will Be Opened To-Morrow," *Inquirer*, October 4, 1896.

Figure 5.1. *Evening Telegraph* at the Lincoln Building, Broad Street, south of City Hall, photographed by N. M. Rolston, October 4, 1916

CHAPTER 5

Improvements

NEVER A DULL MOMENT: THE ROUGH-AND-TUMBLE
HISTORY OF PHILADELPHIA NEWSPAPER PUBLISHING

When Philadelphia boomed, so did its newspapers. The city's population, about 81,000 in 1800, expanded fifteen-fold over the next century to 1.3 million. This did wonderful things to make Philadelphia a robust newspaper reading and publishing town.

No fewer than a dozen dailies started up in Philadelphia between 1836 and 1880. During the Civil War, Charles Edward Warburton and James Barclay Harding thought afternoon readers could be better served and launched the *Evening Telegraph*, a newspaper with a name that actually meant something. Utilizing the telegraph, editors transmitted news from the first national political convention after the Civil War held at "The Philadelphia Wigwam" directly to their offices. The *Evening Telegraph* compiled and ran editorials from newspapers across the United States and Europe. It commissioned translations and serialized Jules Verne's novels, including his popular *Tour of the World in Eighty Days*.

Run by the second generation of leadership, the *Evening Telegraph* built a promising future by the 1890s. While conducting research for his book *American Journalism from the Practical Side*, Charles Austin Bates toured the paper's new quarters at 704 Chestnut Street and sat down with the owner and publisher, thirty-year-old Barclay Harding Warburton. Bates came away impressed, finding the *Evening Telegraph* "in every respect a model newspaper's home." He recognized that the young Warburton needed to maintain the paper's appeal "to the millionaires, solid business people, and the society people," but he also wanted to broaden the paper's popularity. This Warburton accomplished with an array of new features, including a woman's page; "an amateur sporting page"; pages devoted to art, literature, theater, and "the secret and colonial societies"; and on Saturdays, a "ministerial page." The *Evening Telegraph*, Bates noted, "seems to appeal very strongly to both the classes and the masses." Warburton had increased circulation by 300 percent. "At Broad Street Station and the Reading Terminal," wrote Bates, "more copies of *The Evening Telegraph* are sold than of probably all other papers put together." Warburton had also increased advertising by 60 percent, selling space to every last one of Philadelphia's forty-four banks, twenty-eight trust companies, and all law firms that advertised.

The *Evening Telegraph* thrived in the midst of Chestnut Street's remarkable business district, which included a complex and competitive journalistic community with the offices of eleven dailies between Sixth and Twelfth Streets and Chestnut and Market Streets. To Bates, these newspapers appeared to be thriving; he couldn't quite imagine how fragile the state of Philadelphia journalism would become. In the first decade of the twentieth century, three would fold. By the Great Depression, ten were gone.

In 1911, perhaps sensing the sea change, Warburton sold out to Rodman Wanamaker, his wealthy, dilettantish brother-in-law. Wanamaker may have bought the *Evening Telegraph* as an investment but managed it like a plaything. To run the operation, he installed John T. Windrim, an architect with no experience in journalism or publishing. The paper left its Seventh and Chestnut Street office for the high-priced, ostentatious Betz Building, a stone's throw from both City Hall and Wanamaker's department store. Many things were different on Broad Street, but a few remained the same. Journalists at the *Evening Telegraph* continued their longtime practice of "transmitting" the latest news by scribbling it on blackboards hung at sidewalk level. On October 4, 1916, this included the latest bloodletting from the front lines of World War I (the Battle of the Somme) and the score from a baseball game (Phillies lost to the Boston Braves, 1–6).

Two years after Wanamaker bet on the *Evening Telegraph*, Cyrus Curtis, an even wealthier Philadelphian, started on an ambitious newspaper acquisition and consolidation spree. Between 1913 and 1930, Curtis, who had been hugely successful as a publisher of magazines, purchased five Philadelphia dailies, three of which he would fold. Curtis's second target, the *Evening Telegraph*, acquired for its wire services, was bought and closed on June 28, 1918, after fifty-four years of publication.

As it turned out, Curtis's publishing acumen didn't quite translate to the world of daily journalism. His last acquisition, a $10.5 million purchase of the *Philadelphia Inquirer* in 1930, was meant as a savvy final stroke in Curtis's plan. It turned out not to be terribly savvy. After Curtis died in 1933, his company was forced to sell the *Inquirer* at a loss. It wouldn't be the last time such a thing happened.

————

Sources: Charles Austin Bates, *American Journalism from the Practical Side* (New York: Holmes, 1897); John Henry Hepp, *The Middle-Class City: Transforming Space and Time in Philadelphia, 1876–1926* (Philadelphia: University of Pennsylvania Press, 2003).

Figure 5.2. "White Wings" at Clean-Up Week parade, Broad and Arch Streets, looking south, April 20, 1914

What with nearly 1.5 million people and the refuse of day-to-day life, cleaning the early twentieth-century city of Philadelphia proved no small task. But for South Philadelphia pig farmer-turned-politician Edwin H. Vare, cleaning up in Philadelphia would become quite the lucrative operation.

Back then, the city didn't clean its streets—private contractors did. And year to year, the political competition to win and hold contracts for the city's six districts grew fierce. Before long, the powerful Vare Brothers obtained contracts for every last city street. And they would hold onto at least several of these handsome contracts until the City Charter of 1919 turned the massive undertaking over to the city.

In the early decades of the twentieth century, cleaning the city also included annual demonstrations of influence, displays of military-style choreography, and campaign advertising. As early as 1900, the newly minted army of 150 uniformed street sweepers—"White Wings," as they became known—passed in review before city officials. "Each man wore a uniform of white; his helmet, jumper and overalls were immaculate, and each was armed with a formidable brush, or about 24 inches callibre," reported the *Philadelphia Inquirer*. Commanding each company were leaders in "neat gray uniforms" issuing orders in Italian, Hungarian, or another native language of the squad at hand. By 1912, these white duck uniforms and pith helmets became standard issue. The parades became an annual event.

"Every citizen is requested to join in the crusade against dirt and filth," proclaimed Mayor Rudolph Blankenburg in April 1914. He asked everyone to do their part "in cleaning out rubbish and waste material from rooms, closets, hallways, garrets, roofs, cellars, fire escapes, yards, all dark corners and out of the way places." And to reinforce the city's commitment, the mayor designated April 20–25 as "Clean-Up Week" and launched it with a parade on Broad Street. At the head of the two-mile-long march, peppered with eight brass bands, rolled a single ash wagon as a parade float. Then came a car packed with contractors, superintendents on foot, and the White Wings—uniformed, helmeted blockmen and gangmen wheeling bag carriers or wielding brooms. They were followed by sprinklers, squeegee machines, flushers, machine brooms, dirt wagons, ash wagons, and rubbish wagons. In all, 2,000 street cleaners and 750 pieces of equipment paraded by.

But the procession was only the half of it. The director of the Department of Public Works sent out 3,400 personal letters to every manufacturer of brushes, brooms, buckets, vacuum cleaners, and advertisers of the same. He wrote to every last civic group and major business. All mail from the city bore gummed stickers in yellow and blue with the words "Remember Clean-Up Week, April 20–25, 1914." Police handed out 260,000 four-page printed bulletins. School children were issued blue-and-yellow buttons. More than 20,000 display placards appeared in the windows of department

stores and retail merchants. Every one of the 700,000 Philadelphians viewing films at any one of the city's 205 "moving picture houses" would see
images directing their attention to "Clean-Up Week." And inside the city's
3,200 streetcars were posted neatly designed placards featuring the figure
of William Penn wielding a broom from atop City Hall.

As to the metaphor of the broom signifying sweeping political reform?
Apparently, that hadn't yet caught on.

———

Sources: "'White Wings' Pass in Review Before City Officials," *Inquirer*,
January 3, 1900; "Spick and Span City Is Aim of Clean-Up Week," *Inquirer*,
April 12, 1914; "White Wings Will Herald Clean-Up Week's Approach: Men
and Equipment to Be Shown in Parade Today," *Inquirer*, April 18, 1914;
"White Wings in March Clean-Up Week's Prelude: 2000 Street Cleaners,
Spick and Span, Seen in Parade," *Inquirer*, April 19, 1914.

Figure 5.3. Street-cleaning machine, Elgin Motor Sweeper, October 31, 1917

Great twentieth-century cities demanded forward-looking solutions. When Philadelphia announced its intentions to join the City Beautiful movement, grandiose cleanups called for something more than the pith-helmeted army of "White Wings," the marching, uniformed broomsmen who were more reminiscent of nineteenth-century colonial conquests than twentieth-century urban efficiency.

The new solution would be a machine—and the more newfangled, the better. Sprinkling and sweeping devices were horse-drawn and required abundant supporting labor on foot. Squeegee machines were moving in the right direction. They slicked down miles of asphalt, but anything pulled by a horse was still old school, manure producing, and self-defeating. What could maintain the explosion of new highways and byways and blend in with booming vehicular traffic? It would need to be something self-contained that looked and played the part.

In 1911, the first internal combustion–powered sweeper *seemed* to have it all, even though it was limited by too small a collecting capacity. And its steel-rimmed wheels were out of step with the latest rubber tire technology. This sweeper did accomplish twice the work "at half the cost of the horse-hauled machine sweeper," but its engine moved it along at a snail's pace, and its inability to maneuver led to traffic jams.

John M. Murphy, an Illinois farmer-turned-windmill-maker and Elgin, Illinois, city father crafted the solution with a new and improved "street sweeping machine." Murphy's device was agile; it kept up with automobile traffic. It didn't damage the pavement, raise dust, or leave debris behind. The Elgin Motor Sweeper received U.S. Patent number 1,239,293 on September 4, 1917. And a month later, a Philadelphia city official called for the city's new acquisition to be parked at the northeast corner of City Hall, where he struck a pose on it.

No question: the Elgin Motor Sweeper would cost-justify itself in Philadelphia, just as it had in beta testing on the streets of Boise, Idaho. There, the sweeper worked two, eight-hour shifts and cleaned 275,000 square yards of pavement per day—twice as much as the horse-drawn method. The operating cost? Nine cents per 1,000 square yards compared with a whopping 31.5 cents using the old technique, according to the company history. "News of the fantastic new sweeper spread to Pocatello, Idaho—to Portland, Oregon" and, of course, to Philadelphia. "Fifteen Elgins were produced and put to use in 1915, twenty-three in 1916, and forty-two in 1917."

The days of the "White Wing" army were over. Machines with names like "Gutter Snipe" would clean city streets in the twentieth century. Mechanization—made elegant by innovation and compelling by fiscal responsibility—had taken command.

———

Sources: William A. Richmann, *The Sweep of Time* (Elgin: Elgin Sweeper Company, 1962); J. M. Murphy, Street Sweeping Machine, U.S. Patent 1,239,293, filed August 21, 1913, issued September 4, 1917.

Figure 5.4. Kensington Labor Lyceum Hall, Second Street, north of Cambria Street, 1898

Of all the places where Mother Jones might have started her famous 1903 protest known as the March of the Mill Children, which did she find the most strategic? Philadelphia's Kensington Labor Lyceum at Second and Cambria Streets. Mother Jones also advised a thousand young seamstresses on the verge of the "the great Philadelphia shirtwaist strike of 1909" when she visited Philadelphia's Labor Lyceum at Sixth and Brown Streets. Likewise, when Eugene V. Debs came to Philadelphia in 1908 campaigning for the U.S. presidency, he proclaimed, "We are today upon the verge of the greatest organic change in all of history. . . . We are permeated with the spirit of the new social order and of the grander civilization. . . . Here in the United States we are very happily approaching the third revolution." And that revolution would begin on the stages of Philadelphia's Labor Lyceums.

At the Kensington Lyceum in January 1921, thousands of textile workers filled "every seat and windowsill" and "every inch of standing room" before marching up Second Street to support strikers at the textile mills. "Bright-eyed girls," burly men, and "careworn women" were stirred by the silver-tongued labor leader Abraham Plotkin and his warnings: "The fellow who hasn't a job and is cold, and whose stomach hurts all the time from hunger is dangerous. . . . Out of the unemployed come the tramps, out of the tramps come the criminals, and out of the criminals, the jails. We've learned this from hard knocks." The Labor Lyceums were places were free speech reigned, where *all* ideas were welcome.

The idea of the Lyceum was first presented at a Labor Day picnic in 1889, the brainchild of Frederick Wilhelm Fritzsche, a self-described "labor agitator" from Germany. The city's first Labor Lyceum thrived in rented quarters at 441 North Fifth Street and served as both a headquarters for unions and a home away from home for workers. Members would come for meetings, votes, and "mental and moral improvements" in the form of classes in typewriting, singing, drawing, cabinetmaking, and English. When Lyceums had the space, they'd also offer libraries packed with books in German and English.

In 1893, the congregation Keneseth Israel vacated its ornate 126-by-96-foot 1860s building on Sixth Street just north of Brown for a larger synagogue on Broad Street, where Temple University's law school stands today. Lyceum leaders immediately stepped in and bought the building.

"Labor's New Home," read the *Inquirer* headline describing the move to the new quarters. "Over three thousand men were in line with banners and brass bands . . . [and] entered the new building." The Fresco Painters' Union led the procession with its "blood-red flag and badges," followed by the Typographers' Union, with its banners displaying Guttenberg and Franklin. Then came the Metal Workers', Carpenters', Cigar Makers', Cigar Packers', Dyers', Leathers Workers', Blacksmiths', Wheelwrights', Harness Makers', Barkeepers', Waiters', and the Socialist Labor Unions. They arrived at the new building and "crowded into the big hall . . . decked with greens and flags."

The Lyceum was so successful that, less than two years later, the city's textile unions hired architect A. C. Wagner to design and build the Kensington Labor Lyceum in the heart of the city's textile district on Second Street just north of Cambria.

When Fritzsche died in 1905, the Lyceum on Sixth Street became the site of his memorial service. "Thousands Mourn Dead Socialist," read the headline. Fritzsche's body lay "in state in the hall" as "five thousand men and women trudged through the rain and icy streets" to pay last respects. "The auditorium had been decorated with long streamers of red bunting, the symbol of socialism. Over the catafalque hung the inscription: 'Arbeiter Aller Lander Vereinigt Euch.'" "Workers of the World Unite."

What's left today? No buildings. No historical markers have been installed. Only faded memories remain, plus a handful of archived images and newspaper articles. And a whole lot of history.

————

Sources: Murray Dubin, "Baby Steps: Philadelphia Strike in 1903 Gave Rise to 'Children's Army,'" *Inquirer,* June 24, 2003; Mary Harris Jones,

Autobiography of Mother Jones (Mineola: Dover Publications, 2012), Google Play Books; Daniel Sidorick, "The 'Girl Army': The Philadelphia Shirtwaist Strike of 1909–1910," *Pennsylvania History* 71, no. 3 (Summer 2004): 323–369; J. Spargo, "Child Slaves of Philadelphia," *The Comrade* 2 (1903); "The Labor Lyceum," *Inquirer*, November 4, 1891; "Labor's New Home," *Inquirer*, April 23, 1893; "World of Labor," *Inquirer*, October 15, 1899; "Thousands Mourn Dead Socialist," *Inquirer*, February 13, 1905; "Debs Talks in Philadelphia," *New York Times*, October 12, 1908; "Textile Workers Hear Strike Talks," *Evening Public Ledger*, January 28, 1921.

Figure 5.5. German Society of Pennsylvania, Marshall and Spring Garden Streets, northwest corner, ca. 1890

There was a lovely little installation about the German Society of Pennsylvania (GSP) at the Philadelphia History Museum in 2015. In addition to books and manuscripts, beer steins and photographs, Revolutionary War pistols and Civil War swords, there was an eight-hundred-pound gorilla in the gallery. Unlike the other artifacts, the giant gorilla had no label.

The GSP has been around for 250 years, which means there was plenty to say and show about its history and plenty more that had to be left out. But some chapters in history just can't be brushed aside.

The society was founded in 1764 when German settlers, feeling a need to circle the wagons, met for the first time in a charming Lutheran schoolhouse at Fourth and Cherry Streets. In the nineteenth century,

Philadelphia's German community built a serviceable meeting place on Seventh Street, just across from the Philadelphia History Museum. In 1888, the day after Christmas, the society moved to Seventh and Spring Garden Streets, where architect William Gette designed a three-story palatial clubhouse. The plan was to get closer to the heart of the booming Philadelphia German community. After all, in 1890, 28 percent of foreign-born Philadelphians were German. How German they would remain was the question.

Membership in the society didn't take off; in fact, never again would it surpass 1,000 members, where it peaked in the late 1870s. For the balance of the nineteenth century, the numbers would fall to as few as 700. By 1914, at the start of World War I, it dwindled to 624. By the end of World War II, there were only 350 members. By the mid-twentieth century, according to Birte Pfleger, "with reduced membership contributions and low investment returns, the GSP was more or less ruined financially." Decimated membership was a symptom. But of what? The story of the society's near demise was about something other than money.

World War I, the rise of the Third Reich, and World War II brought about conflicted loyalties and diplomatic disasters. Bombs were thrown, and board members were attacked, detained, tried and even imprisoned. This was a toxic stretch of time for the organization. This was the eight-hundred-pound gorilla, essentially ignored by Harry W. Pfund in his *History of the German Society of Pennsylvania* (1944), only referring to this time as the organization's "most tragic." But instead of facing this historical moment head on, Pfund advocated a collective willingness "to bear this grief in silence."

Yet silence and history aren't compatible. About sixty years after Pfund, Pfleger finally took a step to shed the long silence in a chapter titled, "Hitler's Shadow in Philadelphia: The GSP from the 1930s through the 1960s."

The 250th anniversary of German settlement in Philadelphia coincided with Hitler's rise in 1933. The society took five more years to publicly disavow Nazi sympathies and join with the city's other German American associations to create the anti-Nazi German American League of Culture.

In February 1938, only one month after the anti-Nazi declaration, the society displayed a swastika flag at its annual charity ball. And a month after that, according to Pfleger, "as many as 1,500 German Americans gathered" at the society's building "to celebrate Hitler's annexation of Austria." Sigmund von Bosse, "a Lutheran pastor and prominent GSP leader, gave a rousing speech, and almost everyone in the audience gave him the Hitler salute at its conclusion." Old habits die hard. Old loyalties die harder.

For its library, the society had acquired copies of Hitler's speeches as early as 1924. They added *Mein Kampf* in 1930 and ordered "books by Joseph Goebbels and subscribed to pro-Nazi periodicals." They added Julius Streicher's "notoriously anti-Semitic weekly *Der Sturmer*" and the SS publication *Das Schwarze Korps*. Nazi propaganda arrived "through the Volksbund fur das Deutschtum in Ausland (League for Germandom Abroad) and whatever the Nazis published and sent abroad to their Volksdeutsche, 'Germans outside of the Reich.'" All of these materials and more were available in the reading room at Seventh and Spring Garden.

After the war, the society finally became less German and more American. Meetings and programs were held in English, by then the society's official language. As years passed, the scholarly range and value of the GSP's library—more than sixty thousand books—became increasingly apparent. After all, many books made rarer by wartime losses in Europe were on the shelves in Philadelphia, which was something to be proud of.

But what would become of the cache of Nazi literature? In the postwar period, according to Pfleger, the GSP "decided to keep all Nazi periodicals and books in a dark and dirty storage room on the third floor of the building." This closet, known as the *Giftschrank*, or "poison cabinet," was a way to "bestow a general amnesia on the organization."

An amnesia that, even as the society presents its history in public, continues to this day.

Sources: James Bergquist, "German Society of Pennsylvania," in *Germany and the Americas: Culture, Politics, and History,* ed. Thomas Adam (ABC-CLIO, 2005); Birte Pfleger, *Ethnicity Matters: A History of the German Society of Pennsylvania* (Washington, DC: German Historical Institute and German Society of Pennsylvania, 2006); Harry W. Pfund, *A History of the German Society of Pennsylvania* (Philadelphia: German Society of Pennsylvania, 1944).

Figure 5.6. Inasmuch Mission, northeast corner of Warnock and Locust Streets, January 8, 1917

"Born and brought up a true son of the tenderloin," George Long survived as a child by pickpocketing in Madison Square Park in New York City. At the age of fourteen, having "been thoroughly schooled in the ways of the underworld, he launched himself upon his career as a 'grafter.'" Long grew addicted to cocaine and morphine and, for the next two decades, lived as "a habitué of the dens of vice in the large cities . . . repellant even to the keepers of the lowest resorts." He had "time and time again" been thrown out of even "the filthiest brothels."

George Long "floated about the country for years," arriving in Philadelphia "on the 'hobo's' common carrier, the freight train." On Skid Row, Long lived as "a wreck of a man . . . dissipated and disheveled, unshaven, unkempt, and saturated with liquor . . . a 'bum' of the uttermost, guttermost type."

Then Long found religion. He "fell upon his knees at Philadelphia's Galilee Mission and gave his heart to God," dedicating himself to saving the souls of others. "It takes a 'down and outer' to reform a 'down and outer,'" declared Long. "Social workers try hard, but they can't realize that feeling the other fellow has." He could talk with "them in their own language." He met them where they lived, "in the heart of the city's most disreputable and filthy sections" like Philadelphia's Hell's Half Acre—a place even more desperate than Skid Row.

Falling between Spruce and Walnut Street and Tenth and Eleventh Streets, Hell's Half Acre was then "cut up by many small thorough fares filled with dilapidated houses. No less than 65 were being used for immoral purposes," including three gambling dens, two opium joints, many pool rooms, and speakeasies.

At the heart of it, on Locust Street east of Eleventh, real estate developer George Woodward owned twenty "vacant, ramshackle houses." Worse than ramshackle, they constituted a public menace: "Each was connected with the other by an underground passage, so that if a crime was committed in one, the perpetrator could easily make his way from that house to another, and so on to the street and to safety. One building in this group was known as the 'get-away house.'"

Long convinced Woodward of his plans, and the wealthy Chestnut Hiller turned over the houses, rent free. Long and his associates cleaned them up, removing "eleven wagonloads of beer bottles, playing cards, discarded frills and burbelows [furbelows?] of feminine wearing apparel, and other rubbish." They remade the former getaway house into Long's headquarters. The Inasmuch Mission (named for the biblical passage Matthew 25:40: "And the King shall answer and say unto them, Verily I say unto you, Inasmuch as ye have done it unto one of the least of these my brethren, ye have done it unto me") was born.

Inasmuch offered help to "any man in need, providing that the beneficiary showed the desire to help himself." In the first six months of operation in 1911, more than 14,000 attended services, 8,731 meals were served, and more than 2,000 took lodging. The mission placed 96 reformed men in paying jobs. At the second anniversary celebration, the first three rows were packed with men whose testimony so inspired Mrs. Woodward that she offered to donate funds for "a suitable building in which Mr. Long might carry out his original dream."

Inspired by London's Rowton Houses for working men and New York's Mills Hotel, Philadelphia architects, Duhring, Okie, and Ziegler designed a severe, four-story fireproof facility with a chapel for three hundred, an office, a restaurant, a kitchen, and four hundred beds. In March 1914, Long and others dedicated the Inasmuch Mission "as a place where men will be cleansed, both mentally and physically."

Meanwhile, Long's evangelistic career grew in scope and scale. With a "large touring car," another gift Mrs. Woodward, Long began a series of "automobile meetings"—sermons accompanied by musical entertainment—on street corners "throughout the Tenderloin." As a rising evangelist, Long soon preached to gatherings of one thousand in a giant Inasmuch tent pitched at Sixtieth and Locust Streets. In the midst of World War I, Long railed about the kaiser, food profiteers, and rent gougers. "Hell is too good for them," Long shouted to cheering followers.

In the summer of 1918, Long determined to break a preaching record. For ten weeks straight, he packed tent meetings with as many as three thousand listeners. Long moved indoors to the nearby Imperial Theatre, at 219 South Sixtieth Street, while his architects drew up plans for a new five-thousand-seat evangelistic tabernacle. Now more confident than ever, Long pivoted from the pulpit to politics: "There are more gamblers, thieves, pickpockets and prostitutes in this city than ever before, and it depends upon our next mayor as to whether they are to remain here."

Long "censured women who wear immodest attire," claiming they "were responsible for much of the widespread immorality" adding "more men are being sent to hell today owing to women's immodest dressing than ever before." And he critiqued preachers less fiery than himself: "The she-man in the pulpit, with his soft voice and ladylike manners, has been driving red-blooded men away from the church." One headline declared, "Evangelist Flays 'Sissies' in Pulpit."

Long, it seemed, was only getting started.

———

Sources: G. Grant Williams, "Hells Half Acre and Inasmuch Mission," *Philadelphia Tribune*, May 18, 1912; "Rose from Underworld," *New York Times*, May 12, 1913; "Inasmuch Mission and Founder Have Done Great Work," *Inquirer*, September 1, 1912; "To Conduct Street Missions in Auto," *Inquirer*, January 15, 1913; Blair Jaekel, "The Inasmuch Mission" in *The World's Work: A History of Our Time*, vol. 25 (Garden City: Double-day, 1913); "Inasmuch Mission Will Provide Home for Men Desiring Reform," *Inquirer*, January 24, 1914; "Inasmuch Mission Now in New Home," *Inquirer*, March 24, 1914; "Inasmuch Mission: A Work of God Made Manifest," *Church News of the Diocese of Pennsylvania* (1915), https://philadelphiastudies.org/2014/08/02/inasmuch-mission-a-work-of-god-made-manifest-1915/; "Scores Food Gougers," *Inquirer*, July 8, 1918; "Tent Meetings Overflow," *Inquirer*, July 27, 1918; "Evangelist Flays 'Sissies' in Pulpit," *Inquirer*, August 4, 1919.

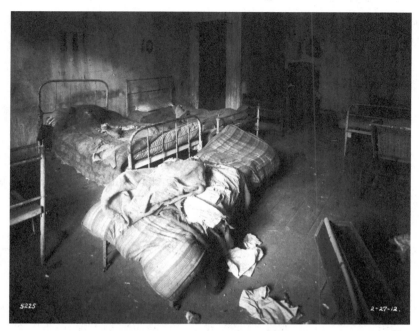

Figure 5.7. Lodging house, 531 Delancey Street, second floor front, February 27, 1912

Mayor J. Hampton Moore knew better when he remarked in 1933 that "Philadelphia was too proud to have slums." Indeed, the city had some of the worst housing conditions anywhere in America. Philadelphia's labyrinth of courts and alleys were lined with tenements going back a long, long time—despite efforts to deny their existence.

Ignoring slums had been just about impossible since 1909, thanks to a citizens' action group that called itself the Philadelphia Housing Commission (later the Philadelphia Housing Association). The commission "recruited an army of volunteer housing inspectors" who "combed the city's courts and alleys looking for noxious heaps of manure . . . fouled privies, structurally unsafe houses, and other threats to public health and safety." They filed complaints by the thousands. And they spread the word about the city's slum conditions, advocating for reform in lectures, leaflets, meetings, and—maybe most effectively—in photographs.

But advocates hit a wall in 1913, when the state legislature created— and the city council ignored—the Division of Housing and Sanitation within the Department of Health and Charities. "Better government in Philadelphia is being slowly strangled," editorialized the *Evening Public Ledger* in October 1914. The "cold fingers" of "Philadelphia's Tammany twisting dexterously through a pliable majority in Councils" are failing to require landlords "to keep their properties in such repair as to make them healthy places to live in. By refusing to appropriate funds necessary to put the law into effect the majority members completely nullified it. It is now as good as dead, killed by Councils." City slums remained intact; housing reform in Philadelphia would have to wait.

Without funding, tenement occupants without water would continue to live without water; those without connections to sewers would have no sewers. Their unsafe stairways would stay unsafe; broken plumbing, leaky roofs, flooded cellars, and windowless rooms would remain as they were. Poor, largely immigrant families "caught on the treadwheel of life," argued the *Evening Public Ledger*, lived with "darkness, impure air, dampness, dirt and dilapidation." But the city's slum conditions were mostly out of sight and out of mind. So photographers hired by the Philadelphia Housing Commission documented them and commandeered a storefront window on one of the city's busiest streets to show exactly how bad the conditions were.

In November 1914, the Philadelphia Housing Commission's display in a storefront window at the Sharswood Building, at Tenth and Chestnut Streets, opened eyes of those who would never otherwise see slums themselves. And in the center of the window, the Commission mounted the *Evening Public Ledger*'s editorial demanding reform. The photographs attracted attention from hundreds of "shoppers, merchants, ministers, physicians, lawyers, laborers and visitors." Many were "surprised to see that conditions such as pictured . . . actually existed in the 20th century in this city" and were disturbed that the conditions "told by the camera" were of homes only a few blocks away from the exhibition.

"Welfare Workers Charge Councils with Responsibility for Evil Conditions," read the *Evening Public Ledger* headline about the display. The next year, the Philadelphia Housing Commission would prevail with the passage and the funding of the city's first comprehensive housing code. But as housing advocates knew so well, implementation would require monitoring: ongoing data collection, filing of complaints, and vigilant public information campaigns.

Despite laws, agencies, and ongoing advocacy, the rising number of poor residents in Philadelphia resulted in more, not less, one-room tenements. In 1922, the Philadelphia Housing Commission filed more than eight thousand complaints with the city and wrote of the ongoing problem: "The City knows that families, like rats, have taken to cellars to cook, eat and work . . . The City knows that the 4,837 tenements and the 2,465 rooming houses recorded are far below the actual number . . . The City knows there is a teeming population . . . in narrow alleys and courts and minor streets, approximating 60,000 persons."

Philadelphia's first housing code was not nearly enough to make a real difference. More powerful, comprehensive, and systemic interventions would be needed to mount an effective war on poverty. But the citizens' campaign of 1914 had been a start. And in time, government would again follow their lead.

Sources: "The Hands of Esau, Councils Sets Itself against Better Living Conditions for Tenants," *Evening Public Ledger*, October 28, 1914; "Welfare Workers Charge Councils with Responsibility for Evil Conditions," *Evening Public Ledger*, November 23, 1914; Edith Elmer Wood, *The Housing of the Unskilled Wage Earner: America's Next Problem* (New York: Macmillan, 1919); Bernard J. Newman, *Housing in Philadelphia* (Philadelphia: Philadelphia Housing Association, 1922); John F. Bauman, "A City of Homes, Housing in Philadelphia," in *Invisible Philadelphia: Community through Voluntary Organizations*, ed. Jean Barth Toll and Mildred S. Gillam (Philadelphia: Atwater Kent Museum, 1995), 411–416.

Figure 6.1. Dyott Glass Works at the Aramingo Canal, 1898

CHAPTER 6

Innovation and Industry

Thomas W. Dyott, Snake Oil, Soda Water, and the
Perennially Seductive Philadelphia Bottle

Everyone in America, it seemed, wanted to wrap their fingers around a
bottle. What poured from the bottle didn't seem to matter that much, so
long as it made the consumer feel good in some way. It might be shoe
polish, patent medicine, or whiskey—anything that was cheap to make
and easily marketable. When it came down to it, the bottle's contents were
almost secondary to a steady, affordable supply of pocket-sized glass con-
tainers. Without them, manufacturers and merchants had no reason to
create, or meet, demand.

Thomas W. Dyott understood this dilemma and overcame it. Although
he called himself a doctor, he was not. But he was an operator, an entrepreneur, and an ambitious visionary who started out as a poor arrival
from England. Dyott polished shoes and mixed and sold his own boot-
black, then added *MD* to his name and bottled, marketed, and sold elixirs
including "Vegetable Nervous Cordial," "Infallible Toothache Drops," and
"Stomachic Bitters." Dyott's drug store at Second and Race Streets became
headquarters for the largest patent medicine businessman in the United
States, with sales agents pounding the pavement in a dozen states.

As long as Dyott depended on others for a steady supply of bottles, his
success was at their mercy. So he bought and breathed new life into the old

Kensington Glass Works, located where Gunner's Run flowed into the Delaware River. Dyott ramped up production with eight thousand pounds of glass every day. He undercut everyone else's prices; he made and supplied quality bottles for his own ventures as well as those of his competition.

By the 1830s, the four-hundred-acre glassworks of T. W. Dyott grew into a company town for his labor force of up to four hundred, about half of whom were apprentices, some as young as six years old. Dyott was demanding, but he also provided housing, health care, education, recreation, religion, and rules. He guaranteed employment all year around. Dyottville's farm helped sustain the workforce. And his factory manufactured bottles in clear and tinted glass with bas-relief images of nearly everything—from the American flag to cornucopia—and everyone—from Washington, Franklin, and the Swedish singer Jenny Lind to Dyott himself.

Dyott became known for excess and extravagance. And when he launched a private bank—the Manual Labor Bank—Dyott brought to bear his skills as a manipulator. He "induced a great many people, principally of the middling interest and poorer classes, to deposit their earnings" and issued paper money with presidential portraits, his own signature, and the assurance that each note was "secured in trust."

When the best banks collapsed during the Panic of 1837, so did Dyott's Manual Labor Bank and, with it, his grand version of the American dream. In the celebrity trial that followed, the commonwealth charged Dyott with "fraudulent insolvency" and "defrauding the community." Sixty-eight witnesses testified against him, and the seventy-year-old was sentenced to a term at Eastern State Penitentiary. The factory closed, and Dyottville became a ghost town.

In the 1840s, a fad for plain and flavored mineral waters spurred new and an even greater demand for bottles, and another immigrant entrepreneur, Eugene Roussel, took over Dyott's shuttered factory. Meanwhile, investors widened Gunner's Run into the Aramingo Canal to support Kensington's burgeoning industrial landscape, which soon produced paint, pottery, rope, stoves, wagons, and ships. At the end of the nineteenth century, Dyott's factory, by then acknowledged as the city's oldest glasshouse, was still producing bottles.

In the twentieth century, I-95 came through the Dyott site, which obliterated the past above ground but left behind opportunities for some interesting industrial archeology. A recent dig reported no bottles but even more important finds among the foundations.

Where are the Dyott bottles today? They continue to have a life of their own. The Philadelphia Museum of Art holds a few, as do bottle and glass collectors. In the twenty-first century, folks still want to wrap their fingers around Dyott's bottles. In 2010, a Dyott "Firecracker Flask" set a world record at auction, bringing more than $100,000.

Dyott bottles have always made their owners feel special.

———

Sources: Ian Charlton, "PhilaPlace: Dyottville Glass Factory" (Historical Society of Pennsylvania, n.d.); Kellie Patrick Gates, "PennDOT Archaeologists Uncover Historic Dyottville Glass Works," PlanPhilly, January 20, 2012; John Thomas Scharf and Thompson Westcott, *History of Philadelphia, 1609–1884*, vol. 3 (L. H. Everts and Co., 1884), 2299; Kevin A. Sives, "Dr. Thomas W. Dyott: A True Renaissance Man," http://www .manheim1762.org/files/Revised_Dr._Dyott_-_2.pdf; James Harvey Young, *The Toadstool Millionaires: A Social History of Patent Medicines in America before Federal Regulation* (Princeton: Princeton University Press, 1961); "'Firecracker Flask' Sets New World Record," *Antique Trader*, April 2, 2010.

Figure 6.2. Coal yard, south side of Washington Avenue, east of Eleventh Street, March 16, 1915

In the 1820s, Philadelphia investors "awoke as if from a dream [to the] immensity of the riches concealed in the mountains and ravines of their native State." As "news of fortunes accumulated by piercing the bowels of the earth, and bringing forth [coal] from the caverns of mountains," wrote Edwin Freedley, the trade in anthracite, which "appeared yesterday but a fly, now assumed the gigantic proportions of an elephant!"

In an optimistic rush, investors who "previously laughed at the infatuation of the daring pioneers of the coal trade" now initiated their own "plans of towns . . . surveys of coal lands . . . railways, canals and . . . other improvements." They poured $5 million into the Schuylkill coalfields to get "black diamonds" to the city, digging more than 800 miles of canals and laying 1,600 miles of railroad track. Investors made out. So did "laborers and mechanics of all kinds from all quarters and nations," who "flocked to the coal region" and "found ready and constant employment." Down on Philadelphia's Schuylkill docks, arrivals from Ireland found ready, if backbreaking, work as "coal heavers," laboring dawn to dark for a dollar a day.

Philadelphia's appetite for coal—a skimpy 365 tons in 1820—flourished at 867,000 tons by 1840. Less than a decade later, the city was consuming five million tons of anthracite. Cheap coal meant cheap heat. Affordable, high-quality anthracite provided the city with a competitive edge. "Inexpensive and abundant coal," according to the *Encyclopedia of Greater Philadelphia*, "helped drive population and industrial growth." Citizens used it "to heat homes, power factories, propel steamships, and smelt iron." Anthracite "enabled Philadelphia to transform itself from a commercial city of merchants into an industrial powerhouse. . . . Canals, coal, and industrial Philadelphia grew together synergistically."

By the last quarter of the nineteenth century, when manufacture was strategically chosen as the theme for the Centennial Exhibition, Philadelphia could display its makeover to the world. By 1876, the question wasn't what Philadelphia manufactured but what it *didn't*.

Expansion—and the fortunes made from it—seemed endless. In the middle of the nineteenth century, the Reading Railroad built a facility in Port Richmond large enough to handle more than 1.2 million tons of coal every year, with wharves capacious enough to handle one hundred ships at a time. After the Civil War, the Pennsylvania Railroad developed its own Greenwich Point Holding Yard along the Delaware in South Philadelphia. By the early 1890s, coal cars stretched as far as the eye could see. Greenwich car dumpers heaved three hundred carloads of coal each and every day. Clearly, King Coal had rubbed his gritty elbows with those of the City of Brotherly Love. What could *possibly* go wrong?

———

Sources: Edwin T. Freedley, *Philadelphia and Its Manufacturers* (Edward Young, 1859); Christopher F. Jones, "Canals," *Encyclopedia of Greater Philadelphia* (Camden: Rutgers, 2015); John C. Van Horne et al., *Traveling the Pennsylvania Railroad: Photographs of William H. Rau* (Philadelphia: University of Pennsylvania Press, 2002); Russell F. Weigley, *Philadelphia: A 300 Year History* (New York: W. W. Norton, 1982).

Figure 6.3. The standpipe at the Spring Garden Water Works, near Thirty-Third and Master Streets, after 1882

In a quirky burst of engineering, aesthetics, and memory in the middle of the nineteenth-century, Philadelphia built itself a great, 130-foot spiral column. The idea was complicated and ambitious: provide water pressure for the emerging neighborhood of Mantua with a standpipe wrapped in an ornate, circular staircase and topped off with a 17-foot-wide public viewing platform and a 16-foot statue of George Washington. Everything would be custom engineered, locally manufactured, and except for the stone base, made from cast iron.

Engineers Henry P. M. Birkinbine and Edward H. Trotter drove the scenario that saw the "fairy like" Gothic structure to completion. "Eight cluster columns opposite each angle of the stone base support . . . a railing of Gothic scrollwork," read one official report. "The upper platform, surrounded by a Gothic railing, is sustained by ornamental brackets springing from the columns; these are continued above the platform, where, by flying buttresses, they are connected together, and to the standpipe, which is surmounted by a spire and a flag staff, the whole of iron except the base." In the fall of 1854, the eight-foot Gothic doorway at ground level was thrown open for the public to venture up the 172 narrow steps, follow "the continuous Gothic scroll railing" and enjoy a spectacular view of the growing city.

By then, plans for the Washington statue had fallen by the wayside. Anyway, the job of remembering the father of the country was being taken care of elsewhere. Philadelphia long had its wooden Washington at Independence Hall, carved by William Rush in 1815. Baltimore installed its statue-capped column in 1829. Congress commissioned Horatio Greenough to sculpt a twelve-ton, white-marble, bare-chested emperor, installed at the Capitol rotunda in 1841. Washington, DC, also had its longtime in-progress Washington Monument, which had declared bankruptcy the year Philadelphia built its standpipe. (The national monument wouldn't be completed until 1888.) All of these were done, more than less, in the classical style with classical materials. Philadelphia's standpipe also had its models in ancient Rome's venerable columns for Trajan and Marcus Aurelius, monuments with spiral stone steps on the inside and spiral stone friezes on the outside.

But here in mid-nineteenth Philadelphia, something in addition to the Classical Revival was in play.

Technology afforded an unprecedented opportunity to leap beyond old-world models and explore up-to-date materials—in ways that deployed them to grand effect. Above its thirty-five-foot stone pedestal, the standpipe reached new heights by utilizing "modern" cast iron.

Expressed in contemporary forms that were soon to become a part of everyday life, the structure was evidence of Philadelphia's burgeoning engineering culture.

By the 1850s, Philadelphia's engineers had come to appreciate "excellence of material, solidity, an admirable fitting of the joints, a just proportion and arrangement of the parts, and a certain thoroughness and genuineness." These are the qualities, wrote Edwin T. Freedley, "that pervaded the machine work executed in Philadelphia, and distinguished it from all other American-made machinery." In the standpipe, we see more than engineering: there's an engineering aesthetic spilling over into the mainstream. The London-published *Civil Engineer and Architect's Journal* profiled the standpipe. So did *Gleason's Pictorial Drawing-Room Companion*, a popular national magazine of the day whose editors presented an illustrated feature in the spring of 1853. "When completed," they promised, "the structure will form one of the most notable curiosities . . . an object of much scientific interest" for engineers *and* the general public.

It would take a few more decades before this sort of thinking would collide in the imagination of the architectural genius Frank Furness. He grabbed hold of Philadelphia's "industrial repertoire" and conducted daring feats of "structural panache." The University of Pennsylvania's Fisher Fine Arts Library of 1890 confirms broadly what Philadelphia's leaders and engineers had come to relish in the world they manufactured.

That world was ever changing. Meant to be a stand-in, the standpipe became obsolete after a reservoir came online fifteen years later. The standpipe sat abandoned until the early 1880s, until—in yet another display of derring-do—engineers moved it in a single piece to the opposite side of the Schuylkill River at the Spring Garden Water Works. There also, permanence proved fleeting and fickle. Philadelphia's spiral column, its monument to industry, innovation, and history, was last seen sometime at the end of the nineteenth century. Its ultimate demise took place without fanfare. Meanwhile, in Rome, the standpipe's ancient progenitors remain standing—two millennia and counting.

———

Sources: "Philadelphia Water Works," *Gleason's Pictorial,* March 26, 1853, 201; *Civil Engineer and Architect's Journal* 17 (1854); Edwin T. Freedley, *Philadelphia and Its Manufacturers* (Edward Young, 1859); *Annual Report of the Chief Engineer of the Water Department of the City of Philadelphia,* vol. 74, Water Department, Philadelphia, 1876; *Journal of Select Council of the City of Philadelphia* (1876); Michael J. Lewis, "The Pennsylvania Academy of the Fine Arts as Building and as Idea," *Pennsylvania Academy of the Fine Arts: 200 Years of Excellence* (Philadelphia: University of Pennsylvania Press, 2005), 63–73.

Figure 6.4. Keystone setting, east portal of the tunnel near Twenty-First and Hamilton Streets near Knickerbocker Ice Company, December 17, 1898

Because they could, the American Ice Company encased Old Glory in a five-ton slab of ice, propped it up on a wagon, and hauled it down Broad Street. Delighted spectators at the Founder's Week Industrial Parade cheered the chilly float, awed at the impressive chunk from the same source that supplied their own kitchens. Five tons wasn't an outlandish amount of ice. Many customers would buy as much before a year was out—fifty pounds at a time—and they'd buy as much again in 1909. And yet again in 1910. America had an ice addiction.

It all started at Sixth and Market Streets in the 1780s at the Presidents House's eighteen-foot-deep, stone-lined, octagonal ice pit that supplied the elite with pristine river ice all year round. By the late 1820s, Philadelphia's appetite had grown to more than nineteen tons per day, or about seven thousand tons every year—more than could be cut from the Schuylkill River, even venturing as far upstream as Norristown. In the 1830s, the city's major ice harvester, Knickerbocker, searched out sources along the Perkiomen Creek and up the Lehigh River—anywhere cold met water. And when those sources fell short during unseasonably warm winters, they packed ice in schooners and shipped it down from Maine.

By the 1840s, Philadelphians used 30 tons of ice every day. Harvesters cut as much as they could, imported the rest, and stored aggressively, anticipating warm winters and hot summers. Knickerbocker's icehouses in Maine held 400,000 tons from the Kennebec and Penobscot Rivers. By 1880, the addiction grew even more intense. Each and every Philadelphian consumed 1,500 pounds. Eighty-one companies employed nearly 1,300 workers who kept the city chilled with five hundred ice-filled, horse-drawn wagons. Still, demand outgrew supply until the invention of "artificial ice." Pennsylvania had five ice plants by 1889. Thirty years later, it had more than two hundred.

Knickerbocker's at Twenty-Second and Hamilton and Ninth and Washington were said to be the largest ice plants in the world. The company had yet another facility along the Schuylkill at Spruce Street. There seemed no end to the demand or the supply. Indeed, between 1880 and 1914, American ice consumption more than tripled. It provided an opportunity for a monopoly with an "ice trust" created in 1899 by merging Knickerbocker and others into the grandly named American Ice Company. Ice bribed officials and doubled prices in New York City. Distraught citizens heckled the mayor with cries of "Ice! Ice! Ice!" Next election, they froze him out of office.

As Philadelphians awaited the announcement of their price hike, an *Inquirer* reporter interviewed an American Ice official. "Prices for the coming summer have not been fixed yet," he hedged, "and if I were to hazard a guess I would not know whether to say they were going up or going down." The ice factory superintendent dismissed worries: "But that is all bosh." He saw no reason to increase prices in Philadelphia and no reason not to share his observations with the reporter. "In New York there is practically no competition," he said. "Here in Philadelphia there is plenty of it. Outside of the Knickerbocker Company there are four independent natural ice companies capable of furnishing an almost unlimited supply if called upon to do so. . . . I can name no less than twelve artificial ice companies already in operation . . . Of the artificial ice companies output the trust controls probably thirty per cent. So you see, the trust hasn't everything its own way here, as it has in New York, and there will be no doubling up on prices, I assure you."

Yet ice prices did rise. It wasn't so much a matter of supply as it was a matter of power. The Ice Trust and its successors had it; they would keep it and wield it until the electric refrigerator short-circuited their vast, frozen empire.

––––––

Sources: Vertie Knapp, "The Natural Ice Industry of Philadelphia in the Nineteenth Century," *Pennsylvania History* 41, no. 4 (October 1974); Jonathan Rees, *Refrigeration Nation: A History of Ice, Appliances, and Enterprise in America* (Baltimore: Johns Hopkins University Press, 2013); Independence Hall Association, "The First Icehouse in America?," USHistory.org, http://www.ushistory.org/presidentshouse/history/icehouse .php; "New Ice Making Plant in the 'City of Brotherly Love,'" *Industrial Refrigeration*, vol. 6 (Des Plaines: Nickerson and Collins, 1894), 13–16; "No Advance in Price of Ice: Philadelphia Will Not Follow New York's Example," *Inquirer*, April 12, 1900.

Figure 6.5. "This Modern Ice Man Calls Once with Frigidaire," Frigidaire electric refrigerator exhibit at the sesquicentennial, 1926

Frigidaire wanted to freeze the iceman out of America's kitchens. To accomplish this, it took him on, appropriating the folksy icon of home delivery as the centerpiece of its lavish art deco display at Philadelphia's Sesquicentennial Exposition in 1926. But instead of a block of ice, this giant iceman statue had on his shoulder the final delivery—a new, compact electric refrigerator.

Four years earlier, the *Inquirer* had predicted the iceman's demise, happily looking forward to relief from years of mopping up footprints and spills from overflow pans. The new, electric "iceless refrigerator," it said, "spelled doom for the iceman." Soon he would be "an [extinct] species; a veritable Dodo." Dethroning Big Ice wouldn't come fast or easy.

In Philadelphia, one ice company, Knickerbocker, had massive plants, one with 125 employees and the storage capacity for a million tons. With the help of 1,200 horses and mules, Knickerbocker drivers kept more than 500 delivery wagons on the streets. And as the nation's iceboxes multiplied at the start of the twentieth century, America seemed to need every last one its 1,320 ice plants. Between 1889 and 1919, icebox manufacturing in the United States increased more than sixfold.

Eventually, electric refrigeration would become bigger, but not as long as the cost of the product remained high and its performance poor. In 1920, a household refrigerator cost $600 (more than $7,500 in today's dollars) and broke down about every tenth week. Once the price dropped and reliability increased, utilities recognized the potential goldmine in household refrigeration. Since units were always running and consumed far more electricity than any other appliance, home refrigeration could more than double their revenues. Realizing that promise, utilities didn't want to leave marketing and sales up to the manufacturers. By the mid-1920s, they were selling nearly a third of all new electric refrigerators.

In the same decade, Frigidaire, a subsidiary of General Motors, also engaged in aggressive, creative, and even whimsical marketing—and became America's refrigerator of choice. "How do you do, Mrs. Prospect?" Frigidaire's door-to-door sales script began in 1923. Once in the kitchen, the salesmen would take the temperature of the family's icebox. "Mrs. Prospect," continued the pitch, "we find that the average ice box maintains a temperature of about 55 degrees, and I think you will agree with me that this will keep food properly for only a short time." But, the salesman proceeded, sharing his thermometer with the housewife, "the temperature in your refrigerator is ___ degrees. This is slightly warmer than I expected. If you had Frigidaire, the temperature would certainly be ___ degrees colder than you now have in your icebox. . . . Won't you please talk this matter over with your husband tonight as, in all probability; I or one of our men will call upon him tomorrow afternoon and tell him the benefits of owning a Frigidaire."

Between 1920 and 1925, the number of refrigerators in American kitchens rose from 4,000 to 75,000. In 1926, it boomed to 248,000 units, and by 1928, 468,000. The following year, Frigidaire manufactured its millionth refrigerator. By 1930, the sales of electric household refrigerators surpassed those of iceboxes.

In the middle of the Great Depression, Americans still cleaned up after 350,000 iceboxes. They had also grown accustomed to the hum and chugging of 1.7 million plugged-in refrigerators. By 1940, 63 percent of all households had refrigerators—13.7 million of them. Four years later, 85 percent of America's kitchens were equipped. As Jonathan Rees, author of *Refrigeration Nation* put it, "The electric household refrigerator symbolized modernity. When filled with food, it symbolized abundance." After World War II, when just about every kitchen had one, size of the American refrigerator conveyed another kind of status—prosperity.

By 1953, when the last U.S. icebox manufacturer went out of business, the young, virile deliveryman carrying dripping, often dirty, blocks of ice into millions of clean American kitchens—the man whose proximity to wives and daughters fueled countless rumors, would-be scandals, and jokes on stage and screen—finally found a new home and a new role in nostalgia purgatory.

––––––

Sources: Jonathan Rees, *Refrigeration Nation: A History of Ice, Appliances, and Enterprise in America* (Baltimore: Johns Hopkins University Press, 2013); W. C. Fields, *The Dentist*, directed by Leslie Pearce (Hollywood: Paramount Pictures, 1932); "The Newest Ideas of Invention and Industry: The Passing of the Iceman," *Inquirer*, September 17, 1922; Frank Hamilton Taylor, "Knickerbocker Ice Company," in *The City of Philadelphia*, ed. Frank Hamilton Taylor (Philadelphia: Philadelphia Chamber of Commerce, 1900).

Figure 6.6. Front and Spring Garden Streets, November 18, 1915

How should someone safely exit a building on fire? The fire exit, of course. But what was the solution before the law required buildings to include the familiar "iron skeleton" fire escape? In the greater part of the nineteenth century, when fire struck in the rising city, urbanites were often at the mercy of fate. On more than one occasion, when Philadelphia's garret sweatshops and New York's tenements went up in flames, those trapped inside upper stories perished in "galleries of certain death."

Inventors heeded the calls for help. In March 1849, the Franklin Institute exhibited for public admiration a now-lost model of "a very ingenious contrivance," a "new fire-escape." There was no word as to how it might save lives or if it ever did. Nor do we know exactly how many such contrivances, either ingenious or ridiculous, promised the trapped and doomed freedom to walk, jump, or even fly to safety. But as we know from the city's deadliest fires, even after buildings were equipped with exterior

fire escapes, their inadequacies and awkward design contributed to the
fatalities.

Philadelphia passed an ordinance creating a fire-escape regulatory
board in 1876 and endowed it with the authority to order their installation
"upon such buildings as they may deem necessary . . . to secure life and
property." Three years later, Pennsylvania passed a sweeping law declaring
that any building "three or more stories in height, shall be provided with a
permanent, safe external means of escape therefrom in cases of fire." The
list of specific building types seemed comprehensive: "every building used
as a seminary, college, academy, hospital, asylum, or a hotel for the accom-
modation of the public, every storehouse, factory, manufactory, workshop
of every kind, in which employees or operatives are usually employed at
work in the third or higher story, every tenement house or building in
which rooms or floors are usually let to lodgers or families, and every public school building." Somehow the 1879 list missed theatres. That oversight
was corrected in 1885.

To some, a greater mistake lay in the assumption that the exterior iron
fire escape would be effective. According to Sara Wermeil, Philadelphia
architect Samuel Sloan "condemned the 'iron ladders clamped against the
wall' as 'worse than useless, because they are deceptive; giving the appearance of an escape without the reality.'" They were, Sloan wrote in 1868,
"'a most stupid contrivance' because women, children, the aged and the
disabled could not use them. With fires lapping out the window, he asked,
'would not those balconies be turned into gridirons to roast the unhappy
victims?'" Sloan's choice? Wall off internal stairwells with iron doors—a
solution that became standard, though not until the twentieth century.

In the nineteenth century, building owners and landlords took advantage of a culture of noncompliance and inadequate enforcement. A full
decade after passage of the 1879 law, "the lives of fully 100,000 children are
in danger," reported the *Inquirer*. "City Councils have failed to obey the laws
plainly laid down by the legislature of Pennsylvania. There are over 113,000
school children in Philadelphia distributed among 262 schoolhouses. Only

17 of these buildings are provided with fire escapes . . . The remaining 245 schoolhouses, with over 100,000 pupils, are totally without any means of escape in case of fire."

No surprise, really. Compliance failures continued for decades, as we know from the landmark disaster at the Triangle Shirtwaist fire of 1911 in New York, which killed 146 garment workers in less than half an hour. Did Philadelphia somehow manage to avoid such a pivotal and devastating event? Hardly. Who could forget the Market Street fire of 1901, where 22 died? (See pages 223–225.) And a full thirty years before the Triangle Shirtwaist fire, Philadelphia endured the tragic and scandalous Randolph Mill fire. (See pages 219–222.)

––––––

Sources: "The Model of a New Fire-Escape," *Inquirer*, March 26, 1849; "Tenement Traps," *New York Times*, February 4, 1860; "The City's Safety, Annual Meeting of the Board of Fire Commissioners. Report of the Chief," *Inquirer*, February 11, 1880; "School Houses and Fire Escapes" (editorial), *Inquirer*, October 7, 1889; "Fire Escapes Few," *Inquirer*, October 7, 1889; Sara E. Wermiel, "No Exit: The Rise and Demise of the Outside Fire Escape," *Technology and Culture* 44, no. 2 (April 2003): 258–284.

Figure 6.7. Officer Guy Parsons and another officer with team gas equipment, 1923

"I rob banks," Willie Sutton famously quipped, "because that's where the money is." Sutton didn't realize that's also where the tear gas was. Early one morning in February 1933, Sutton and a partner, disguised as postal messengers, gained entrance to the Corn Exchange National Bank and Trust, located at Sixtieth and Ludlow Streets. They tied a guard to a chair, but the guard freed himself, managed to release tear gas—and foiled the robbery.

Tear gas had become an accepted law enforcement tool—one of the more successful technology transfers from the battlefields of World War I to urban America. Months before the Treaty of Versailles, military leaders were gung ho to demonstrate the potential of tear gas in places like Philadelphia. "More effective than clubs, and less dangerous than bullets," they boasted.

The Army Chemical Warfare Service promised that tear gas had positive "psychological impacts." It could offer police "the ability to demoral-
ize and disperse a crowd without firing live ammunition." According to
a more recent history in the *Atlantic*, tear gas "could evaporate from the
scene without leaving traces of blood or bruises, making it appear better
for police-public relations than crowd control through physical force."

However, getting taxpayers to pay for the deployment of gas-filled
bombs on their hometown streets was a hard sell. After all, as early as 1899,
the Hague Conventions prohibited "projectiles filled with poison gas."
And then there was the recent horror of poison gas on the battlefields of
France. But military chemists claimed they had reconstituted formulas,
making them tame enough for use in peacetime urban America. At least
that's what Major Stephen Delanoy promised, fresh back from France,
"where he had been for more than a year perfecting various gases for the
government."

To demonstrate "how efficacious gas could be," Delanoy came to Philadelphia, where he had a friend in Philadelphia police superintendent William B. Mills. Together, they choreographed a high-profile experiment
where two hundred "volunteers" from the Philadelphia police force would
be gassed at the city's model farm near Fort Mifflin in South Philadelphia.
On July 19, 1921, according to the *New York Times*, "Police Supt. Mills took
a battalion of his huskiest men into a roped-off enclosure with instructions to capture six men who were armed with 150 tear gas bombs. Three
times they charged but each time we're driven back weeping violently
as they came within range of the charged vapor."

"Before they entered the mimic battle," Delanoy "assured the men that
the substance was 'absolutely not dangerous.' It is merely a tear-producing,
choking, nauseating gas," he said. "But be careful you don't swallow too
much." Philadelphia's guinea pigs apparently swallowed just the right
amount. The "sham attack" sold them on the stuff.

"The effectiveness of teargas as a mob dispeller received the emphatic
endorsement of 200 stalwart Philadelphia policemen today," reported the

Times. "Police officials said the test had undoubtedly proved the value of tear gas in police work. Not only is it immediately effective in disbursing a mob, but it might be used to drive a fugitive from a barricaded building." They imagined how a "container . . . placed in a bank vault . . . would also thwart burglaries."

"Bullets as mob-quellers now belong to the Dark Ages," declared the *Literary Digest.* Police would get "gutta-percha hand-grenades containing chemical gas," and their victims would choke with copious tears flowing. "One of these bombs or grenades is equal to a hundred police clubs in a riot," declared the officer in charge after the Philadelphia test. "This method of dealing with offenders against the peace has many obvious advantages," claimed the *Inquirer.* "It is humane, for one thing. Riding down or shooting into a mob may cause needless injuries or deaths, sometimes of innocent bystanders."

Within a few months, the city council approved a $2,500 appropriation to supply equipment for a new fifty-man "gas battalion" for the Philadelphia police. Amos Fries, chief of the U.S. Army's Chemical Warfare Service, who had been working "to redeploy the technology for everyday uses," provided "chemicals, material and equipment free of cost to the city." Philadelphia taxpayers only needed to purchase masks. Within a few years, police departments from New York to San Francisco were stocking up on tear gas and related supplies.

Philadelphia police, eager to make good on their investment, considered ways to put tear gas to work fighting a spate of robberies. Officials ordered their "bandit-chasing squad" to carry "tear bombs" as well as "sawed-off shotguns . . . to end the robbers' activities." They didn't have to wait long.

On October 7, 1922, police learned of an afterhours "ransacking" at the dress shop of R. A. and J. A. Brown at 1530 Sansom Street. One officer fired his pistol at the suspects and missed. They had hidden behind packing cases. No problem. Police "hurled a tear bomb against the wall directly above" their hiding spot. For the first time in an American city, plumes of tear gas filled the air. One suspect crashed through a window and escaped into a side alley.

Police captured the other suspect. According to the *Inquirer*, "When the air cleared sufficiently, the policemen entered the room and found George Rex, colored, twenty years old, of 18th and Lombard streets, in a stupefied condition, temporarily blinded."

Trench warfare had come home.

———

Sources: "Tear Gas for Mobs, U.S. Colonel's Plan," *Inquirer*, February 26, 1919; "New Gas with K. O. Wallop May Help Police in Battles," *Inquirer*, July 19, 1921; "200 Philadelphia Policeman Weep in Flight from Tear Gas in Sham Attack," *New York Times*, July 20, 1921; "Knockout Gas for Mobs," *Literary Digest* 70, August 20, 1921; "City Police to Use Gas Bombs Shortly," *Inquirer*, October 26, 1921; "Gas Bombs Prove Nemesis to Bandits," *Inquirer*, October 8, 1922; Anna Feigenbaum, "100 Years of Tear Gas: A Chemical Weapon Drifts off the Battlefield and into the Streets," *The Atlantic*, August 16, 2014; *Some of Willie Sutton's Heists*, document, http://williesutton.com/Willie%20Sutton%27s%20Robberies.pdf.

Figure 7.1. Second Street market, butter and egg stall, June 14, 1935

CHAPTER 7

Food

MISTY-EYED FOR MARKET SHAMBLES

As early Philadelphia expanded, the city's spine of market shambles in the center of High (later Market) Street kept growing. "The market could . . . be conveniently extended in the same plan," wrote an observer in 1809, giddy that Philadelphia might be able to maintain century-old shopping traditions. But nineteenth-century growth would outpace everyone's expectations, rendering the last remaining shambles a quaint and shabby vestige.

The nineteenth-century "market mania" ushered in an era of grand market halls that modernized food buying with a collection of block-long, light-filled, state-of-the-art venues for hundreds of vendors and thousands of shoppers. Many Philadelphians liked these markets and the bragging rights they offered, while others preferred to shop at the city's vestigial vintage shambles.

"There were three phases in the logical development of a market," explained the author of a 1913 study. "First, the curbstone market; second, the open shed; and third, and the modern enclosed market house. Strange as it may seem, Philadelphia's municipal markets are in the second phase—namely, open sheds. The North and South Second Street markets are all that remain to us of Philadelphia's once well-developed market system." The eighteenth-century design had been updated with "sheet iron roofs, cement floors and the systematizing of the numbering of the stalls."

Otherwise, "they [stood] as they were built," just the way many Philadelphians, who were exceedingly proud of their old market shambles, and
their old marketing ways, liked it.

"Few cities can boast of markets better supplied with the bounties of
nature than Philadelphia," claimed the guidebook *Philadelphia as It Is
in 1852*.

> Let the reader, particularly if a stranger, take a tour of observation
> through them, especially on Wednesday and Saturday mornings, and he
> will behold an exceedingly interesting and gratifying spectacle. He will
> find those buildings well supplied with all kinds of meat, poultry, game,
> fish, vegetables, fruit, &c., while the streets in the immediate vicinity are
> crowded in all directions with well-filled baskets.
>
> These markets, distributed throughout the city, embrace altogether
> over forty entire squares, in addition to the range of wagon stands on
> Market Street and Second Street, which of themselves form a line equal
> in extent to three miles.

Here's where the market shambles stood, according to the guide:

> **High Street Market.**—Those long ranges of buildings that line this
>   noble avenue, were not contemplated in the original plan of the
>   city. Penn designed Centre Square for this purpose. The first of
>   these houses was erected in 1710; it extended half way up from
>   Second Street. In 1729, it was carried up to Third Street, where,
>   for a long period, it was marked with the appendages of Pillory,
>   Stocks, and Whipping Post. . . . [Before the Revolution, the mar-
>   kets were extended to Fourth Street and eventually stretched all
>   the way to Eighth Street. At the easternmost end stood a fish mar-
>   ket and a New Jersey Market with a domed head house flanked
>   by cornucopia. West of Broad Street, the markets extended from
>   two more blocks.]

South Second Street Market extends from Pine to Cedar (South) Street.

North Second Street Market extends from Coates (Fairmount Avenue) to Poplar Street.

Callowhill Street Market is situated in Callowhill Street, between Fourth and Seventh Streets.

Shippen (Bainbridge) Street Market extends from Third to Fifth Street.

Maiden (Laurel) Street Market, Kensington, Maiden Street, between Broad and Manderson Streets. This is Laurel and Frankford Ave at Delaware Avenue.

Spring Garden Market, Spring Garden Street. Extensive ranges of light and graceful market-houses line this elegant avenue, from Sixth to Twelfth Street. [The 1862 Philadelphia atlas shows another block of market sheds from Thirteenth to Broad.]

Girard Market, Girard Avenue, between Tenth and Lewis (Warnock) Streets. [The 1862 atlas shows market sheds from Lawrence Street (between Fourth and Fifth) to Seventh and then also from Tenth to Twelfth.]

Moyamensing Market, extends from Prime (Ellsworth) to Wharton Street.

Franklin Market, Franklin (Girard) Avenue . . . consists of two ranges; one extending (a block east to) Hancock Street to the Germantown Road (now Avenue), the other from Crown (Crease) Street to the Frankford Road (Avenue).

Eleventh Street Market, Moyamensing. Eleventh Street, extends from Shippen (Bainbridge) to Fitzwater Street. [The 1862 atlas shows four blocks from Bainbridge to Carpenter Streets.]

The old system lasted, though not forever. "If retail markets are to succeed," worried Clyde Lyndon King in 1917, "they must change their locations as population centers shift. Public markets have evidently not adapted themselves to these changes as quickly as have private stores." And by 1917, market watchers knew that more than 1.5 million Philadelphians, living in hundreds of miles of row house neighborhoods, visited markets about twenty-five thousand times every day. More and more, these visits were shifting to new marketing habits focused on the neighborhood grocery store. And by then, Philadelphia had no less than 5,266 retail groceries and 2,004 butchers—about one for every fifty citizens—located at corners throughout the spreading city.

———

Sources: "Some Account of the Markets of Philadelphia," *The Port Folio*, vol. 2 (1809): 508–511; R. A. Smith, *Philadelphia as It Is in 1852* (Philadelphia: Lindsay and Blakiston, 1852); Achsah Lippincott, *Municipal Markets in Philadelphia*, vols. 49–50 (Annals of the American Academy of Political and Social Science, 1913); R. A. Smith and E. M. Patterson, "Co-operation among Grocers in Philadelphia" (PhD diss., University of Pennsylvania, 1915); Clyde Lyndon King, *Public Markets in the United States* (Philadelphia: National Municipal League, 1917).

Figure 7.2. Dock Street fish market, April 28, 1914

"The completion of the market between the two rivers will probably take place in the present generation," wrote an anonymous commentator in 1809, adding "a uniform, open arcade mathematically straight, two miles in length, perfect in its symmetry . . . will never be a contemptible object." In time, a generation of Philadelphians wouldn't be nearly as patient, or appreciative, of the vision for Philadelphia as an urban village. While the anonymous writer worried some "pragmatical architect" might come along and "destroy this symmetry, by adopting new dimensions as to height or breadth, and taking a different curve for his arch," the public would soon move on and advocate total demolition.

By the middle of the nineteenth-century, many Philadelphians considered the city's spine of market sheds "a time-honored nuisance," an outdated vestige of William Penn's 1680s vision for a "country town." By 1850, the population exceeded 120,000, and a few years later, the two square miles of the city would consolidate with the roughly 129 square miles of the county. By 1900, Philadelphia's population would explode to nearly 1.3 million. That would demand a sweeping transformation of how this sprawling, modernizing city would supply itself with victuals. As historian Helen Tangires put it, squat, quaint, open-air markets had "no place in the emerging vision."

The new vision demanded an entirely new type of building: spacious market halls with soaring arched ceilings, made possible by modern trusses and accommodating hundreds of vendors and thousands of shoppers. Those market halls would join the repertoire of large urban building types: city halls, schools, museums, libraries, theaters, factories, train sheds, and depots. They'd play a distinct role, explains Tangires, in a nineteenth-century "moral economy," where government and private interests collaborated to support the community's social, political, and physical well-being. And Philadelphia, as it so happened, provided perfect conditions for this market movement to flourish.

Four years after consolidation, "in the wake of the demolition" of Market Street's old sheds, writes Tangires, seventeen market companies were incorporated in the city, leading to a period of "unparalleled construction." Each new corporation issuing stock meant another "unprecedented opportunity for speculation in food retailing" and another new hall with "the latest innovations in refrigeration, lighting, ventilation, and construction." Philadelphia's "market house company mania" turned out an impressive collection of state-of-the-art "market palaces."

One by one, they opened. At the northeast corner of Sixteenth and Market Streets in April 1859, architect John M. Gries's Western Market Company invited in the public and received praise for its arched roof and clerestory above a 170-by-150-foot interior featuring "280 stalls with Italian marble counter tops" divided by commodious aisles. At each end were galleries devoted to "the sale of flowers, seeds, and ice cream." Iron-framed doors with "wicker inserts for air circulation lined the entire perimeter."

Seven blocks away, vendors bid in an auction for 431 stalls at the Eastern Market, a 100-by-300-foot hall at Fifth and Commerce Streets. Higher prices than expected spurred more confidence and additional investment citywide. When the market opened in November 1859, a company of top-hatted hosts served a feast in the center of the main floor.

Center City soon had its share of new market houses. So would neighborhoods that only a few years before were beyond the city proper. The Fairmount Market Company, incorporated in March 1859, raised $100,000 by selling two thousand shares at fifty dollars apiece. Before long, they started construction of a 100-by-300-foot hall at the northwest corner of Twenty-Second Street and Pennsylvania Avenue.

Throughout the city, from Northern Liberties to Point Breeze, from West Philadelphia to Germantown, the city's appetites launched a golden age of market construction. And that was only the first round. "The market house company mania that began in Philadelphia in 1859 continued unabated through the rest of the state, particularly during 1870s and 1880s," writes Tangires. "They grew up like mushrooms in every part of the city." In North Philadelphia alone, market halls cropped up at Ninth and Girard, Tenth and Montgomery, Broad and Columbia (Cecil B. Moore), Seventeenth and Venango, Eighteenth and Ridge, and Twentieth and Oxford—to mention but a few of the thirty-nine listed in a city directory from 1901.

It was a glorious, unsustainable expansion. "Too numerous and costly," observed Thomas De Voe as early as 1862, citing "false confidence," false starts, and early failures due to "overcapitalized and highly speculative" projects. The Franklin Market at Tenth and Marble (now Ludlow) had to be repurposed as the Mercantile Library. Neither the Eastern nor the Western Markets survived. Nor did the Fairmount Market. Gone are the Black Horse, the Union, the Fidelity, the Globe, the Red Star, and the Red Lion. It could be that the Green Hill Market at Seventeenth and Poplar stands as the city's last remaining hall of those chartered in 1859.

Ask anyone today about the city's great food halls, and they'll point you to the Reading Terminal Market, a ground-level emporium under the 1892 train shed at Twelfth and Filbert Streets. It stands where, not one, but two of the grand original market halls once stood, side by side, in the heady days of Philadelphia's market mania.

A proud, lone survivor.

———

Sources: "Some Account of the Markets of Philadelphia," *The Port Folio*, vol. 2 (1809): 508–511; "Laws of the General Assembly of the Commonwealth of Pennsylvania, Passed at the Session of 1859" (Harrisburg, 1859); "A Digest of Titles of Corporations Chartered by the Legislature of Pennsylvania, Between the Years 1700 and 1873 Inclusive" (Philadelphia: J. Campbell and Son, 1874); "Gospill's Philadelphia City Directory for 1901" (Philadelphia: James Gospill's Sons, 1901); Helen Tangires, *Public Markets and Civic Culture in Nineteenth-Century America* (Baltimore: Johns Hopkins University Press, 2003); Helen Tangires, "Public Markets," *Encyclopedia of Greater Philadelphia* (Camden: Rutgers, 2016).

Figure 7.3. Interior of slaughterhouse (abattoir), 5319 Westminster Avenue, January 16, 1909

"If we do not want to eat the stuff ourselves," declared veterinarian Charles Allen Cary in 1887, "we had better bury or burn it." Experts of the American Veterinary Association called for more and better inspections of dairies and slaughterhouses to reduce the amount of tubercular meat and milk reaching consumers.

At the turn of the twentieth century, tuberculosis remained a leading cause of death in the United States. Approximately 10 percent of cases resulted from exposure to infected cattle or cattle products. Most distressing was the fact that cattle caused 25 percent of the childhood cases of the disease, and the rates were highest in cities. It seemed a losing battle to Franklin K. Lowry, Philadelphia's official "meat detective." In 1904, Lowry's office conducted nearly 6,400 visits to slaughterhouses and about 700 to the city's stores and markets. His team inspected more than 205,000 cattle and calves. Too many were infected.

Lowry augmented his team with a graduate of Penn Veterinary School, Dr. Albert Fricke Schreiber, who he named chief meat inspector. Schreiber ramped up the search for violators and condemned even more meat, sending it up to M. L. Shoemaker's Fertilizing Plant at the foot of Venango Street. Even so, with few arrests and even fewer convictions, Philadelphia's cattle drivers and meat packers continued to conduct business as usual.

Schreiber and his team of inspectors visited nearly forty-four thousand butchers, slaughterhouses (known as abattoirs), storage houses, and markets in 1909. By dropping in "quite unexpectedly, late at night, on two small downtown abattoirs," they found "a tubercular beef carcass, from which the affected tissues had been carefully, if not deftly, trimmed out . . . being dressed for market." Condemning that meat was a good day's work for the inspectors but also an unusually successful one. With a "small and inadequate force," Schreiber had little chance of keeping up with the violations among the city's 150 or so small abattoirs spread far and wide, about half of which had been cited for unsanitary conditions. Nearly 375,000 pounds of meat was condemned and destroyed in 1909 alone. But it resulted in only a single fine and a single guilty plea—business kept on as usual.

For Philadelphia to have "something remotely related to intelligent supervision," Schreiber promoted New York's solution: confining its abattoirs to a single section of the city. He pleaded that his force of six inspectors (only two of whom were veterinarians) be expanded to twelve, including a total of four veterinarians, a team "approximating the scope of the problem with which we have had to deal." Only then could Schreiber hope to seriously address the tuberculosis problem, not to mention many other infractions, including "the handing of meat outside in the open air, uncovered and exposed to street dust, refuse and insects."

In 1910, attrition caused by low pay reduced Schreiber's team to three, "a force obviously and absurdly inadequate" if the city was "to prevent the killing of tuberculous cattle, measled hogs and immature calves" and provide "systematic surveillance" of the city's stores and markets. The case for more staff had merit on several fronts. In 1910, Philadelphia's population stood at just over 1.5 million, and the city was still growing and diversifying. The meat inspectors needed to not only catch up but keep up.

When the city's meat inspection unit did expand to eight (not the requested twelve) in 1911, Schreiber *still* felt overwhelmed. Now, in addition to the ongoing problem of killer cattle, he wanted his inspectors to turn their attention to the city's "'pest' sections" and address "persistent offenders," which he described as a "class of dealers, who keep dirty shops in congested localities overrun with street stands, barrow venders, and other features of like character peculiar to the sections of the city inhabited by people of foreign birth." According to Schreiber, these newer arrivals, "vendors of the curbstone and push cart variety . . . bring in partially decomposed rabbits, heated and unwholesome poultry, and other products." Schreiber found them "pitifully poor, woefully ignorant of the plainest rudiments of sanitation, and not infrequently belligerently obstinate in their opposition to hygienic regulations." He likewise found their shops to be "badly kept, lacking in equipment . . . without order or intelligent direction, and sometimes [a] jumble [of] two or more lines of trade obviously not compatible under one roof."

In a city with a new and growing immigrant population and a persistent unsolved problem of tuberculosis in cattle—with curbstone vendors who "litter the roadways, gutters and sidewalks with refuse" and allow "street dirt [to be] blown over and upon exposed meats, poultry and fish"—the inadequate number of meat men had no choice but to do their jobs one day at a time.

———

Sources: "Annual Report of the Meat Detective for the Year 1904" in *Second Annual Message of John Weaver, Mayor of the City of Philadelphia,* vol. 1 (Philadelphia: 1905), https://books.google.com/books?id=u1Q5AQAAMAAJ &source=gbs_navlinks_s; "Annual Report of the Division of Meat and

Cattle Inspection for the Year 1911," *First Annual Message of Rudolph Blankenburg with the Annual Reports Issued by the City of Philadelphia*, vol. 3 (Philadelphia, 1912), https://books.google.com/books?id= YUwwAQAAMAAJ&printsec=; "Annual Report of the Division of Meat and Cattle Inspection for the Year 1910," in *Annual Reports of the Director of the Department of Public Health and Charities and Chief of the Bureau of Health* (Philadelphia, 1910), https://books.google.com/books ?id=svY3AAAAYAAJ&dq; "Annual Report of the Division of Meat and Cattle Inspection for the Year 1911," *Annual Message of the Mayor of the City of Philadelphia with the Annual Reports of Directors of Departments* (Philadelphia, 1911), https://books.google.com/books?id=svY3AAAAYAAJ &printsec=; Mitchell V. Palmer and W. Ray Waters, "Bovine Tuberculosis and the Establishment of an Eradication Program in the United States: Role of Veterinarians," *Veterinary Medicine International* 2011 (2011).

Figure 7.4. Macfadden's Physical Culture Restaurant, 25 South Ninth Street, photographed by M. Rolston, March 15, 1915

"Weakness is a Crime." With those four words, Bernarr Macfadden launched a media empire built on health in 1899. Within a year, his *Physical Culture* magazine brought its growing readership a number of articles covering many topics, including arguments for fitness and against refined foods, for contraception and against the corset. Macfadden also wrote and published tomes with seductive titles: *Virile Powers of Superb Manhood* (1900) and *Power and Beauty of Superb Womanhood* (1901). His boldly shared opinions on health, sex, exercise, diet, and hygiene became famous; his name became a household word. Circulation of Macfadden's *Physical Culture* magazine topped 150,000 in its first year. In time, it would reach 500,000.

Macfadden's ambitions extended beyond publishing. In 1902, he opened a vegetarian restaurant in New York City, also named Physical Culture. Before long, he opened restaurants in Boston, Buffalo, Pittsburgh, St. Louis, Cleveland, Chicago—and Philadelphia, at 25 South Ninth Street. By 1911, the year Macfadden published his first *Encyclopedia of Physical Culture*, his health-food restaurant chain had twenty locations nationwide. Macfadden opened Physical Culture sanatoriums and health resorts and even planned a Physical Culture City. The man had presidential aspirations.

"We need stronger, more capable men; healthy superior women," wrote Macfadden in 1915, introducing *Vitality Supreme*, another of his popular books. He continued:

The great prizes of life come only to those who are efficient. . . . The body must be developed completely, splendidly. The buoyancy, vivacity, energy, enthusiasm and ambition ordinarily associated with youth can be maintained through middle age and in some cases even to old age. . . . Why not throb with superior vitality! Why not possess the physical energy of a young lion? For then you will compel success. You will stand like a wall if need be, or rush with the force of a charging bison toward the desired achievements. . . . Adherence to the principles laid down herein will add to the characteristics that insure special achievements. They will increase the power of your body and mind and soul. They will help each human entity to become a live personality. They will enable you to live fully, joyously. They will help you to feel, enjoy, suffer every moment of every day. It is only when you are thus thrilled with the eternal force of life that you reach the highest pinnacle of attainable capacities and powers. Hidden forces, sometimes marvelous and mysterious, lie within nearly every human soul. Develop, expand and bring out these latent powers. Make your body splendid, your mind supreme; for then you become your real self, you possess all your attainable powers. . . . It will be worth infinitely more than money. . . . Adhere to the principles set forth and a munificent harvest of physical, mental and spiritual attainments will surely be yours.

What did they serve at Macfadden's Physical Culture restaurants? Foods "in their natural condition." Ahead of his time, Macfadden believed "the process of 'refining' is the great food crime of the age." He believed conventional methods of food preparation had "a destructive effect" upon their "nutritive value." He pointed out the evils of "white bread," where "the best part of the wheat has been eliminated in the process of milling." Likewise, nutritional value is "removed from our vegetables in the process of boiling" and from rice in the process of polishing. "Trying to secure adequate nourishment," Macfadden observed that many Americans consumed "an excessive amount of the refined defective foods." Bread is "supposed to be the 'staff of life,'" he noted, but "it might reasonably be termed to be the 'staff of death.'"

Macfadden urged his followers "to select only natural foods," arguing that "unquestionably, a perfect diet is furnished by nuts and fruits." In their raw state, "foods . . . possess a tremendous amount of vitality-building elements." Macfadden relied on salads of "celery, lettuce, tomatoes, onions, water-cress, parsley, cucumbers" with spinach and dandelion, dressed in olive oil and lemon juice. He wouldn't serve vinegar "partly because it is seldom pure, and one can never tell what combination of chemicals it contains."

Bernard Adolphus Macfadden (at some point, he changed his first name to Bernarr for effect) barely survived a miserable childhood to build America's first public bodybuilding empire. He survived four marriages, founded his own religion—Cosmotarianism—made and lost fortunes, and planned to live to 125. Judging from his confidence and physique in middle age, Macfadden might have actually believed he could.

Macfadden didn't achieve his ultimate goal of longevity. In 1955, the *Washington Post* and *Times Herald* summarized the accomplishments of the eighty-seven years he lived. Macfadden's most "proudly avowed aim" was "to rescue sex from the stuffy and unhealthy atmosphere of the smoking room and the honky-tonk into the clean sunlit world of outdoors, and also perhaps to dignify it as a subject of serious and high minded conversation in physical culture restaurants over a nut-and-spinach ragout and a magnum of chilled carrot juice." In the end, Bernarr Macfadden got credit for what he really was: a twentieth-century American lifestyle pioneer.

———

Sources: Mark Adams, *Mr. America: How Muscular Millionaire Bernarr Macfadden Transformed the Nation through Sex, Salad, and the Ultimate Starvation Diet* (New York: HarperCollins, 2010); Kathleen L. Endres, "The Feminism of Bernarr Macfadden: Physical Culture Magazine and the Empowerment of Women," *Media History Monographs* 13, no. 2 (2010); Ben Fanton, "Strange before His Time in Trying to Live 125 Years, Bernarr Macfadden Made the Most of the 87 He Had," *Buffalo News*, October 31, 1993; Bernarr Macfadden, *Vitality Supreme* (Physical Culture, 1915); Ben Yagoda, "The True Story of Bernarr Macfadden: Life and Loves of the Father of the Confession Magazine," *American Heritage*, December 1981; Joseph F. Wilkinson, "Look at Me: As Far as Bernarr Macfadden Was Concerned, the Main Aim in Life Was to Be Noticed," *Smithsonian*, December 1997; "Bernarr Macfadden," *St. James Encyclopedia of Popular Culture* (Farmington Hills: Gale, 2013).

Figure 7.5. White Tower, Broad and Race Streets, southeast corner, photographed by Wenzel J. Hess, January 10, 1944

White Tower opened its ninth location at Broad and Race Streets in 1932,
only two years after expanding into Philadelphia. The Milwaukee-based
company founded in 1926 by the father-son team John E. and Thomas E.
Saxe produced restaurants at a fast-food pace. By the middle of the 1930s,
the griddles of more than 120 White Tower restaurants in eleven American
cities had forever changed the urban American foodscape. Day or night, so
long as there was a nickel in your pocket, you were never far from a "pure
beef" hamburger.

White Tower built its business model copying that of White Castle, a chain launched in Wichita, Kansas, in 1921. No detail went unnoticed as the Saxes studied and then assiduously replicated White Castle restaurants. They adopted a similar name, menu, and pricing. The Saxes lured away White Castle staff to create a mirror operation. They even the co-opted the slogan: White Castle urged customers to "Buy 'em by the sack"; White Tower told theirs to "Take home a bagful." From Boston to Norfolk, Minneapolis to Philadelphia, both companies populated intersections with whitewashed crenellated clones—or, in the case of White Tower, clones of clones.

By the time bags of burgers started flying out of the door, White Tower and White Castle were three years into a lengthy court battle that would determine which company had the right to do what and where they could do it. Two years later, the decision from the Michigan Court came down: White Tower's copying would have to come to an end. In Detroit, where the chain had forty-six restaurants, White Tower had to "change its name, architecture and slogan."

Emboldened by this win, the founder of White Castle offered White Tower conditions for a settlement. According to David Gerard Hogan in *Selling 'Em by the Sack*, White Tower could continue using the name if the Saxes would pay a sizable lump sum and lose the crenellated, castle-like battlements. The Saxes agreed to an immediate payment of $65,000 plus a subsequent payment of $17,000—a total worth more than $1.3 million in today's dollars. Plus, they would document their compliance in photographs. In its transformation, White Tower abandoned its attachment to the ancient building style. Crenellations didn't particularly say much about purity and service, anyway. But what would?

As Paul Hirshorn and Steven Izenour observed in their book *White Towers*, this quandary called for a "strong architectural idea." And as it turned out, the 1930s offered up some potent choices. American architects and their corporate clients were experimenting with the sleek, streamlined Art Deco style and the newly arrived International style. Without missing a beat, White Tower became an adjudicated proving ground for a reinvigorated image of cleanliness, consistency, and modern service. One by one, the crenellated White Towers, including the one at Broad and Race Streets, were replaced with modern towers and clean cubes of white porcelain enamel, pristine billboards lit with goose-necked lamps deftly announcing that hamburgers were to be had. As far as White Tower was concerned, the modernized hamburger was well-done—and done well. By the 1950s, the chain had expanded to 230 restaurants, including seventeen in Philadelphia.

———

Sources: Paul Hirshorn and Steven Izenour, *White Towers* (Cambridge: MIT Press, 1981); David G. Hogan, *Selling 'Em by the Sack: White Castle and the Creation of American Food* (New York: New York University Press, 1999); Philip Langdon, *Orange Roofs, Golden Arches: The Architecture of American Chain Restaurants* (New York: Alfred A. Knopf, 1986); "White Tower System Inc. v. White Castle System of Eating Houses Corp. Appeal from the District Court of the United States for the Eastern District of Michigan; Edward J. Moinet, Judge," HeinOnline, May 4, 1937, accessed March 10, 2018.

Figure 7.6. Dock Street between Front and Water Streets, north side, November 5, 1955

All Don and Peggy Kleinschmidt wanted was a nice family dinner. The *last* thing they expected was for their three-year-old son, Dale, to become the poster child in a frenzied food-tainting scandal.

On Tuesday, March 24, 1959, Peggy went shopping at her local supermarket in Haddon Heights, New Jersey, and arrived home with two pounds of flounder fillets. As her four children played nearby, Peggy unwrapped the fish; slathered it with breadcrumbs, salt, and pepper; and set about cooking. Dale, the Kleinschmidt's three-year-old, loved fish and couldn't wait. As soon as Peggy fried the first fillet, she gave it to him with a glass of milk. Dale scarfed down his meal and ran off to visit with his grandmother, who lived nearby. The rest of the Kleinschmidt family then sat down to eat.

Almost immediately, Dale's grandmother sensed something wrong. At first, she attributed it to Dale having missed his usual nap. But within a few minutes, he was crying and vomiting. Then he started turning blue. The Kleinschmidts called their family physician, who arrived quickly. The doctor saw Dale "lying on a chair with no detectable blood pressure, eyes rolled back, and absent reflexes." By the time he arrived at Cooper Hospital in Camden, Dale was dead. And other family members were also suffering symptoms of food poisoning. What could it be? "The fish didn't taste quite right," observed Don Kleinschmidt. But for more than twenty-four hours, no one knew for sure.

Police ordered the flounder removed from the supermarket fish counter. And as word spread and reports came in, local, state, and national health officials and the Food and Drug Administration investigated. The next morning, the *Inquirer* reported several women becoming ill after eating fillet of flounder "in a well-known restaurant in Philadelphia." The city health department "issued a warning on a teletype service" that reached "newspapers, radio and televisions stations." By five p.m. on Wednesday, March 25, every last radio announcer in the Philadelphia area was cautioning, "All flounder purchased yesterday and today is poisonous." Don't eat it; Destroy it.

"Poisoned Fish Hits East; Baby Dies," read a front-page headline in Gadsden, Alabama. "Boy's Death Sparks Poison Food Search," declared another in Sarasota, Florida. The alarm had spread up and down the East Coast. Throughout the city, the suburbs and beyond, flounder-lovers crowded emergency rooms requesting antidotes and pleading to have their stomachs pumped.

Quickly, the investigation pointed to a single source, Dan DiOrio's Universal Seafood Company, a fish processor at Water and Dock Streets on the Philadelphia waterfront. And investigators identified the additive that had killed Dale Kleinschmidt: sodium nitrite. Just as the warnings were going out, DiOrio himself stood in front of news cameras denying the fish industry "had or would use sodium nitrite." And even after his firm was identified as the likely processor, DiOrio held firm to his denial: "sodium nitrate is not used in his plant operations." DiOrio felt "just as sorry as anyone" about the loss of life.

At first, Food and Drug Administration district director Robert C. Stanfill found nothing to contradict DiOrio's repeated denials. But upon further investigation, Stanfill's team found "evidence of nitrites . . . on the concrete floor, and on the cutting table." Digging deeper, they traced several transactions. The day before Dale Kleinschmidt's death, a nearby chemical supply house made "an early-morning delivery of 400-pounds of sodium nitrite" to DiOrio's facility. He "personally authorized the order and personally accompanied" the clearly labeled drum "from the truck to the filleting room," where 1,800 pounds of fish—that would kill the youngest Kleinschmidt and sicken at least forty others—were treated. Three-year-old Dale Kleinschmidt died after consuming an estimated 460 milligrams of sodium nitrite, more than 2.5 times the amount that would "induce hypotension, pallor, sweating, nausea, dizziness, and loss of consciousness" in an adult.

Dan DiOrio pleaded nolo contendere. Sentenced to a month in jail, he served sixteen days and remained on probation for three years. Burdened by scandal and lawsuits, Universal Seafood soon closed.

————

Sources: Associated Press, "Boy's Death Sparks Poison Food Search," March 25, 1959; Albert V. Gaudiosi, "Area Warned of Poisoned Flounder," *Inquirer*, March 26, 1959; Robert Greenberg, "U.S. Aide Links City Distributor to Tainted Fish," *Inquirer*, March 26, 1959; Associated Press, "Poison Philadelphia Flounder Causes Panic," March 26, 1959; "Poisoned Fish Hits East; Baby Dies," *Gadsden Times*, March 26, 1959; "Fish on Sale Now Are Held to Be Safe," *Baltimore Sun*, March 27, 1959; Robert C. Stanfill, "A Case Study of a Chemical Food Poisoning Involving Fish," quarterly bulletin, Association of Food and Drug Officials of the United States, vols. 24–26, 1960; Thomas L. Singley III, MD, "Secondary Methemoglobinemia Due to the Adulteration of Fish with Sodium Nitrite," *Annals of Internal Medicine* 57, no. 5 (November 1962).

CHAPTER 8

Fires and Disasters

THE RANDOLPH MILL FIRE: DISASTER, INDIGNATION, AND RECOGNITION

The Landenberger's Dress Goods Manufactory's two front doors on Randolph Street were locked tight. "This practice," according to a news account, "prevails extensively in that neighborhood among the mill managers—partly to keep intruders out, and partly to keep the male hands in" during work hours and "prevent their slipping around the corner to get a drink." In spite of the three-year-old law requiring fire escapes, the five-story mill building had not a one. On the night of October 12, 1881, when fire struck the factory, destruction multiplied into horror and death.

A little before 10 p.m., neighbors heard "shrieks of agony and despair . . . issuing from the building." They looked to the windows on the third and fourth floors to see "the forms of men and women gesticulating frantically and screaming for aid, their retreat being cut off and the flames sweeping around them."

"Don't jump," shouted someone on the ground. "We will get ladders."

The fire spread faster. As an eyewitness described it, "The first thing we knew, down came a girl, and then another and another. When the first was picked up it was found that she had broken her back over the railing of the iron steps. The next leaped from the fourth story and was crushed out of shape upon the pavement. And so the work of desperation went on until nearly a score of victims had been cruelly and in most cases fatally injured."

Mattie Conlan was somewhat luckier since she was "let down by a shawl from the third story window." With the smoke "rising round her and the flames streaming upward," she let go. Thankfully, Conlan's injuries weren't fatal. Kate Schaeffer and Annie Brady "jumped hand-in-hand from the third floor window. Brady died instantly."

What became of the thirty-five others working the night shift? According to newspaper reports, no one even knew exactly who they were: "Landenberger's people positively refused to furnish the list of those who were in the building when the fire broke out." And without a list, loved ones were at loose ends: angry, confused, and grieving.

The following morning, as the coroner searched the ruins, relatives "begged pathetically to be allowed to enter the building and look for missing husbands or sons." Five victims were retrieved that day, including the sixteen-year-old Elizabeth Franck, who had lived with her family at 1706 Waterloo Street. Her funeral services would be held at St. Jacob's Evangelical Lutheran Church at Third and Columbia (now Cecil B. Moore). "Six young ladies clad in white" were Lizzie Franck's pallbearers.

Two days after the fire, searchers continued to look for bodies "but discovered none." James McMunn's wife waited nearby, sadly watching. So did Joseph Glazer's mother. Annie Straub's brothers looked on "with anxious hearts."

At the morgue, George Matheson barely recognized the body and polka-dotted, blue-and-white dress of his fifteen-year-old daughter Mary. He had her remains transferred home to 1419 Hope Street. Later the same day, authorities sent a contingent "to see whether the body was not really that of the missing Annie Straub." Matheson angrily turned them away, refusing access to Mary's body. What he had expected was a visit by Charles Landenberger. The mill owner "might have come to see the family, as any gentleman would have done," the grieving Matheson snapped to a reporter.

"The feeling around the neighborhood was intense, and many people, while they unreservedly condemned the owner of the building, Joseph

Harvey" also challenged Landenberger's denials of culpability. He knew the upper floors had no emergency egress, though he claimed to have urged Harvey, time and time again, to install fire escapes. "Why did he send so many people up there to work?" they asked. The streets filled with expressions of distress: "Knots of employees of other mills" gathered "earnestly discussing the sad event, and strongly denouncing the false economy which failed to provide suitable means of escape."

"Popular sentiment, urged on by the atrocity of this case, with its ugly exposure of indifference to human life and human suffering and sorrow" inspired an "indignation meeting" attended by six hundred mourners who crowded onto a lot adjacent to "the scene of slaughter."

The coroner's inquest into the fire and the nine deaths it caused produced an undisputed verdict: "The fire was caused by the improperly constructed and inefficiently managed apparatus for lighting the building . . . Joseph Harvey, owner of the mills, is criminally responsible for the loss of life, in neglecting to furnish proper means of escape in case of fire." In addition, "the city of Philadelphia is responsible for not enforcing the laws in compelling Joseph Harvey to erect proper fire-escapes."

In fact, the Randolph Mill Fire turned out to be a pivotal disaster. A specially appointed committee of the Franklin Institute examined technologies and design possibilities for fire escapes and elevators and, as historian Sara Wermiel tells us, made several "farsighted recommendations" leading to "an important advance in the field of life safety."

Do we remember and recognize any of this at the site today? No—not yet, anyway.

———

Sources: "Another Horror: Fatal Result of a Mill Fire," *Inquirer*, October 13, 1881; "A Holocaust: The Mill Fire Disaster," October 14, 1881; "Around the Ruins," *Inquirer*, October 14, 1881; "At the Hospitals: How the Wounded Are Faring," *Inquirer*, October 14, 1881; "The Man-Trap: More about the

Mill Disaster," *Inquirer*, October 15, 1881; "Last Week's Horror: The Disaster and Its Results," *Inquirer*, October 17, 1881; "Report of Committee of the Franklin Institute on Fire-Escapes and Elevators," *Journal of the Franklin Institute* 113, no. 667–672 (July–December 1881): 408–414; Sara E. Wermiel, "No Exit: The Rise and Demise of the Outside Fire Escape," *Technology and Culture* 44, no. 2 (April 2003): 258–284.

Figure 8.1. Five-alarm fire at Hunt-Wilkinson Company, Twelfth and Market Streets, October 25, 1901

Walls of the Hunt, Wilkinson, and Company furniture emporium came tumbling down the morning of October 25, 1901. By lunchtime, firefighters declared the conflagration of the eight-story, fourteen-year-old building at 1219–1221 Market Street under control. Twenty-two were dead, ranking this Philadelphia's deadliest fire. (It is missing from the top "25 Most Deadly Building Fires in America," where it would have ranked as twenty-fourth with the 1929 Detroit Study Club dance hall disaster.)

"Never in its history has Philadelphia experienced a fire which spread with such great rapidity," reported the *Inquirer*. Never before were so many victims "speeded through gates of eternity," reported the *Atlanta Constitution*. "Rows of charred bodies at the morgue, a score of homes made desolate, a gaunt pile of twisted, steaming ruins on Market street between Twelfth and Thirteenth, are monuments to a fire" that was "swift as a whirlwind, sickening in its horrors." First responders were quick, "but the flames were quicker." The fire rose quickly "from cellar to roof, eating into adjoining buildings and hanging in a seething, spark-dotted canopy over Market street." Hell reigned outside and in:

> Sixty or more men, women and children were at work on the upper floors of the building. The roaring flames and the suffocating smoke that cut off retreat were their first and only warnings. Madly they groped for windows and the fire escapes, many meeting death where they stood, others reaching the iron railed balconies, only to find themselves and like rats in a trap, confronted with the alternative of being gridironed or the chance of being crushed on the stones below. Most of those killed were at work on the sixth floor, where women were engaged in sewing. It was reported that goods were stored against the windows, which prevented the women from getting out on the fire escapes, but this was positively denied by a member of the firm.

> Thousands from the streets below witnessed tragedy upon tragedy, powerless to help. They saw women penned in by flame tearing out their hair in their frenzy. They saw men struggle on wires and gratings and burn as they hung between earth and sky. They saw others plunge from the windows or turn and stagger back into the pitiless cauldron. The stones of Commerce street, the narrow highway at the rear of the building, rang the dirge of more than one victim who jumped blindly and missed the net.

> Squares away the screams of the dying could be heard. Tongues cannot tell the horrors that eyes saw.

At one point, "all eyes turned to the fire escapes" outside a seventh-story window, where upholsterers "were running down the escape pell-mell."

> The smoke ascending in their faces was growing blacker and blacker. A man appeared at the window with a woman. He put his arm around her waist. They began to climb down the escape and reached the sixth

floor. He seemed to faint. They stopped to rest, and then made another struggle.

Cheer after cheer went up from the street at this. But the situation was growing more desperate every second. When the next wave of smoke passed the woman was seen standing alone on the landing. It was impossible for her to get down through the flames beneath her. She heard the shouts and knew the net had been spread below to catch her. . . . She had one chance in a hundred to save her life by a leap. The firemen grasped their net and looked up. They could not see her. The woman peered down. She could not see them. Persons farther away tried to shout directions. It was a guess. It was her only chance. She leaped. Her form came straight through the air, feet foremost. She jumped well and clear. Thousands of eyes watched the flying form. They saw it strike the iron rail of the awning. She dropped a little to one side of the net outstretched to save her and struck the pavement.

Such was the death of Susan Gormley, 42 years of age, of 1727 Filbert street.

A special jury of experts convened by the city coroner collected evidence, reviewed testimony, and found the structure in compliance with the safety codes that existed. They couldn't zero in on what started the fire, suggesting that only the deceased "could probably explain the direct cause." And they recommended sweeping changes aimed at prevention, mitigation, and "providing proper and sufficient means of escape."

––––––––

Sources: "Flames Starting in Basement of Hunt, Wilkinson and Co.'s Furniture Store, 1219–21 Market Street," *Inquirer*, October 26, 1901; "Story of the Fire Told in Detail," *Inquirer*, October 26, 1901; "Eight Story Building Fire," *Atlanta Constitution*, October 26, 1901; "No Cause Found for Fatal Fire," *Inquirer*, November 21, 1901; "The 25 Most-Deadly Building Fires of All Time," Fire Science Degree, Firesciencedegree.com.

Figure 8.2. Break in sewer, Thompson Street, west of Eighth, September 19, 1913

That morning, just like any other Thursday morning, John Connor stepped out of his family's two-story row house, near Thirteenth and Moore Streets, and made his way up Passyunk Avenue to his job in Center City. Summer still lingered in the sunny September air, and the twenty-three-year-old Connor looked forward to another day behind the wheel of Merchant and Evans's brand-new, custom-made delivery truck.

Merchant and Evans had just about outgrown its building at 517 Arch Street. The company had done quite well since the Civil War, when Clark Merchant retired from the Navy and built a business in brass, bronze, copper, and tin. Over time, he aligned the firm with the building trades. And in 1913, with Powell Evans of International Sprinkler Company fame at the helm, even more success was certain. Under Evans, the firm expanded its offerings. Its fireproof products would soon be standard everywhere, if the insurance companies had anything to say about it—and they did. Soon, few large structures rose without sprinklers and fireproof metal doors and shutters. But Evans also saw potential in the automobile market and turned the company's talents to the manufacture of clutches, alignment joints, rear axles, jackshaft transmissions, grease cups, and metal tire cases. Before long, Merchant and Evans would build its own motor trucks, not unlike the models assembled for deliveries and pickups in Philadelphia. The company was "one of the premier metal houses of the United States," with plants in Philadelphia, Chicago, and Wheeling, West Virginia, and offices from New York to Kansas.

Back on the street, as Connor approached Merchant and Evans's loading dock on the Cuthbert Street side of the building, his delivery truck was already packed. This September morning, just as he did every day, Connor headed out from company headquarters with a full load of metal products that just about doubled the weight of his three-ton truck.

He navigated the grid in Philadelphia, making stops and gradually unburdening some of the load. In Northern Liberties, Connor skirted the well-known stretch near Second and Germantown where, in the 1880s, a cave-in of the Cohocksink was supposed to have swallowed a horse-drawn streetcar. Connor knew this was no rumor. This wily underground creek-turned-sewer had nearly claimed a trolley car filled with passengers only one year before. And it would grab him too if he made the wrong turn, on the wrong street, on the wrong day. Especially in a truck more than two-and-a-half times heavier than a Model-T Ford.

By late afternoon, Connor trundled through the busy traffic of North Ninth Street, stopping, as his work orders dictated, at building sites, mills, wagon works, machine shops, and hardware factories. As he approached the Girard Avenue Farmers Market and the new Girard Avenue Train Station, Connor knew from experience that he had to avoid the intersection of Ninth and Girard. And so he made a left turn onto Thompson Street.

Heading east to quieter quarters, with Seyferts's Foundry and the American Smelting Company fading in his rearview mirror, Connor passed narrow Darien Street and glimpsed two church steeples straight ahead at Thompson and Franklin. Then in front of Heickhaus's Groceries and Provisions, Connor saw out of the corner of his eye a "hump in the cobblestone paving." He swerved his truck too little and too late. With no further warning, Connor "felt the street suddenly sinking beneath him" as he "plunged head-on into a collapsing mass of cobblestones and dirt." As the truck dropped, Connor didn't have time to think, he just "threw himself backward." Then as the debris-covered front of the truck shuttered and steamed, he saw water shooting from the front and back of the chasm. Worse, he smelled natural gas. Connor "clawed his way upward along the tilting surface" of the truck. "The odor of escaping gas was so powerful Connor had barely enough strength to climb over the edge . . . and stagger to safety." But stagger he did. Connor escaped "scarcely a minute" before a great explosion echoed throughout the neighborhood.

As for Merchant and Evans, they survived too and rolled onward. Within a few years, Powell Evans moved the entire Philadelphia operation to a new plant near Twentieth Street and Washington Avenue. And the company proclaimed in advertisements that "rapid motor trucks" of their "own manufacture" were "used daily to make free delivery in all parts of the city."

No word as to whether John Connor ever got behind the wheel again.

———

Sources: "Huge Truck in Sewer Cave-in, Large Vehicle Falls through Street When Old Cohocksink Collapses," *Inquirer*, September 19, 1913; "Merchant and Evans Co., Fiftieth Anniversary," *Metal Worker, Plumber, and Steam Fitter*, vol. 85 (New York: D. Williams, 1916).

Figure 8.3. Break in Cohocksink sewer, Germantown Avenue, north of Second Street, May 29, 1894

With an investment of $100,000—the equivalent of millions in today's dollars—city leaders assured Philadelphians that the "noisome" Cohocksink, the creek that drained much of North Philadelphia, had finally been contained. No longer would its "fetid and polluted waters" meander in plain sight, sluggishly making their way to the Delaware. It was 1871, and this country creek-turned-urban sewer would forever be "closed from view . . . shut off from further sight and further mischief." City life could continue unimpeded above.

Or so they thought.

In spite of the best of intentions, this "work of magnitude and importance" would not tame the wily Cohocksink. With runoff from the expanding grid of north-central Philadelphia, this underground "solution" gained power as it flowed to the Delaware. By the time its waters got to Northern Liberties, the Cohocksink became much more mischievous, especially when swollen with storm water.

Time and time again, the Cohocksink dramatically carried away bits and pieces of the city. In November 1888, the horses and delivery wagon of wholesale grocer Henry Graham were saved only by tremendous efforts on the part of the driver and a handful of pedestrians, who managed to pull a half-swallowed horse onto solid ground at Germantown Avenue near Second Street. Before workmen could repair that gaping hole, another storm opened it up even more, just as a horse-drawn streetcar passed over. The driver, "realizing their peril" as the ground was rumbling and sinking, "lashed his horses into a gallop, and . . . got onto firm ground" before "the earth beneath the tracks gave way."

Engineer Frank Seaville, who had been pumping water out of the earlier hole, slipped into the "yawning chasm." If not for the efforts of fellow workmen, Seaville would have "fallen into the malodorous and swift rushing waters" to certain death. William F. Keppler wasn't so lucky. When another storm caused a collapse over the Cohocksink, he was swept away.

The gorge at Second Street soon extended "from curb to curb," compromising homes and ruining businesses. Clothiers P. Ostheim and Sons lost their Christmas trade. Store-keepers along nearby Girard Avenue—a baker, a butcher, a tobacconist, and a pair of saloonkeepers—lost goods and customers. Rising waters extinguished cellar furnaces as far away as Fourth and Girard.

Sinkholes opened in nearby streets with increasing frequency. "A mighty stream of water poured through the Cohocksink sewer last night," reported the *Inquirer* in January 1889, "and near the big break at Germantown and Second Street masses of earth and masonry were heard giving way as the torrent swept toward the river." That rainy summer, the *Inquirer* reported yet "Another Big Cave In." The waters "carried away sidewalks, and threatened to undermine houses." Frustrated residents above the

Cohocksink pleaded with the city council "to take immediate measures to prevent further breaks," but repairs would take years.

As work continued, so did the storms. In September 1894, a nighttime deluge led to another familiar "deep rumbling" that was heard throughout Northern Liberties. Everyone knew what was happening: the Cohocksink had reclaimed yet another chunk of the city.

———

Sources: "Municipal Improvements," *Inquirer*, January 4, 1871; "Work of the Storm," *Inquirer*, November 12, 1888; "Like a Yawning Chasm," *Inquirer*, December 18, 1888; "Another Break in the Cohocksink Sewer," *Inquirer*, January 10, 1889; "Snow, Rain and Slush," *Inquirer*, January 21, 1889; "Cohocksink Sewer Again," *Inquirer*, March 22, 1889; "Another Big Cave-In," *Inquirer*, July 31, 1889; "Cohocksink Sewer," *Inquirer*, May 23, 1894; "City Deluged by Heavy Rain," *Inquirer*, September 9, 1894; "The Earth Dropped," *Inquirer*, July 29, 1899.

NUCLEAR APOCALYPSE AT TWELFTH AND ARCH

As the tenth anniversary of the Hiroshima and Nagasaki bombings approached in 1955, horrors of nuclear war seemed closer, not farther away. Millions of Cold War Americans were rattled to see the disfigured "Hiroshima Maidens" visiting the United States for reconstructive surgery on protoreality television (an episode of *This Is Your Life*). Even more frightening—if such a thing was possible—the arms race with the Soviet Union turned out ever larger and more destructive weapons.

The Soviets tested their first atomic bomb in August 1949. Four years later, they claimed to have the hydrogen bomb. In November 1955, they detonated it. Americans also had also been developing larger and more powerful warheads. In 1952, the United States detonated "Mike," a 10.4-megaton hydrogen bomb with twice the explosive power of the weapons used during World War II. Two years after that, the Americans tested "Bravo," a 15-megaton hydrogen bomb that resulted in an explosion more powerful than anticipated. Bravo contaminated seven thousand square miles of the Pacific and blanketed the globe with fallout.

The possibilities of deploying nuclear weapons seemed very real. In 1950, President Truman admitted A-bombs were being considered in the Korean War. Five years later, President Eisenhower wouldn't rule them out in the Formosa Straits Crisis. Americans grew increasingly distraught about the possibility—the probability, it seemed—that the United States would attack or come under attack. And if this were to happen, when this happened, known society would be over, replaced by a decimated, fragmented version somehow managed by a government hidden deep underground.

The transition to this new, postapocalyptic world would begin a few minutes before the bombs hit America's soon-to-be-devastated cities. If all went well, the apocalypse would begin with the wail of air-raid sirens signaling a mass exodus from the targets. And civil defense authorities figured that any city with a population of more than fifty thousand would be a target.

Operation Alert took place on June 15, 1955, a day that otherwise seemed like any other Wednesday. "Imaginary atom bombs 'blasted' Washington and 60 other American cities to theoretical rubble," reported the *Inquirer*. "Thousands of officials, led by President Eisenhower, fled the capital and set up a scattered, skeleton government at sites up to 300 miles away." A Secret Service motorcade escorted the president and his entourage from the White House to "an undisclosed hideaway in a 'mountainous, wooded area.'"

Philadelphia, too, "was brought face-to-face with the grim realities of atomic war. A 'surprise bomb' hit the city at 2:11 p.m., striking at 12th and Arch Sts. and theoretically making a wasteland of many square miles." Operation Alert "brought traffic to a standstill throughout the Philadelphia area. . . . Sidewalks were emptied of pedestrians and the city's full complement of Civil Defense personnel and equipment went into action."

"Mayor Joseph S. Clark and members of his Cabinet left City Hall . . . to take command at the secret central control station set up in the Northeast. . . . Philadelphia 'evacuees' were moved out of the city . . . to previously prepared reception centers in Bucks, Delaware and Montgomery counties." Police led convoys from Bridesburg to Council Rock High School in Newtown and from Germantown to Abington High School. More than 1,600 people evacuated West Philadelphia in three hundred cars and buses.

Casualties would be devastating. Officials estimated 760,340 dead and 363,860 injured in Philadelphia, reported the *New York Times*. More than three quarters of a million would be homeless. Across the nation, according to the Civil Defense Administration, "a partial presumed toll of more than 5,000,000" had died; nearly as many were injured. Other officials projected even more: 8.5 million Americans dead, 8 million injured, and 10 million displaced. Best guesses had 25 million without food or water.

"Staggering," said Eisenhower. The former general admitted that "if war comes, it will be horrible. Atomic war will destroy our civilization. It will destroy our cities. . . . [it] would not save democracy. Civilization would be ruined . . . No one was going to be the winner. . . . The destruction might be such that we . . . go back to bows and arrows."

Even so, the Eisenhower administration supported the policy known as MAD—mutually assured destruction—and the idea that Americans were "better dead than red."

Not everyone bought into Operation Alert, and not everything worked as planned on June 15, 1955. Schoolchildren spotted Eisenhower's supposedly "secret" caravan and shouted, "Hey Ike!" as it sped by. In New York, resisters refusing cover occupied park benches across from City Hall. One insider, an official in the District of Columbia declared, "The test will teach us nothing." Another in Peoria, Illinois, refused to cooperate, questioning the point of having "a lot of people running around with armbands on." And in Flint, Michigan, the siren system was broken. In Flint, everyone "died" without even hearing the piercing, futile wail of the Cold War sirens.

———

Sources: "The 36-Hour War," *Life*, November 19, 1945; "President Leads Flight of Officials to Hideaway Capital in Atom Test," *Inquirer*, June 16, 1955; "202,000 'Casualties' Listed in City in Mock A-Bombing," *Inquirer*, June 16, 1955; Anthony Leviero, "'H-Bombs' Test U.S. Civil Defense: 61 Cities 'Ruined,'" *New York Times*, June 16, 1955; Federal Civil Defense Administration, *Annual Report for 1955* (USG Printing Office, 1956); Dee Garrison, *Bracing for Armageddon: Why Civil Defense Never Worked* (Oxford: Oxford University Press, 2006); "Civil Defense, 1955," Highway History, U.S. Department of Transportation, Federal Highway Administration, updated November 18, 2015, https://www.fhwa.dot.gov/infrastructure/civildef.cfm.

CHAPTER 9

Riots, Upheaval, and Protest

The Gangs of Philadelphia

"Armed to the teeth [with] pocket pistols, knives, or those horrible inventions known as 'slung-shot,'" Philadelphia's gangs dominated the streets of Southwark and Moyamensing in the 1840s, raining bricks and creating terror. How had the streets gotten out of control? The lack of policing beyond the city's southern border, then South Street, and the give-and-take of street warfare were causes. Cycles of violence began when a gang member escapes an incident

> barely with his life, and mangled, wounded, and bleeding, makes his appearance among his confederates and companions, details a vivid account of the manner in which he was assailed . . . A spirit of vengeance is kindled . . . threats of retaliation are uttered, and an early opportunity is sought, to pay back in the same coin, with bricks, bludgeons and knives, the attack upon their brother. When the fight is once commenced under these circumstances, the feelings become inflamed, the mind is maddened, the blood heated, and the scene is often of the most fearful character. This, we believe, is the whole story with regard to most of the collisions which have recently taken place.

"What is the remedy?" asked the *Inquirer* in desperation during the hot summer of 1849.

All hell had broken loose. "We are told there are no less than five gangs of organized ruffians, either in the county, or on the outskirts of the city." Columnist George Foster identified even more—eleven "squads or clubs" in Southwark and Moyamensing populated by "loafers" who gave themselves "outlandish titles"—the fiercer, the better. Marauding the streets were Killers, Bouncers, Rats, Stingers, Nighthawks, Buffers, Skinners, Gumballs, Smashers, Whelps, Flayers, "and other appropriate and verminous designations." They marked their territories by fighting, rioting, and writing "in chalk or charcoal on every dead-wall, fence and stable-door." They held their "nightly conclaves on the corners of by-streets or in unoccupied building-lots, sneaking about behind the rubbish-heaps, and perhaps now and then venturing out to assault an unprotected female or knock down a lonely passenger." And worse.

On the night of Election Day, October 9, 1849, the Killers and the Stingers corralled a few hundred of their allies and attacked the California House at Sixth and St. Mary Streets (now Naudain), a tavern operated by an interracial couple. The battle "raged for a night and a day" before casualties were counted. "Dreadful Riot," read one of several headlines, "Houses Burned, and Several Persons Killed and Wounded." By early December, George Lippard published *The Killers*, a novel loosely based on the event and gang life in Philadelphia.

For years, the newspapers had been crying out for "the law efficiently and vigorously administered," no matter the cost. "Is it not possible for the authorities of the immediate districts concerned, to secure one or two of the ringleaders?" they demanded. "Are the citizens of that district content to live in such a state of anarchy?"

Apparently the citizens had little choice in the matter. According to David R. Johnson in *The Peoples of Philadelphia*, the *Public Ledger* reported on the doings of no less than fifty-one gangs. In an effort to be even more comprehensive—from sources listed below as well as the *Inquirer*—I located an additional fourteen.

Here are Philadelphia's sixty-four gangs, listed in alphabetical order: American Guards; Bleeders; Blood Tubs; Blossoms; Bouncers; Buffers; Bugs; Bulldogs; Centre Street Boys; Chesapeakes; Crockets; Darts; Death-fetchers; Dogs; Dog-Towners; Flayers; Fly-By-Nights; Garroters; Gumballs; Hyenas; Jack of Clubs; Jumpers; Juniatta Club; Kensington Blackhawks; Kerryonians; Keystone No. 2; Killers; Lancers; Molly Maguires; Neckers; Nighthawks; Orangemen; Pickwick Club; Pluckers; Pots No. 2; Privateer Club No. 1; Rangers; Rats; Reading Hose Club; Rebels; Red Roses; Reed Birds; Schuylkill Rangers; Shifflers; Skinners; Smashers; Snakers; Snappers; Spiggots; Spitfires; Sporters; Springers; Stingers; Stockholders; the Forty Thieves; the Vesper Social; Tormentors; Turks; Vampyres; Wayne-towners; Weecys; Whelps; Wild Cats; Wreckers.

Their heroes were the toughest of Philadelphia's volunteer firemen, who, according to Bruce Laurie, they "gazed upon and followed in awe and reverence." Unlike the gangs, which served as firefighting farm teams, fire companies adopted names without bite or even growl. They found resonance and cover in sweet, civic-sounding names: Assistance, Diligent, Friendship, Good Intent, Good Will, Hand-in-Hand, Harmony, Hope, Humane, Perseverance, Reliance, and Vigilant—even though they were basically grown-up versions of the same street gangs.

Ah, branding.

———

Sources: David R. Johnson, "Crime Patterns in Philadelphia, 1840–70," in *The Peoples of Philadelphia: A History of Ethnic Groups and Lower-Class Life, 1790–1940*, ed. Allen F. Davis and Mark H. Haller (Philadelphia: University of Pennsylvania Press, 1998), 89–110; Bruce Laurie, "Fire Companies and Gangs in Southwark: The 1840s," in Davis and Haller, *Peoples of Philadelphia*; George Lippard, *The Killers: A Narrative of Real Life in Philadelphia*, ed. Matt Cohen and Edlie L. Wong (Philadelphia: University of Pennsylvania Press, 2014); Peter McCaffery, *When Bosses Ruled Philadelphia: The*

Emergence of the Republican Machine, 1867–1933 (University Park: Penn State University Press, 1993); George Rogers Taylor and George G. Foster, "'Philadelphia in Slices' by George G. Foster," *The Pennsylvania Magazine of History and Biography* 93, no. 1 (January 1969): 23–72; "Fireman's Triennial Parade," *Inquirer*, March 27, 1849; "News/Opinion," *Inquirer*, August 7, 1849; "Bouncers and Killers," *Inquirer*, August 11, 1846; "Dreadful Riot," *Inquirer*, October, 10, 1849.

Figure 9.1. Thirteenth Street and Washington Avenue, northwest corner, B. F. Hill and Company, coal supplier, September 20, 1914

There wasn't much to the life of a Schuylkill coal heaver. Bosses hired fresh arrivals from Ireland to unload canal boats at the coal yards, and by the hundred, crews manned wheelbarrows on the riverbanks from dawn to dark, six days a week, for a dollar a day. This racked up to as many as fourteen backbreaking hours per day during the summer months. The men were allowed a one hour break for breakfast and another for supper.

Philadelphia's appetite for anthracite had mushroomed. More than 6,500 tons passed through the docks in 1825. Nine years later, the coal heavers moved 227,000 tons. As days grew longer in the spring of 1835, coal-laden canal boats lined up along the Schuylkill's banks. Laborers in Pittsburgh and Boston had tried and failed to get a ten-hour work day. A few trades in New York City had appealed for shorter working hours and won their bid. Now, in the spring of 1835, Philadelphia's laborers seized their moment to organize and to strike.

All three hundred coal heavers walked off the job, abandoning seventy-five coal-laden vessels at the Schuylkill docks. Marching along the river-bank, strikers threatened anyone intent on replacing them. Mayor John Swift visited as many as four times, reported the *Inquirer* on May 29, and found the strikers "quiet but determined" and absolutely unwilling to back down.

The "Working Men of Schuylkill," as they called themselves, had an evolving, two-pronged strategy. As they marched, especially at the start of their strike, their fearsome leader brandished a sword. When they spoke, their words were impassioned yet reasonable. In an "Appeal to the Public," they wished "for nothing but peace, quietness and good order." Under the "present aristocratic system" that required work "from daylight to dark," the coal heavers claimed to be worse off than "galley slaves." They asked not for more pay, only the guarantee of a twelve hour day—a ten-hour workday—with two breaks, one for breakfast and another for dinner.

The coal merchants mulled over the strikers' demand and presented their counteroffer. The dawn-to-dark working hours would remain in place and so would the pay. Laborers would be granted a third hour-long break. The strikers were unimpressed.

More than a week into their walkout, the coal heavers had captured the entire city's attention and an increasing amount of sympathy. The humane logic of the "Six to Six" campaign had gained broader follow-ing. After the coal heavers rejected their bosses counteroffer, on Saturday, June 6, they marched from the Schuylkill to the very heart of the city—Independence Square.

Led by fifes and drums, coal heavers chanted "From Six to Six," a slogan heard on the streets and seen in the headlines, on broadsides, in store win-dows, and even "scrawled in chalk on fences." They marched with it on ban-ners, along with another slogan: "Liberty, Equality and the Rights of Man."

As the procession closed in on Independence Square, workers from other trades joined in, some carrying tools as they marched. In the shadow of the state house, speeches called for a ten-hour day in not one but *all* trades. Philadelphians heard a fiery reading of the "Ten-Hour Circular" from Boston, which argued that "the odious, cruel, unjust, and tyrannical system" left workers unable to do anything "but to eat and sleep." Work prevented them from performing "duties . . . as American Citizens and members of society." "We cannot, we will not, be mere slaves to inhuman, insatiable and unpitying avarice," it proclaimed.

"The effect was electric," wrote John Ferral, an organizer from Manayunk. And in the days following, coal heavers were joined by hod carriers, brick layers, plasterers, carpenters, smiths, sheet iron workers, lamp makers, plumbers, painters, and leather dressers—twenty thousand workers from twenty trades. What started as a strike on the Schuylkill docks had grown into the first general strike in the city—the first in American history.

"The hum of business is hushed; the coal yards are deserted and shut; and every kind of business is completely at a stand," reported the *Niles Register* on the day of the march. "The militia looks on, the sheriff stands with folded arms," observed a visitor from France. "The times," worried editors at the *Philadelphia Gazette*, "are completely out of joint."

The public had aligned with the strikers. By June 8, the *Inquirer* reported that "the opinion is almost universal that the term of ten hours per day during the summer season, is long enough for any industrious man, whether mechanic or otherwise." Historians Scharf and Westcott would later write of the "strong feeling that the demand was just . . . that the concession ought to be made to toiling men."

And one by one, the city's largest employers, from the City of Philadelphia to Eastern State Penitentiary, the Commissioners of Southwark, and the Cornelius and Son lamp and chandelier manufacturer adopted "six-to-six" work days. The coal heavers, and thousands of other advocates of "Six-to-Six," had won a quick and "bloodless revolution."

———

Sources: Leonard Bernstein, "The Working People of Philadelphia from Colonial Times to the General Strike of 1835," *Pennsylvania Magazine of*

History and Biography 74, no. 3 (July 1950); John R. Commons et al., *History of Labour in the United States*, vol. 1 (New York: Macmillan, 1921); Tom Juravich, William F. Hartford, and James R. Green, *Commonwealth of Toil: Chapters in the History of Massachusetts Workers and Their Unions* (Amherst: University of Massachusetts Press, 1996); Philip Yale Nicholson, *Labor's Story in the United States* (Philadelphia: Temple University Press, 2004); J. Thomas Scharf and Thompson Westcott, *History of Philadelphia, 1609–1884*, vol. 1 (Philadelphia: L. H. Everts and Co., 1884), 641; "The Strike," *Inquirer*, May 30, 1835; "Councils," *Inquirer*, June 6, 1835; "From Six to Six," *Inquirer*, June 6, 1835; "From Six to Six," *Inquirer*, June 8, 1835; "From Six to Six," *Inquirer*, June 11, 1835.

Mother Jones and the Fight against Child Labor in Kensington's Textile Mills

"During the Philadelphia textile workers' strike in 1903," wrote reformer John Spargo in his 1916 book, *The Bitter Cry of the Children*, "I saw at least a score of children ranging from eight to ten years of age who had been working in the mills prior to the strike. One little girl of nine I saw in the Kensington Labor Lyceum. She has been working for almost a year before the strike began, she said, and careful inquiry proved her story to be true."

Spargo was trying to do something about the fact that, in the second half of the nineteenth century, urban industrialization had turned cities into giant child labor pools. American textile companies employed more than eighty thousand children, and Pennsylvania was among the worst offenders. As historian Walter Licht explains in *Getting Work in Philadelphia*, between 1860 and the end of the century, the percentage of fourteen-year-olds put to work jumped from 8 percent to more than 40 percent. In Philadelphia, the mills of Kensington were ground zero for child labor.

It hardly mattered that the employment of children younger than twelve years of age had been illegal since the 1840s. State officials, mill owners, and parents figured that fifty thousand working children was simply an economic necessity, even if it meant that there'd be no time for education or that the lives of children would be in danger. "Children who work in the dye rooms and print-shops of textile factories, and the color rooms of factories," wrote Spargo, "are subject to contact with poisonous dyes, and the results are often terrible."

"Progressive era reformers quickly singled out Pennsylvania as the worst offender," wrote historian Joseph M. Speakman. As early as 1890, Florence Kelley noted that child labor in Pennsylvania, flourished "almost unchecked." And Jane Addams pointed to Pennsylvania in 1905, noting that "there were more children employed in manufacturing industries in the state than in all of the cotton states of the South."

"The high point of publicity on the issue," according to Licht, came in late 1906, when "more than 25,000 Philadelphians crowded into the city's Horticultural Hall" on Broad Street to see "'an Industrial Exhibit,' which dramatized with shocking photographs the use and state of child labor in Philadelphia Industry." Advocacy organizations were embarrassing Philadelphia, the city promoting itself as the "Workshop of the World," with the equally well-earned and dubious title, "The Greatest Child Employing City."

But it took a special effort to move the issue of child labor to the forefront, ahead of other pressing concerns. In April 1903, wrote Philip Scranton, "all the unions in the textile industries of Philadelphia met in convention at the Kensington Labor Lyceum" and agreed that they would strike for better pay and a reduction from a sixty-hour to a fifty-five-hour workweek. Within a few months, more than ninety thousand textile workers had walked off the job. A quarter of this striking workforce was younger than fifteen years of age.

Enter Mary Harris, a.k.a. Mother Jones. "I'm not a humanitarian. I'm a hell-raiser," she claimed. Knowing full well that at least ten thousand of the textile strikers were children, Jones imagined the power of a spectacle: an army of children in protest. She quickly organized one in the center of Philadelphia.

"A great crowd gathered in the public square in front of the city hall," wrote Mother Jones in her autobiography.

> I put the little boys with their fingers off and hands crushed and maimed on a platform. I held up their mutilated hands and showed them to the crowd and made the statement that Philadelphia's mansions were built on the broken bones, the quivering hearts and drooping heads of these children. That their little lives went out to make wealth for others. That neither state or city officials paid any attention to these wrongs. That they did not care that these children were to be the future citizens of the nation.
>
> The officials of the city hall were standing in the open windows. I held the little ones of the mills high up above the heads of the crowd and pointed to their puny arms and legs and hollow chests. . . . I called upon the millionaire manufactures to cease their moral murders, and I cried to the officials in the open windows opposite, "Some day the workers will take possession of your city hall, and when we do, no child will be sacrificed on the altar of profit."
>
> The officials quickly closed the windows, as they had closed their eyes and hearts.

On July 7, 1903, Mother Jones and her sign-carrying "children's army" embarked on a ninety-two-mile March of the Mill Children, departing the physical and spiritual home of organized textile labor in Philadelphia: the Kensington Labor Lyceum at Second and Cambria Streets. Its destination was Oyster Bay in Long Island, New York—the vacation home of President Theodore Roosevelt. The trek would become famous, if delayed in its impact. Not until 1909 did the state raise the minimum age of employment to fourteen and reduce the workweek to fifty-eight hours.

––––––

Sources: Mary Harris Jones, *Autobiography of Mother Jones* (Courier Dover Publications, 2012), Google Play Book; Walter Licht, *Getting Work in Philadelphia, 1840–1950* (Philadelphia: University of Pennsylvania Press, 2000); Philip Scranton, *Figured Tapestry: Production, Markets and Power in Philadelphia Textiles, 1855–1941* (Cambridge: Cambridge University Press, 1989); Joseph M. Speakman, "The Inspector and His Critics: Child Labor Reform in Pennsylvania," *Pennsylvania History* 69, no. 2 (Spring 2002).

Figure 9.2. Tenth Street and Washington Avenue, northeast corner, September 15, 1914

Looking at the six lanes of blacktop on Washington Avenue today, you wouldn't know that locomotives once trundled along, hauling hundreds of thousands of tons of anthracite to thirty coal yards between Second and Twenty-Fifth Streets. Every day of winter, coal cars supplied the city's lifeblood. Until they didn't.

Coal once powered most factories and heated nearly every shop, school, theater, and home—a quarter of a million buildings. One large public school of the city's 231 would consume as much as 10 tons on an extremely cold day. The University of Pennsylvania needed 150 tons to stay open. In all, the city would burn as much as 19,000 tons per day. And on the first frigid week of January 1918, it ground to a halt.

The temperature dropped below zero in the final days of December 1917 and would remain in the single digits for more than a week. The flow of coal from upstate stopped and soon much of the city itself did as well. Frigid, coal-less Philadelphians turned to the dealers of Washington

Avenue, but their stockpiles were quickly exhausted. At Tenth Street, William Bryant had been promised a shipment of fifty tons, but by the time the cars arrived, four-fifths of their contents were gone. The coal famine of January 1918 turned citizens into coal thieves and coal hoarders. As mobs, they would decimate the coal supply of Washington Avenue.

City officials estimated that as much as "half the population was without coal." Mayor Thomas Smith urged "public recreation centers, school buildings, churches, theaters, moving picture houses and hospitals be thrown open to receive suffers and keep them warm." As schools and factories began to close down, he appealed to "good Samaritans to take cold neighbors in." Philadelphia's coal famine threatened "social and economic catastrophe." On January 2, 1918, the coal-less poor, many of whom were newly arrived immigrants, took the matter into their own hands.

"Driven to desperation after burning fence rails, old furniture and every bit of available fuel, the poor began a series of raids on coal cars on Washington avenue," reported the *Philadelphia Tribune*. "Men, women and children with buckets, bags, push carts, baskets, toy express wagons and even baby buggies, worked like beavers in and among the switching crews carrying the precious fuel to their homes. There were at least 2,000 persons in these crowds and the police and railroad crews did not interfere, as the people were freezing and desperate . . . Women and children, for days, had stood shivering at the yards weeping and begging for coal."

"We're almost starving, my babies and me," a widow sobbed to an *Inquirer* reporter. "It's all right to almost starve. We're pretty near used to that, but we can't freeze. I could, but my babies can't." "You must help us!" shouted cold and hungry women and children to the police called in to stop them. "The officers shrugged their shoulders and turned their backs" on the crowd and the coal cars. The mob took that as encouragement. Youngsters "crawled over the heads of the police . . . on the coal cars. . . . In a second . . . a black shower descended upon the ground near the cars. As fast as the bits of coal struck the ground they were picked up and stored carefully away in a bag or a bucket or an apron."

"What can we do?" asked one of the policemen. "The poor devils are hungry and cold. . . . When a woman, lugging a baby to her breast, pushes me aside . . . why, I am not going to be the one to stop her." He added, "I've seen more real misery in the last few days down here around these coal cars than I ever saw in all my police experience."

More than 150 tons of anthracite would be liberated from Washington Avenue's coal-yard corridor in the first week of 1918. According to the *Inquirer*, "most of the coal stolen was consigned to the J. W. Matthews Coal Company, Tenth street and Washington avenue; William A. Bryant, of Tenth street and Washington avenue, and S. Margolis, of 815 Washington avenue." At Twelfth and Washington, men and boys were seen completely emptying a coal car.

While the police turned the other way, the railroad did not. "In the midst of the raid on one of the cars came the chugging of a freight engine. No one paid the slightest attention. The engine was hastily coupled to the car. It drew away. Not one of the coal-seekers jumped. They still continued to toss out bucket after bucket of coal." On the ground, "those . . . left behind followed the slow-moving engine and car, picking up fuel as it was thrown to them. This was only one of several raids by persons driven frantic by the want of fuel . . . who, armed with buckets, bags, wheelbarrows and pushcarts, defied the police and railroad guards and mobbed trains of coal when they arrived along Washington Avenue."

South Philadelphia's "coal-hunters were undaunted."

———

Sources: "Coal Lack Closes 43 Public Schools . . . Severe Weather Conditions Halt Coal Train on Way Here," *Inquirer*, January 3, 1918; "Suffering Crowds Storm Coal Yards; Railroads Helpless," *Inquirer*, January 4, 1918; "Coal Famine Grips Our City: Much Suffering," *Philadelphia Tribune*, January 5, 1918; "R.R. Stockholders . . . Ask Refuge for 100,000 Suffering from Cold Here," *Inquirer*, January 5, 1918; "Men, Women and Children Empty Cars of Fuel despite Efforts of Policemen and Guards," *Inquirer*, January 6, 1918.

Figure 9.3. Ellsworth Street, south side from Twenty-Ninth Street, December 6, 1965

Adella Bond figured the 2900 block of Ellsworth Street would be a safe place to live.

She figured wrong.

Described as a "short, young woman of light brown color, with a quiet but emphatic manner," Bond worked by day as a probation officer in municipal courts. As an African American, she knew that racial tensions played out poorly in some neighborhoods. She knew of the incidents in early July 1918, when local "ruffians" welcomed a new family to the 2500 block of Pine Street with racial epithets before burning their furniture in the street. No, Adella Bond wouldn't be looking at any houses near Fitler Square.

About a mile to the southwest, an African American real estate agent was showing 2936 Ellsworth Street, a two-story brick row house near the end of a block wedged between the Henry Bower chemical factory and the U.S. Arsenal. Bond "supposed colored people were welcome." She heard another woman of color, a Mrs. Giddings, who had previously occupied the very same residence.

Bond wasn't told that real estate managers were systematically terminating the eleven dollar-per-month leases held by working-class Irish Americans and offering rents of fourteen or even sixteen dollars-per-month to incoming working-class African Americans. And if the new renters wanted to buy, all the better.

"We had a perfect right to dispose of our properties if we wanted to," later recalled real estate agent A. D. Morgan.

> These white tenants have been trying to "run this block" for some time . . . We have had trouble with them for two years. They were always behind in their rent. . . . We got tired of dealing with these people. Yes, I employed a negro agent and sought to dispose of the eight houses I owned down there. We almost "begged" the white tenants to buy the properties. They would not.
>
> When we got a chance to sell the house to Mrs. Bond we did so. We have sold six of the houses. Yes, all to colored people. We have two more houses on the market. I would like to see them go to colored tenants for they are far better tenants than the element which is there now. . . . they'll have to get out as soon as their leases are up. And when they are all gone and the colored people take their places, there will be no more trouble there.

But there *would* be trouble.

"The second time I went down that street, I was stoned," Bond later testified. "If I had known that there was any objection to colored people in the block I wouldn't have taken the house . . . It was only after I had bought the house that I knew of any objection. But since I could not get my money back, what else was I to do except to live there?"

On Wednesday, July 24, the movers arrived with Bond's furniture. Cautious and fearful, she answered her door brandishing a gun. The day went smoothly. On Friday, as Bond later told it, about 100 white men and boys gathered in front of my house. I heard them talk about having guns, and I saw the guns and cartridges. At last a man came along with a baby in his arms. He handed the baby to a woman, took a rock and threw it. The rock went through my parlor window. I didn't know what the mob would do next, and I fired my revolver from my upper window to call the police. A policeman came, but he wouldn't try to cope with that mob alone, so he turned it into a riot call.

The rock thrower, Joseph Kelly, twenty-three, lived a few blocks away on Carpenter near Twenty-Third and had been shot in the leg. Both he and his brother, William, would be held without bail, pending investigation. Police arrested Bond for "inciting to riot."

"Lone Woman Holds a Mob of 500 White Brutes at Bay," read the page one headline in the *Philadelphia Tribune*. "The plucky little probation officer . . . shot to kill in defense of her honor and home," ran the caption below a standing, full-length photograph of Bond. "Can you blame citizens of color for mobilizing at 29th and Ellsworth Sts. to protect one of their own . . . ?" wrote G. Grant Williams, the *Tribune*'s editor.

Just as American soldiers were being shipped abroad to fight for freedom, Bond's attorney, G. Edward Dickerson, contemplated the irony of this and other incidents. "How can a colored man go to France with a clear conscience?" he asked. "How can he willingly give his life for a country that will not protect his family during his absence?"

Unable to move back home for a week, Adella Bond worried about the same thing—and more. Police were supposedly guarding her house, but in Bond's absence, "white hoodlums" broke in, "robbed her of . . . valuables and . . . demolished her furniture."

————

Sources: "Dixie Methods in Philadelphia," *Philadelphia Tribune*, July 6, 1918; "Man Shot in Race Riot over Negro Resident," *Inquirer*, July 28, 1918;

"Mrs. Bond Determined to Occupy Her House," *Inquirer*, July 31, 1918; "Lone Woman Holds a Mob of 500 White Brutes at Bay: Adella Bond Shoots into Mob Attempting Violence," *Philadelphia Tribune*, August 3, 1918; "The So-Called Race Riot," *Philadelphia Tribune*, August 3, 1918; "White Policeman Clubs a Race Riot Victim on Hospital Cot," *Philadelphia Tribune*, August 10, 1918.

South Philadelphia Erupts: The Race Riot of 1918

"Can you blame citizens of color for mobilizing . . . to protect one of their own . . . ?" wrote *Tribune* editor G. Grant Williams after the attack on Adella Bond near Twenty-Ninth and Ellsworth.

Earlier the same summer, responding to the stoning of the home of a Mrs. T. Lytle at 2504 Pine Street and the burning of two wagon loads of furniture owned by newcomers to 2524–2526 Pine, Williams struck the same chord of warning: "We favor peace but we say to the colored people of the Pine Street warzone, stand your ground like men. This is a free city in a free country and if you are law abiding you need not fear. Be quiet, be decent, maintain clean, wholesome surroundings and if you are attacked defend yourself like American citizens. A man's home is his castle, defend it if you have to kill some of the dirty, foul-mouthed, thieving Schuylkill rats that infest that district."

One month later, sparked by the incident at Ellsworth Street, the war of words escalated into a war with weapons and became one that quickly spread. "2 Slain, 20 Injured as 5000 Fight Race War in South Philadelphia," read one startling headline.

In a series of street battles waged for twenty-four hours yesterday . . . covering about two square miles, two white men, one a policeman, were shot and killed, several others, both white and colored, are believed to be in a dying condition and scores were seriously injured in the most terrific and bitter race riot that has ever taken place in this city. Half a hundred men were placed under arrest.

The rioting . . . began with the killing of a white man by a negro early yesterday morning [Sunday, July 28, 1918], grew in intensity throughout the day with individual fights and mobs engaged in gun fire on nearly every other corner of a section bounded by Washington avenue, Dickinson street, 23rd and 30th streets.

Facts and rumors swirled after the fatal shooting of Hugh Lavery, forty-two, of 1234 South Twenty-Sixth Street by Jesse Butler near Twenty-Sixth and Annin Streets. Did Lavery's pregnant wife die of grief? No. Was their unborn child also a casualty? Untrue.

No matter. "From 9 o'clock in the morning until almost midnight the streets of the district were converted into a battle ground. For several hours it appeared as though the police of five downtown districts would be unable to cope with the situation." Fury only grew the next day after Henry Huff shot and killed police officer Thomas McVey, twenty-four.

In bands of thirty and fifty men the whites and the colored men met in the streets and waged their fight, using guns, razors, knives clubs or any weapons which were certain of inflicting injury. These encounters were taking place over every street in the district.

Federal Street was a seething mass of black and white bodies, swinging from one side of the street to the others. Men were trampled underfoot and left unconscious and bleeding. . . . The sight of men falling, dying and bleeding, failed to stop the rioting and it took a hundred policemen, sparing no heads or bodies, to scatter the men.

Police closed off the streets, stopping and frisking every male and arresting many bearing weapons. In front of the Naval Home, "the fighting became so terrific that Commander Payne . . . offered the police the use of two hundred marines to aid in quelling the riot. By that time, there were more than 150 uniformed policemen struggling with the rioters, supplemented by half a hundred detectives from the Central Station and downtown station houses."

"From barred windows and doors the women and children of the neighborhood listened to the progress of the battle. Shutters were closed tight, but in many instances this fact did not deter the rioters from venting their bitterness. They used axes to chop away the woodwork and then shattered the glass with bullets." Some women and children, determined to attend church in spite of the situation, "ran screaming through the streets to places of safety when the shooting started."

During a brief pause in the rioting at dusk, a reporter looked up and noticed "in several small streets between Federal and Washington avenue, there were few houses which had windows left." Then as nightfall came, chaos returned.

———

Sources: Vincent P. Franklin, "The Philadelphia Race Riot of 1918," *Pennsylvania Magazine of History and Biography* 99, no. 3 (July 1975): 336–350; "Dixie Methods Now in Vogue in Philadelphia: White Residents of Upper Pine St. Adopt Tactics of South against Colored Tenants," *Philadelphia Tribune,* July 6, 1918; "2 Slain, 20 Injured as 5000 Fight Race War in South Philadelphia," *Inquirer,* July 29, 1918.

THE RIOT CONTINUES: TARGETING AFRICAN AMERICANS ON TITAN AND STILLMAN STREETS

"The fighting spread yesterday," reported the *Inquirer,* to include a giant swath of South Philadelphia from Twentieth to Thirtieth Streets and from Lombard to Dickinson. Pawnbrokers were forbidden to sell "weapons of any kind until further notice," and saloons were ordered closed. Streets were roped off and police stationed at corners, allowing access only to residents.

Still, on Monday, July 30, 1918, the violence grew more intense. "With the coming of night the rioting continued unabated, while the police made feeble and frantic efforts to scatter the throngs which gathered in the streets armed with every sort of weapon. Some even carried hatchets but the most frequently used instrument was a blackjack. Hundreds carried bricks with jagged edges." Mayor Thomas Smith "confessed that he did not know how order was going to be restored."

"One of the most serious acts of the infuriated white mob took place at the home of Henry Huff," at 2743 Titan Street near Twenty-Eighth and Wharton, when Huff was charged with killing police officer Thomas McVey. While Huff sat in a cell in Moyamensing Prison, reported the *Inquirer*, about fifty men, "many of them neighbors and friends of the dead bluecoat marched into Titan Street, armed with clubs, knives, bricks and revolvers."

> With wild cries they descended upon the Huff home. The door had been locked and the windows barred. Inside were two women and three children, said to be the children of Huff. . . . They smashed the [door] panels with axes, tore open the windows and climbed in, one after the other. . . . Meanwhile the women and children inside the house at fled through the rear gate to the home of neighbors. Once inside, the vengeance seeking crowd started to wreck the place. A piano was shoved through the windows and hurled by willing hands into the centre of the street. Beds followed from the upper floors; chairs were tossed through windows, carrying away sash and glass. Everything removable in the house was sent flying into the street where it was made into a huge pile. Matches were applied to oil soaked mattresses and in an instant the furniture was in flames. Inside the house other members of the raiding party had started a fire.

When there was nothing left to destroy at the Huff house, the mob turned to other homes of African American families. "Mobs of white men" rampaged, wrecking residences in their path. Police did show up, according to reports, but "only after the damage had been done." "Hundreds of colored residents are leaving the danger zone for places of safety," police told reporters. "Several men were found fleeing . . . [disguised] in women's garments."

Four blocks southeast of the attack on the Huff home, someone thought a shot might have been fired from a window at 1522 South Stillman Street, the two-story home of Eleanor Grant, an African American. "Within a few minutes a struggling, fighting throng had forced its way into the Grant home and swept everything before it."

"The crowd became a mob of five hundred within a short time." A dozen policemen "were powerless before the swaying mass of bodies locked in deadly struggle. Every window in the house at 1522 Stillman street was broken. The furniture was cast into the street and broken with axes. From the Grant home the crowd entered houses of five other colored residents, repeating their actions. The street was soon filled with broken furniture and glassware. Half an hour later a mounted squad of twelve policemen arrived and, by sending their horses directly into the crowd managed to break it up."

Soon after, William Duberry, thirty-three, an African American resident who lived nearby at 1511 South Stillman Street, returned home. "A crowd of white men who still lingered in defiance of the police" spotted Duberry, chased him through his house, then through the alley behind Stillman Street and across a nearby lot to Dickinson Street. With the mob "at his heels . . . Duberry ran into the office of the National Alloy Company and sought refuge behind the desk of the president of the company, Henry P. Miller. The crowd demanded admittance, and as Mr. Miller went to the door it gave way before the pushing of the crowd. Duberry managed to evade capture . . . by scaling the fence."

But by the time police arrived, the mob had caught and was "pummeling" the now-unconscious Duberry. "With their revolvers the policeman held the crowd at bay while they put Duberry into an automobile and took him to St. Agnes hospital," where he was admitted with internal injuries and a fractured skull.

———

Source: "Race Riots Grow in Fury as Police Fail to Curb Mobs, Negro Is Slain at Door of Station House," *Inquirer*, July 30, 1918.

AFTERMATH OF THE RACE RIOTS OF 1918

After a weekend of rioting, the likes of which Philadelphia had never seen, families of the deceased planned funerals for two of the men killed in the mayhem. Grieving for their fallen twenty-four-year-old patrolman, the McVeys would have Requiem Mass sung at St. Anthony's Catholic Church, located at Twenty-Fourth and Fitzwater Streets. "Thousands of persons, hours before the services started, began assembling along the route of the funeral procession," reported the *Inquirer*. Lieutenant Harry Meyers of the Seventeenth Police District at Twentieth and Federal Streets would send a thirty-man "guard of honor" and the largest floral wreath. Six officers from the station stepped up as pallbearers. They would attempt to console McVey's bereft mother, who told them, "I have but one wish . . . to live long enough to see my poor boy's death avenged. He didn't deserve to meet with such an end, to be killed by the bullet of a negro."

Even though he was officially on vacation, one of the pallbearers, patrolman John Schneider, reported for duty that Monday, the day after the death of Thomas McVey and two days before his funeral. The streets of South Philadelphia still seethed with a toxic mix of mob violence and martial rule, which again and again proved nearly fatal for African American men—even those going about their business.

That morning, Preston H. Lewis visited his brother, hoping "to find new living quarters because the family with whom he boarded, at 2739 Titan Street, was moving on account of the riot," reported the *Inquirer*. Lewis "was met on the streets by Officers Ramsay and Schneider," who stopped and frisked him and "finding a small pocket knife, beat him about the head inflicting about 20 wounds." Ramsay and Schneider pummeled Lewis "until he was semiconscious" before sending him to the Polyclinic

Hospital at Eighteenth and Lombard Streets. There, with his face and head "a mass of bruises," Lewis "was laid on a cot to await his turn to have his wounds dressed."

But Officer Schneider wasn't finished. He "walked into the hospital . . . went to the Accident Ward, and without a word of warning, knocked down Miss Applegate, one of the nurses in attendance" and began to beat Lewis with his fists and then with his black jack. Lewis was "knocked unconscious."

William Watson, an African American officer from another district present in the hospital "made an attempt to get his gun . . . when several white officers present wrenched [it] from his hand." The head nurse telephoned the police of the Nineteenth Police District—purposely not Schneider's own stationhouse—and two other officers arrived. "I tried to stop [Schneider] but could not," resident physician William M. Cooperage later testified, "It took the efforts of three other policemen to drag him from the helpless victim."

Schneider would later be charged and tried, but that day, right after the incident at the Polyclinic Hospital, Schneider returned to the Seventeenth District station house at Twentieth and Federal and rejoined Robert Ramsey, his partner. Schneider and Ramsey would soon be back on the streets, looking for more trouble.

———

Sources: "Pays Fine Tribute to Victim of Riot—Rev. Francis A. Brady Praises Policeman McVay [*sic*] for Dying at Duty," *Inquirer*, August 2, 1918; "White Policeman Clubs a Race Riot Victim on Hospital Cot," *Philadelphia Tribune*, August 10, 1918; "Policeman Tried for Brutal Action," *Inquirer*, August 30, 1918; G. Grant Williams, "Cop Schneider on Trial," *Philadelphia Tribune*, September 7, 1918; "Echo of Race Riot—Policeman Schneider to Be Tried for Deadly Assault," *Inquirer*, September 25, 1918.

A day after riots shook the city and a few hours after the Polyclinic incident, patrolmen Robert Ramsey and John Schneider were back to patrolling the streets. Within minutes, they encountered Riley Bullock, a thirty-eight-year-old African American who lived at 2032 Annin Street.

Bullock would soon be dead.

According to one account, Bullock "was being attacked by a crowd of white men when the two policemen came to his rescue and arrested him." According to another, Ramsey and Schneider "arrested Bullock while he was going on an errand and committing no crime." The officers struggled with Bullock, who, they later claimed, "wielded a razor."

No one would challenge the fact that Ramsey and Schneider severely beat Bullock. According to one witness, they "beat him with all their might and force for about two squares until he reached the station" at Twentieth and Federal Streets. Mrs. Williams, a witness, "testified that she saw Ramsay and Schneider beating Bullock at the corner of Titan and Point Breeze Avenue; that they held both of Bullock's arms up as he walked . . . Schneider was beating him with a black jack and Ramsey was beating him with the butt of a revolver." Then "just as soon as they entered the station house door, she heard a shot."

At first, police claimed "the bullet which ended Bullocks life was really intended for one of the white policemen." As police escorted Bullock into the station's rear door, he was "shot by 'a colored man' [who] was detected running away from the scene of the murder with a revolver in his hand."

The story soon changed, and Lieutenant Harry Meyers issued a statement: "As they came up the steps of the police station on the Point Breeze Avenue side, Ramsey, who still had his gun in his hand to keep the pressing crowd at bay, suddenly slipped. The revolver was accidentally discharged and the bullet struck Bullock in the back, piercing his lungs." Meyers added, "Ramsey did not shoot the negro because of any malice resulting

Figure 9.4. Seventeenth District,
police station and engine house
#24, Twentieth and Point Breeze
Avenues and Federal Street,
November 9, 1896

from the killing of Policeman McVey by Negroes." Then Meyers "ordered all newspaper men from the station house and forbade them to return."

During the following days, "delegations of Negro clergymen and business men" attempted to meet with the mayor and police officials to send the message that "Afro-Americans of this city are tired of legalized murder." They "put responsibility for the rioting squarely up to the police of the 20th and Federal Streets station, whom they charged with showing sympathy for the white residents of the turbulent area." They and others organized "The Colored Protective Association," which retained attorney G. Edward Dickerson "to prosecute Policeman Ramsey," who was being held at Moyamensing Prison.

Dickerson depended on the testimony of two African American policemen in the station house when Ramsey shot Bullock. One had even "helped put out the fire which the pistol shot started in Bullock's clothes;" both had "heard Policeman Ramsey acknowledge that he shot [Bullock]." But when it came to the trial, they didn't turn out to be reliable witnesses. One of the officers even "swore he never saw Ramsey before."

Testimony from the coroner's physician proved the most damaging to Meyers's story: "The ball entered into the small part of Bullock's back and took a downward course through the pelvis [indicating] . . . that the bullet could not have been accidentally fired when Ramsey slipped going up the steps." Judge Henry N. Wessel refused bail for Ramsey, who remained in his cell at Moyamensing. Wessel criticized the police for their apparent looseness in the investigation and expanded it to include "every policeman who was in the station house at the time of the shooting."

A month later, Lieutenant Meyers would be transferred to the Fishtown station at Girard and Montgomery Avenues, and a week after that, in an unprecedented move, "the entire force of policemen at the 17th District Station House" was transferred. "May the good Lord have mercy on the neighborhood to which this king of thugs has been assigned," editorialized the *Tribune* about Meyers's move. A week later, they were able to report: "Now we have a mixed force of colored and white officers."

"For the first time in six weeks colored children have been able to play in front of their homes . . . colored people can walk home and feel safe."

Ramsey and Schneider lost their jobs and went to trial, but they would never serve time for the murder of Riley Bullock. Two years later, they were tried and found "not guilty." The jury deliberated for thirty minutes.

———

Sources: "Race Riots Grow in Fury as Police Fail to Curb Mobs, Negro Is Slain at Door of Station House," *Inquirer*, July 30, 1918; "Race Riot Area Dry; Detain Policeman in Shooting Probe," *Inquirer*, July 31, 1918; "Policeman Is Held after Rioter's Death," *Inquirer*, August 10, 1918; T. D. Adkins, pastor of the Mt. Carmel Baptist Church, letter to the editor, "Philadelphia Gripped by a Race Riot," *Philadelphia Tribune*, August 10, 1918; G. Grant Williams, "Meyers Kicked Out 17th District," *Philadelphia Tribune*, August 31, 1918; "Entire 17th District Police Transferred," *Philadelphia Tribune*, September 7, 1918; "Cop Schneider on Trial," *Philadelphia Tribune*, September 7, 1918; "Judge Rebukes Police for Killing of Negro," *Inquirer*, September 21, 1918; G. Grant Williams, "Coroner Holds Patrolman for Grand Jury," *Philadelphia Tribune*, September 21, 1918; "Schneider Is in the Jail

House Now; Prisoner Held Bullock While Ramsey Shot Him," *Philadelphia Tribune*, September 2, 1918; "The Colored Protective Association," *Philadelphia Tribune*, September 18, 1918; "Ex-Policemen Freed," *Inquirer*, December 16, 1920.

JOHN AVENA AND SOUTH PHILADELPHIA'S "BLOODY ANGLE"

As he liked to tell it, John Avena had "friends" at the Thirty-Third District police station. The thing was, Avena, a.k.a. "Nozzone" or "Big Nose John," was a Sicilian-born gangster who'd eventually head the Philadelphia mob. And if he didn't have friends at the station, exactly, Avena did have allies.

Avena's interests included dope dealing, extortion, passing counterfeit notes, numbers, and two high-stakes gambling houses at Eleventh and Christian and Ninth and Washington.

When federal agents set out to arrest Avena in June of 1922, the gangster bragged that he got tipped off by a policeman from the police station at Seventh and Carpenter. He got the word to "beat it," and Avena disappeared for a few days.

Later, when they caught up with Avena and arrested him, the bail was set at $10,000. It wouldn't be the last time. There was a lot going on in the 1920s in the vicinity of "Dope Row" (the 800 block of Christian Street). And cornering prohibition, gambling, and the protection rackets would grow fierce as Avena made his way to become the biggest numbers man in South Philadelphia.

A decade-long war would claim as many as twenty-five lives in the neighborhood surrounding the police station. The area would earn the nickname the "Bloody Angle" (the same as the most fatal places on the Civil War battlefield at Gettysburg). And along this stretch of Passyunk from Christian Street to Washington Avenue, Avena himself would survive several assassination attempts in the 1920s.

The report of Avena's demise in the *Bulletin*, published August 17, 1936, provides some insight:

The first time came early in 1926, when police had marked him as a boot-legger. They missed that time, missed altogether. Then it was July 29, a few months later. Avena was running a cigar store at 12th and Webster streets. It was night. Outside the store "Big Nose" heard a persistent whistling, a peculiar whistle, short and sharp, as though someone were calling. He went out. He met a burst of fire, and three shots ploughed into his back as he turned around to see where the whistling visitor was. An innocent woman bystander was wounded that night.

The word went out that they had "Big Nose" at last. Three shots. The boys shook their heads. But he made the grade, and then came March 10, 1927. He was in a restaurant on 8th street near Catharine. It was night again. He stepped out and two men, lurking in the shadows, sent twin streaks of fire across the pavement. They missed. A bootleggers' feud.

"South Philadelphia's Public Enemy No. 1" would become famous for denying death. "He'd been news for years. Always, they said: 'Well, Big Nose beat 'm again. He's going to live.'"

"And always, when he was shot, or shot at, or whenever he was on the police records, the cops used to ask him: 'Come on Nosey, who did it?' And what did 'Nosey' always say?"

"I like to settle these things myself."

———

Sources: George Anastasia, *Blood and Honor: Inside the Scarfo Mob, the Mafia's Most Violent Family* (Philadelphia: Camino Books, 1991); Philip Leonetti, *Mafia Prince: Inside America's Most Violent Mafia Family and the Bloody Fall of la Cosa Nostra* (Running Press, 2012); Celeste Morello, *Before Bruno: The History of the Philadelphia Mafia*, vol. 1 (Philadelphia: self-pub., 1999); "'Big Nose' Avena Slain by Gunmen in South Philadelphia," *Philadelphia Bulletin*, August 17, 1936.

Figure 9.5. Joseph Ida, John Avena, and Luigi Quaranta (left to right) in a police lineup after the Zanghi-Cocozza murders, May 1927

The third attempt on John Avena's life took place on March 10, 1927, as the thirty-two-year-old gangster stepped out of a restaurant at 822 South Eighth Street.

Avena knew exactly who was behind the failed hit. And he had no intention of turning anyone in. "I like to settle these things myself," Avena liked to say.

Avena worked for Salvatore Sabella, who also liked to settle things for himself. Growing up in Sicily as a butcher's apprentice, Sabella killed his abusive boss. Now in Philadelphia, this seasoned head of the local mob joined Avena and a handful of others to send a message, loud and clear: the streets of South Philadelphia were theirs—and would remain theirs.

This message would be delivered on Memorial Day. Anthony "Musky" Zanghi, twenty-seven, a bootlegger, bank robber, bigamist, holdup man, counterfeiter, and alleged cop killer had been making his mark on the Philadelphia crime scene. He was standing on the very same stretch of sidewalk on Eighth Street where Avena had been shot two months before, talking with his nineteen-year-old brother, Joseph, and thirty-year-old Vincent Cocozza, whose own arrest record included burglaries, robberies, and the sales of narcotics.

As "Musky" Zanghi later told it, Avena walked by and "gave me a Judas greeting." Moments later, a car pulled up, and as many as twenty shots rang out from pistols and sawed-off shotguns. "I saw two men lift shot guns and fire," Zanghi stated. "After the shooting, I saw Cocozza on the ground in a pool of blood. Then I saw my brother had been shot. At the hospital I had found out that they had blown his brains out and he was dead."

According to the *Public Ledger*, Zanghi "was hysterical over the death of his brother." And for the first time "in the history of the police department," a gangster had broken the code of silence.

"I was sent for by Sabella," he told police. "The plan was when they fired at me to take my kid brother, too." Police rounded up Sabella's men, and Zanghi placed each one at the crime scene except for Joseph Ida. Zanghi "was positive in his identification of Avena as the man who fired the fatal shot at Joseph." Zanghi also fingered Luigi Quaranta as the one who shot Cocozza with a shotgun; he identified Sabella as another shooter and John Scopoletti as the driver. In all, Zanghi identified six men involved in the incident.

As "he was taken past the 'lineup' at City Hall, Zanghi paused before Avena, his face turning purple with rage: 'Oh, you rat,' he shouted. 'Why did you fire when my back was turned?'" Zanghi "attempted to assault Avena, but was restrained."

On June 3, the day after the victims' funerals, all six were led to their arraignments through cleared corridors of City Hall. "The faces of the prisoners were covered with heavy growth of beard" as they listened to the charges of murder and manslaughter. Each one responded to the charges through an interpreter. "Twenty four detectives sat on the two benches behind the defendants. The prisoners did not even glance at them. Their eyes were fixed on Judge McDevitt throughout." "A tough, hard-looking lot of thugs," observed Mayor W. Freeland Kendrick, who inspected his police department's unprecedented catch.

But star witness, "Musky" Zanghi, would drop from the scene before the trials started. Word was that he had been offered as much as $50,000 to disappear. The authorities held off on their original plan to try Avena first. On June 13, the district attorney announced and the newspapers reported, Quaranta, described as "a swarthy and rather dapper little man" was "unexpectedly chosen as the first to stand trial." Two days later, Quaranta "nervously twisted his gray-banded straw hat in his hand" and "transferred his gaze to the foreman of the jury" before they read the verdict: "We find the prisoner guilty of murder in the first degree."

Quaranta showed no emotion. He turned away from the jury and stared at the floor. "After a few moments elapsed, he looked questioning at his attorney, but finding the latter's attention engaged elsewhere shrugged his shoulders." Then Quaranta, who would be sentenced to life in prison, "was led from the courtroom and down winding stairs to the waiting patrol wagon" and taken to Moyamensing Prison in a now somewhat safer South Philadelphia.

———

Sources: "Two Murdered by Shots from Speeding Auto," newspaper clipping, May 31, 1927, Temple University Urban Archives, Special Collections Research Center; "Gangsters Slay 2," *Philadelphia Bulletin*, May 31, 1927; "Plead Not Guilty to Gang Slaying," *Bulletin*, June 3, 1927; "100 Seized in Raids to End Gangster Wars," *Public Ledger*, June 6, 1927; "Quaranta on

Trial," June 13, 1927; "Quaranta Guilty in First Degree," June 19, 1927; "John Avena Was 'South Philadelphia's Public Enemy No. 1,'" August 18, 1936.

What Became of Them

What became of the perpetrators of the Zanghi-Cocozza Memorial Day murders after Anthony "Musky" Zanghi named names?

At first, city officials thought their arrests could end the gangster wars in South Philadelphia. In a sweep the Saturday night following the Memorial Day murders, police raided seven "sore spots" and "disorderly houses" between Fifth and Eleventh Streets and Christian and Federal Streets—"all the places where men and women of questionable character congregate"—and hauled in more than one hundred suspects. "We are going to keep up the raids until all habitual criminals have fled from the city," officials declared. "The death dealing warfare must come to an end."

But of the first six men arrested—John Avena and Salvatore Sabella (two of the gunmen on foot), Dominick Sesta and Luigi Quaranta (who wielded shotguns in a car), driver John Scopoletti and Antonio Dominic Pollina, a.k.a. Mr. Miggs (or Migs)—all except Quaranta were soon back on the street. Despite hopes for law and order, more witnesses than perpetrators went to prison—for their own protection.

Innocent bystander Piero Francisco, a down-on-his-luck dancer hired to entertain café clientele at Zanghi's La Tosca Café at Ninth and Fitzwater, spent half of his three years in Philadelphia behind bars. Francisco had the great misfortune of witnessing the Memorial Day murders. After a court appearance and several attempts on his life, followed by twenty months in protective custody, in the spring of 1929, Francisco finally left City Hall under armed guard to return to Italy on an unnamed steamer, never to seen or heard from again.

After his own release from protective custody, "Musky" Zanghi returned to his usual gangland ways until enemies caught up with him in New York City one August night in 1934. Zanghi left behind a widow, Antoinette;

seven children; and a stash of counterfeit one dollar bills with which Antoinette augmented her earnings at an Eighth and Montrose Streets fruit stand.

Instead of being the beginning of the end, the arrests in 1927 were more like the end of the beginning. The list reads like a Who's Who of the emerging Philadelphia mob. From left to right in the illustrated lineup, we see the following people:

Joseph Ida: Zanghi could not place Ida at the murder scene, and he was quickly released. Ida would head up the Philadelphia Family in the 1940s and much of the 1950s, only to flee to Sicily after having escaped arrest and indictment following the famous raid of the Apalachin Meeting in 1957. Ida's successor, Antonio Dominic Pollina ("Mr. Miggs") was also arrested for the 1927 murders. Pollina briefly led the Philadelphia family before Angelo Bruno's reign.

John Avena: "The biggest numbers man in South Philadelphia," whose crime interests ran as deep as they were wide, Avena took charge after Sabella "retired" in 1931. Avena had repeatedly been a target, and on August 17, 1936, he was the first mob boss in Philadelphia to be killed, along with Martin Feldstein, another racketeer. They were standing at Passyunk and Washington Avenues when drive-by shooters, thought to be from the rival Lanzetti brothers, killed both men. Avena left behind a widow, Grazia; two children; $8,000; and a diamond-encrusted wristwatch in a safe deposit. Pius Lanzetti, who ordered the killing, was himself gunned down the following New Year's Eve.

Luigi Quaranta: Despite all hopes and plans for the end of mob domination with the Zanghi-Cocozza arrests, this "dapper little man," as newspapers described him, was the only one to be convicted. In court, Francisco testified that "Quaranta and Sesta fired the shotguns." Quaranta claimed, to no avail, that he was in his "chicken store" at the time of the killings. He found himself quickly sentenced to life in prison. But in 1935, on the eve of his execution for the murder of a policeman, William "Mollyooch" Deni scribbled a note that Quaranta had gotten a "bum rap" and that Zanghi had set him up in an extortion attempt. It was enough to throw Quaranta's life sentence into doubt. In 1938, he was pardoned and released.

A few of those involved with the Zanghi-Cocozza murders lived long and healthy lives. After retirement, Sabella lived in Norristown, Pennsylvania, and died of natural causes in 1962. And Antonio Dominic Pollina, "Mr. Miggs," died in 1993, not long after his hundredth birthday.

———

Sources: "Quaranta Guilty in First Degree," newspaper clipping, June 19, 1927, Temple University Urban Archives, Special Collections Research Center; "'Big Nose' Avena Slain by Gunmen in South Philadelphia," *Philadelphia Bulletin*, August 17, 1936; "Executed Convict Frees Life Termer," *Philadelphia Evening Bulletin*, December 20, 1935; Kitty Caparella, "'Mr. Migs,' Ex-don, Dies at Age 100," *Philadelphia Daily News*, March 4, 1993; "The American Mafia: The History of Organized Crime in the United States, Avena, John 'Big Nose' (1893–1936)," accessed May 12, 2014, http://mob-who.blogspot.com/2011/04/avena-john-big-nose-1893-1936.html.

Figure 10.1. Musical Fund Hall, 808 Locust Street, photographed by Volkert, November 12, 1917

CHAPTER 10

Performance and Entertainment

LANDMARK OR NOT: THE MUSICAL FUND HALL IS A SITE OF CONSCIENCE

Philadelphia has a wide assortment of National Historic Landmarks, the crème de la crème of historic sites. The list is long with sixty-seven in all from Independence Hall to Eastern State Penitentiary and the John Coltrane House. And it would have been longer had the National Park Service let stand their original 1974 ruling in favor of the Musical Fund Hall on Locust Street. In 1989, shortly after developers converted the hall's auditorium into condominiums, the service withdrew the coveted designation. In America's most historic city, the Musical Fund Hall is the only site to hold such a dubious distinction.

Violated or not, this building stands as a genuine American site of conscience—and not because the it hosted the first national convention of the Republican Party in 1856, was the home of one of the nation's earliest musical organizations, and was the preferred venue of soloists (Jenny Lind, "The Swedish Nightingale") and lecturers (Charles Dickens). Maybe Philadelphians have become spoiled or jaded with so much of the past so accessible to them. A good, hard look at the story of the Musical Fund Hall revealed by Scott Gac in his book *Singing for Freedom* suggests reconsideration.

Gac profiles the New Hampshire–based Hutchinson Family, known for twelve-thousand concerts across the United States and abroad. The

Hutchinsons introduced the national conversation about abolitionism into popular culture. In concert, they performed original and provocative songs, including Jesse Hutchinson Jr.'s "Get Off the Track" from 1844, which warned, "Jump for your lives! Politicians, / From your dangerous false positions," and continued with the following:

> Men of various predilections,
>
> Frightened, run in all directions
>
> Merchants, Editors, Physicians,
>
> Lawyers, Priests and Politicians.
>
> Get Out of the Way! Get Out of the Way!
>
> Get Out of the Way! Every station,
>
> Clear the track of 'mancipation.

Wherever they went, the Hutchinsons attracted large, enthusiastic interracial audiences. Three years after their first popular performances in Philadelphia and a few months after a successful tour in England (with abolitionist and public speaker Frederick Douglass), the Hutchinsons returned in the spring of 1847. After several performances before "amalgamated" audiences at the Musical Fund Hall, Philadelphia mayor John Swift stepped in with restrictions. Concerned that continued shows would result in rioting at the Musical Fund Hall, the mayor urged management to adopt a new restrictive policy, starting immediately. All future lessees, including the Hutchinsons, had to agree to two conditions: "That no Anti-Slavery lecture shall be delivered" and "no colored person may form a portion of any audience." (This was the same Mayor Swift who had been unable, or unwilling, to stop rioters who destroyed abolitionists' brand-new Pennsylvania Hall in 1838.)

"The Hutchinson Family Singers refused to play for white patrons alone," writes Gac. And Philadelphians would not see or hear the Hutchinsons for the next fourteen years. America's original protest songsters, "who would not dare" to perform south of Wilmington, Delaware, added Philadelphia to the list of cities where they were unwelcome.

———

Sources: Scott Gac, *Singing for Freedom: The Hutchinson Family Singers and the Nineteenth-Century Culture of Reform* (New Haven: Yale University Press, 2008); Louis Cephas Madeira, *Annals of Music in Philadelphia: And History of the Musical Fund Society from Its Organization in 1820 to the Year 1858* (Philadelphia: J. B. Lippincott Company, 1896); William L. Mactier, *A Sketch of the Musical Fund Society of Philadelphia: Read before the Society January 29, 1885* (Philadelphia: Press of Henry B. Ashmead, 1885); National Park Service, "Musical Fund Society Hall, Philadelphia, PA. Designated a National Historic Landmark," May 30, 1974, Designation withdrawn January 13, 1989, http://www.cr.nps.gov/nhl/DOE_dedesignations/Musical.htm; "Amusements, Music, &c. Concert Hall," *Inquirer*, March 7, 1861; "The Hutchinson Family," *Inquirer*, February 3, 1866.

Figure 10.2. Dumont's Minstrels, northwest corner, Ninth and Arch Streets,
May 7, 1914

A century before one of the last gasps of American blackface minstrelsy played out at the corner of Ninth and Arch Streets, Philadelphia
lawyer-turned-cartoonist Edward Williams Clay pioneered his art of stok-
ing white ridicule. Clay's racist "Life in Philadelphia" caricatures of 1829
targeted African Americans and quickly grew in popularity at home and
abroad. While Clay added insult to injustice in Philadelphia, white actor
and playwright Thomas D. Rice adopted African American vernacular
speech, song, and dance to build his following. In both cases and during
the very same years, art was used to appropriate, exaggerate, entertain, and
suppress. Blackface minstrelsy was born.

"Minstrelsy is the one American form of amusement, purely our own,"
wrote a proud Frank Dumont in 1899. "It has lived and thrived even
though the plantation darkey, who first gave it a character, has departed."
Dumont's early career in minstrelsy before the Civil War culminated at the
turn of the century with this off-stage achievement, the 1905 publication

of his *Witmark Amateur Minstrel Guide and Burnt Cork Encyclopedia.* Dumont's troupe then performed at the Eleventh Street Opera House, near Ranstead Street. By 1911, when Dumont's name had become synonymous with blackface minstrelsy, he had his own venue at Ninth and Arch.

Dumont learned how to keep his material fresh with monologues, sketches, and burlesques adapted to "current fads and follies." His "Scenes at Wanamaker's," "Broad Street Station," "Atlantic City Storms," and "The Trolley Car Party" allowed audiences to see and mock themselves and, with the help of blackface minstrelsy, mock others.

How exactly did Dumont's Minstrels "black up" for every show? One evening, Dumont allowed a reporter to witness the nightly ritual. A written account made its way into *Dumont's Burnt Cork Encyclopedia*: Make a paste of burnt cork and water; put some "into your left hand, [and] rub it over the palms as if about to wash your face; then smear it over the features as if applying a cosmetic. Carefully apply it around the eyes and about the lips . . . when you have applied the cork and left the lips in the natural condition, they will appear red to the audience. Comedians leave a wider, white margin all around the lips. This will give it the appearance of a large mouth, and will look red to the spectator."

Readers of the *Burnt Cork Encyclopedia* did exactly that and followed Dumont's stage instructions and shared scripts for burlesques. They became proficient at lightening eyebrows with chalk, affixing woolen chin whiskers, and finishing off their stage faces with "large brass rimmed spectacles" perched on their blackened noses.

With the face complete, Dumont continued, "I take a small soft brush . . . to rub off the particles of cork from my features to prevent them from falling on my white shirt front and white vest . . . I put on my creamy white shirt . . . a paper or celluloid collar, a small black tie . . . my white vest . . . my swallow-tail coat with a flashy flower or 'boutonniere' in its lapel and I resemble a perfect Beau Brummel. . . . We wear black satin knee pants, black stockings and low cut patent leather shoes. This is very genteel, dressing and in keeping with minstrelsy."

Also in keeping with the minstrelsy was the nightly postperformance ritual of removing the burnt cork. "No hard rubbing is necessary. Plenty of lather and a sponge. Then go over the face once more and . . . rinse your 'features' in a bucket of fresh water . . . and once more you are a Caucasian ready to take up the 'white man's burden.'"

Frank Dumont died in his box office at Ninth and Arch in 1919. Dumont's theater went up for sale in 1928, and the building burned a year later. Live blackface minstrelsy on stage in Philadelphia had come to an end, although the screen version, thanks to Hollywood, was only getting started. Philadelphia's mummer tradition of "blacking up" would continue until 1964, when the courts declared that the practice had finally, after nearly a century and a half, run its racist course.

––––––

Sources: Frank Dumont (1848–1919) Minstrelsy Scrapbook, 1850–1902, Description for Collection 3054, Historical Society of Pennsylvania; Frank Dumont, *The Witmark Amateur Minstrel Guide and Burnt Cork Encyclopedia* (Chicago: M. Witmark and Sons, 1905); John Francis Marion, "On New Year's Day in Philadelphia, Mummer's the Word," *Smithsonian Magazine*, January 1981; Jennifer Wallach, "Minstrelsy," in *Encyclopedia of African American Society*, ed. Gerald D. Jaynes, vol. 2 (Thousand Oaks: Sage, 2005), 545–546.

Figure 10.3. Lincoln Theatre (formerly the Dunbar Theatre), southwest corner, Broad and Lombard Streets, January 11, 1932

"Marian Dawley and a few other girls of color . . . went to the movie theater at 59th and Market Streets" in the spring of 1919. They lined up to buy tickets and were told "all tickets for colored people have been sold."

They left "disgusted," according to the *Philadelphia Tribune.*

Other than the Standard Theatre on the 1100 block of South Street, audiences of color had few options for entertainment in Philadelphia. "The white theatres are and have been for some time drawing the color line," pointed out the *Tribune.* "We have but one theatre owned and controlled by our race in this city, and when it is full, which is at every performance, there is practically no place for our people to go."

But change was coming. "In a few months the new Dunbar theatre will be completed at the corner of Broad and Lombard Streets." This theatre, the Dunbar, would be "owned and controlled by citizens of color" to serve the city's African American theatergoers, estimated at fifty thousand as a result of the recent Great Migration.

"The Quality Amusement Company, of which Mr. E. C. Brown, of the Brown and Stevens Bankers is the head" soon had "ten Negro Theatres . . . in cities including Savannah, Richmond, Washington (The Howard), New York (The Lafayette) and Chicago." Philadelphia's promised to be "the finest theatre in the world owned, managed and controlled by colored people."

"It was a grand spectacle December 29, [1919,] to see the thousands of happy souls, men and women, boys and girls, as they wended through the streets of Philadelphia and filled every available space in the new Dunbar Theatre . . . The colored citizens of Philadelphia have something really their own," something "that they will be and are proud of and can boast about" something "wonderful, marvelous, almost inconceivable, yet so true."

"Within the Law," starring Cleo Desmond and Andrew Bishop, filled the 1,600-seat house twice daily for a solid week. And thanks to the Lafayette Players, the productions kept coming.

John T. Gibson, owner of the Standard Theatre responded by cutting ticket prices. Gibson knew that the Dunbar's parent company "had overextended itself by building the $500,000 Douglass Theatre in Baltimore, as well as the Renaissance Theatre in Harlem." And in September 1921, just a few months after *Shuffle Along* premiered at the Dunbar, Gibson bought the theater.

As the stage of choice, "Gibson's New Dunbar Theatre" hosted the full array of African American talent: Will Marion Cook's International Orchestra and Entertainers in *The Quintessence of Jazz*; Mamie Smith; the Ethiopian Art Theater's version of Oscar Wilde's *Salome* fresh from its run on Broadway; the Lafayette Players productions of *The Shoplifters* and *The Hunchback of Notre Dame*; the Manhattan Players' *Cat and the Canary*, *Sunshine Sammy*, *Runnin' Wild*, *Swanee River Home*, *Struttin' Time*, and *Come Along Mandy*; and *The Chocolate Dandies*, featuring Josephine Baker's first Philadelphia appearance.

The Great Depression forced another sale of Gibson's Dunbar to new (white) owners, who added a giant marquee, dubbed it the Lincoln, and continued to bring in talent, including Duke Ellington and his orchestra, Cab Callaway, "the Heidi Ho King and his original Cotton Club Orchestra," and its performance of *Minnie the Moocher*. Lincoln regulars saw "Fats" Waller, Louis Armstrong, Bill "Bojangles" Robinson, Earl Hines, and Ethel Waters, as well as other headliners. From the beginning, the theater played a critical role in addition to serving as the city's most desirable stage for African American performers. The Lincoln was also often dedicated to issues of race relations, human rights, and outright political protest.

In 1920, the Bramhall Players, an interracial troupe, presented Butler Davenport's *Justice*, described as a "race drama." Where *Uncle Tom's Cabin* "went far to free the Negro's body from bondage," *Justice*, claimed one review, "will go far to liberate the white man's mind from prejudice." Three years later, more than 3,500 people packed a mass meeting in the theater to protest lynching, the "Shame of America," and support passage of Congressman Leonidas Dyer's Anti-Lynching Bill.

And in December 1938, the Lincoln hosted a public meeting denouncing "Nazi Germany's persecutions of racial and religious minorities," warning that "such actions are sympathetically received in some quarters in this country." About five hundred attended the event, sponsored by the United Committee against Racial and Religious Persecutions. It began with a march up South Street from Fifth to Fifteenth, to the Lincoln, where "an effigy of Adolf Hitler, replete in brown shirt, swastika and mustache . . . was publicly burned."

Such was Broad and Lombard Street's niche in history, once upon a time.

———

Sources: "All Seats for Colored People Are Sold Out," *Philadelphia Tribune*, March 8, 1919; "Philadelphia to Soon Have a New Colored Play House," *Philadelphia Tribune*, November 8, 1919; "The Dunbar Theatre Has Swung Open Its Doors to the Public," *Philadelphia Tribune*, January 3, 1920; advertisement for "Justice," *The Crisis: A Record of the Darker Races* 21, no. 2

(December 1920): 87; Anny Boddy, "Phila. Has 'Something New under the Sun,'" *Philadelphia Tribune*, January 3, 1920; "Anti-lynching Bill Support Asked," *Inquirer*, July 3, 1923; "Hitler's Effigy Burned by Crowd," *Inquirer*, December 6, 1938; advertisements for "The Dunbar" and "The Lincoln," *Inquirer*, 1920–1936; Errol G. Hill and James V. Hatch, *A History of African American Theatre* (Cambridge: Cambridge University Press, 2003).

SHUFFLE ALONG BROAD STREET

"Fourteen Thousand Negro Actors in This Country Now Performing," read a headline at the start of the 1922 theatrical season. "In vaudeville alone there are more than six hundred acts, of which about sixty are now in Europe. There are twenty-two Negro minstrel shows touring the south." According to *Billboard*, "368 theaters in the United States [are] devoted entirely to the colored race." Among them, in Philadelphia, were the Standard near Eleventh and South Streets, the Royal near Fifteenth and South, and the Nixon on Fifty-Second Street. Plus, there was the only theater built, owned and operated by African Americans: the Dunbar at Broad and Lombard.

From the moment it opened at the Dunbar on April 11, 1921, Eubie Blake's *Shuffle Along* demonstrated the power of the African American jazz sensation. "A ball of merriment rolling at aero-plane speed," *Shuffle Along* would complete its run on Broad in Philadelphia and return again before opening on Broadway in New York. "The biggest hit New York has witnessed in years," critics raved; it was "a breeze of super-jazz blown up from Dixie" that would, over the next sixty weeks, establish a five hundred performance legacy before going on tour.

"Whether you like jazz or not," admitted the Philadelphia Orchestra's Leopold Stowkowski in 1924, "it is a modern featurization of our hectic times and it is with us to stay." Eubie Blake suggested that jazz's "flash and fire" generated "flamboyant effectiveness" artistically and commercially. It offers up "ingredients of freshness in a world where there must be freshness constantly."

Shuffle Along would become the gold standard for American musical theater. Time and time again, Dunbar managers would mount jazz and vaudeville productions hoping for another hit. They promoted *Liza* as the "musical thrill that won't let your feet behave" and the "logical successor to 'Shuffle Along.'" They opened *Carolina Nights* with choreography by Charlie Davis, the "dancing cop" from *Shuffle Along*. In the first half of the 1920s, Dunbar audiences would enjoy *Creole Follies*, *Harlem Follies*, *Ebony Follies*, and *Charleston Fricassee*. They came out for *Come Along Mandy*, *Runnin' Wild*, *Banville Dandies Revue*, Jimmie Cooper's *All Colored Revue Hotsy Totsy*, and Mamie Smith and her *Syncopators' Revue Cyclonic Jazz Band*. None took off quite like *Shuffle Along*.

"There is no color line in the theater," proclaimed one *Inquirer* critic, claiming it as proof of the broad and sustained appeal of *Shuffle Along*. Yet there *was* a color line, possibly several. Racial discrimination by mainstream theaters was one of the reasons the African American community had built the Dunbar in the first place. And as quickly as the blockbuster found a home at the Dunbar, after its extended Broadway run, it would return to Broad Street, though not at the Dunbar. In May 1923, *Shuffle Along* opened for four weeks at the Forrest Theatre, then at Broad and Sansom Streets, a mainstream venue with a much larger stage and four hundred additional seats for eager ticket buyers. Ironically, the success of African American productions would undercut the success of the Dunbar.

This time "Shuffle Along" came to Philadelphia with the 17-year-old Josephine Baker in its chorus line. One critic raved:

> When the best part of a capacity house singles out one little girl in the chorus and gives her attention every time she appears, it shows the recognition of qualities as stars are made of. There is a girl like this in the all-colored musical success, 'Shuffle Along,' at the Forrest Theatre. She is a sturdy youngster with a winning way and comedy that asserts itself in everything she does. She is one of the happy-honeysuckles and her name is Josephine Baker. Jolly as she seems to be in her work, the stage romping

is serious business with Josephine. . . . Miss Baker has been in the professional only a short time but she has done much during that period. She
knows how to make people laugh and how to sing and dance.

Would Josephine Baker ever debut at the Dunbar? She would. In
November 1924, she performed in *Chocolate Dandies*, another Eubie Blake
show. "With snap and zest and to the tune of much musical melody, 'The
Chocolate Dandies' 'strutted their stuff' into Philadelphia . . . The lid was
off and it was a race all evening," one review said, stating that the double-
jointed "Josephine Baker carries off the honors."

When *Chocolate Dandies* closed, it was Baker's last appearance at the
Dunbar and her next to the last appearance on Broad Street. In February 1928, after Baker had relocated to Paris and performed at the Folies-
Bergère, a clip of her famous "banana skirt" dance made its way into a film
travelogue, "Paris by Night," which was shown at the Academy of Music
at Broad and Locust Streets. No matter that the film had been "viewed
by more than 150,000 people and 15 cities without creating criticism on
its alleged impropriety." One Philadelphia "patron" lodged her complaint
about Baker's "lack of garb," and the censors deleted Baker's performance
from all subsequent screenings.

It wouldn't be the last time official censors would judge African American artists and their work on stage in Philadelphia.

————

Sources: "Dunbar Theatre to Open Monday, December 29th," *Philadelphia
Tribune*, December 27, 1919; "Shuffle Along," *Inquirer*, April 12, 1921; "Shuf-
fle Along: Biggest New York Hit," *Inquirer*, December 11, 1921; "There Are
Many Colored Thespians," *Inquirer*, September 17, 1922; "'Shuffle Along:'
Breezy Musical Show Scores a Big Hit at the Forrest," *Inquirer*, May 8, 1923;
"She Is a Real Comedy Chorus Girl," *Inquirer*, May 20, 1923; "How a Jazzer
Views Such Music," *Inquirer*, November 23, 1924; "Chocolate Dandies
Score at Dunbar," *Inquirer*, November 25, 1924; "Paris Night Life Scene Cut
from Travel Film," *Inquirer*, February 19, 1928.

Figure 10.4. Mayor S. Davis Wilson at the controls, dedication, September 16, 1938

The "people's mayor" or a "political chameleon"? From his flamboyant convention hall swearing-in during a "howling snowstorm" in January 1936 to his indictment fewer than three years later, Philadelphia's mayor S. Davis Wilson wielded power with flair. As historian John Rossi put it, "Hardly a week passed that didn't witness some dramatic gesture" on the part of Mayor Wilson.

Wilson battled the city's privately owned utilities in the courtroom and in the press, claiming the citizens were being robbed. "I'm going to wipe out the whole system," he boasted in a hallway argument with young Richardson Dilworth, a lawyer for the PRT (Philadelphia Rapid Transit), before promising to punch him in the nose. "Like hell you are," Dilworth replied as he shed his coat. "I'd like to see you try."

Wilson grabbed headlines every which way: luring the Democratic Party's presidential convention to Philadelphia and convincing organizers of the Army-Navy football game that Philadelphia should be their city of choice. He urged the Philadelphia Orchestra to produce popular concerts and the Mummers to reschedule their New Year's Day parade to a more spectator-friendly time of year. And just for the sake of yet one more headline, Wilson offered the position of superintendent of Philadelphia police to FBI director J. Edgar Hoover.

Wilson seemed everywhere—and was, actually, with his name "stenciled on all kinds of city property" from "traffic lights to trashcans," earning him the nickname "Ashcan Wilson." As his first year in office came to a close, Mayor Wilson attended the *New Faces* revue at the Forrest Theatre. When actors portrayed the former and current first ladies, Mrs. Hoover and Mrs. Roosevelt, haranguing Girl Scouts "on the delicate subject of babies," Wilson walked out.

"It's a damnable outrage, to poke fun at the President's wife!" he exclaimed. "Take that skit out—or I'll stop the whole show." It didn't seem to matter that *New Faces* had run for months in New York without complaint or that the First Ladies actually appreciated the humor. "Either the skit goes," demanded Wilson, "or the show does." The skit went, and the show continued on.

Theater critic Linton Martin worried what Wilson's "attitude and its enforcement could and would do" to Philadelphia's stage. Several productions of recent years would have been "shorn of their smartest and most smarting shafts of satire." Martin and Philadelphia's audiences didn't have to speculate for long.

Wilson stepped in again as the city's official censor on the eve of the opening of *Mulatto* at the Locust Street Theatre. Langston Hughes's play held the record as the longest-running Broadway production by an African American (before Lorraine Hansberry's *A Raisin in the Sun*). At the New York opening in 1935, critic Brooks Atkinson called *Mulatto* a "sobering sensation." Anticipating its arrival in Philadelphia, the *Inquirer* described the play as "a melodrama of miscegenation in the South," telling the story of "a wealthy Southern planter who philanders with his housekeeper" and sends "his four Mulatto children . . . North to be educated. The Yankee environment instills in them the spirit of equality, so that when they return to the plantation they antagonize their family and neighbors." Advertisements promised a "darling drama of sex life in the South."

"It will probably cure no ills and provoke no race riots," wrote Percy Hammond in New York. And not once did *Mulatto*'s 373 performances there or its three month-run in Chicago stir the hint of a riot. But riots were exactly what Mayor Wilson claimed to fear for Philadelphia. "The show won't go on," declared the mayor, claiming *Mulatto* was "an outrageous affront to decency."

"As long as I am mayor," he remarked to the *New York Herald Tribune*, "I will not permit such shows in Philadelphia." He sought confirmation from his "special censor group," which previewed an edited version of the play. Producer Jack Linder assured the censors and the press that "many changes have been made" and "the objectionable features have been removed." One critic wondered in print whether enough "soap and water has been applied to make it safe for Philadelphia consumption." The mayor's censors came in with a tie: 3–3. One publicly criticized Wilson's last-minute ban as "stupid and unfair" and was relieved of her duties. Wilson enacted his original decision and posted police at the entrances of the darkened theater.

Mulatto found audiences outside of Philadelphia, as close as the Garden Pier Theatre in Atlantic City the following August. And two years later, after Wilson's death of a stroke, the play's producers again attempted to bring *Mulatto* to the Philadelphia stage, this time at the Walnut Street Theatre. But Wilson's successor invoked the earlier decision, continuing the debate. As the courts considered the ban, the Reverend Marshall L. Shepard compared "the play's possible importance to that of 'Uncle Tom's Cabin.'" He couldn't understand "why the play should provoke rioting. It only depicts the truth."

Yet Wilson's censorship stood. And from all I can tell, Langston Hughes's *Mulatto* has still not had its Philadelphia premiere.

Sources: Brooks Atkinson, "Race Problems in the South the Theme of 'Mulatto,' a 'New Drama' by Langston Hughes," *New York Times*, October 25, 1935; Percy Hammond, "The New York Theatre," *Inquirer*, November 3, 1935; Linton Martin, "The Call Boys Chat: New Faces," *Inquirer*, November 15, 1936; "Wilson and Lawyer near Fight over P.R.T.," *New York Times*, February 4, 1936; "Mayor Plays Gallant, Bans Girl Scout Skit," *Inquirer*, November 10, 1936; "The Playbill," *Inquirer*, February 7, 1937; "Mayor Won't Yield; Show Fails to Open," *Inquirer*, February 9, 1937; "Philadelphia Halts the Play 'Mulatto,'" *New York Times*, February 9, 1937; "Mrs. Favorite to Lose Job on Theatre Censor Board," *Inquirer*, February 10, 1937; "Censors Tie on 'Mulatto,'" *New York Times*, February 11, 1937; Linton Martin, "The Call Boy's Chat: Revues in This Land of the Free-for-All," *Inquirer*, February 15, 1936; Linton Martin, "The Call Boy's Chat: Taking the Dare Out of Dubious Drama," *Inquirer*, February 14, 1937; "Indict Mayor of Philadelphia in Vice Inquiry," *Chicago Daily Tribune*; September 10, 1938; John P. Rossi, "Philadelphia's Forgotten Mayor: S. Davis Wilson," *Pennsylvania History* 51, no. 2 (April 1984); Joseph McLaren, *Langston Hughes, Folk Dramatist in the Protest Tradition, 1921–1943* (Westport: Greenwood Press, 1997).

Figure 10.5. Joseph Kiefer and the Philadelphia Police Band, City Hall Tower, 1918

"Those moaning saxophones," fretted John R. McMahon in the *Ladies' Home Journal*, "call out the low and rowdy instinct." And with provocative names like "the cat step, camel walk, bunny hug, turkey trot," McMahon figured jazz dance mocked the dignified traditions of social dance. Most insidious of all was a move they called the shimmy. "The road to hell is too often paved with jazz steps," McMahon wrote in an article titled, "Unspeakable Jazz Must Go!"

The shimmy rode in with Spencer Williams's popular song, "Shim-Me-Sha-Wabble," from 1917. Within a few years, the shimmy had just about taken over white dance halls and cabarets, thriving on stage and in recordings, all the while shaking America's sense of decency.

"With hardly any movement of the feet," described singer and actress Mae West, dancers "just shook their shoulders, torsos, breasts and pelvises." West introduced her version of the shimmy in New York during the fall of 1918, and a year later, her image appeared on the sheet music for "Ev'rybody Shimmies Now." While the shimmy amused people, its boldness also shocked them. Even West noted the "naked, aching sensual agony about it."

By 1919, the shimmy dominated American music publishing, recording, and performing. The Ziegfeld Follies featured it on Broadway. Gilda Gray introduced the shimmy to Philadelphia in the "Shubert Gaieties" at the Chestnut Street Opera House, suggesting that if she hadn't exactly invented the move, she owned it on stage. "I don't know whether my shoulders were made to express the shimmy," Gray told the *Inquirer*, "or whether the shimmy was made for my shoulders to express."

America danced to "an explosion of shimmy tunes," and "everyone seemed to jump on the shimmy bandwagon," wrote Rebecca A. Bryant in "Shaking Things Up: Popularizing the Shimmy in America." The famous "I Wish I Could Shimmy Like My Sister Kate" would be joined by the "Shimmie Waltz," "Let Us Keep the Shimmie," "Shimmying Everywhere," and Irving Berlin's "You Cannot Make Your Shimmy Shake on Tea." Some were worried that Prohibition might kill the shimmy off before it went out of style. But banning alcohol didn't slow the shimmy down. Philadelphia soon shook to its very own song: "All the Quakers Are Shoulder Shakers (Down in Quaker Town)."

Others joined the scandalized Quaker on the illustrated cover of "Shoulder Shakers," chiming in with their opinions. "Dancing Masters Join Clergy to Purify Dance," read one headline, "International Association Blames Wave of Vulgar Dancing on Song Writers." Before long, from New York to San Francisco, moral authorities wanted, and sometimes managed, to ban, restrict, or censor the shimmy.

"The insidious thing," wrote the *Inquirer* in an article confirming "the shimmy dance has been barred from Philadelphia," is that "when one dancer starts the whole place must start, until the room rocks with the shimmy dance. It is more insidious than champagne, it is more insidious than drugs." In the suburbs, the Lansdowne Club designated chaperones as "shimmy sleuths," assigning them to break up both "the bunny-hugging and too affectionate 'toddling.'" In the city, the task of policing the city's four thousand licensed dance halls proved more challenging.

The solution? Dancing—and censoring—in public.

"Police Dance Censor Taboos Street Shimmy," read the headline before the first Philadelphia street dances of 1919. Sergeant Theodore S. Fenn assured that dancers "will do nothing 'suggestive' by way of street dancing while I am around . . . Philadelphia will dance with her feet, and her feet only. The Quaker City . . . will not be disgraced by the 'shimmy' dance." The dancers had other ideas. When fifteen thousand jammed the Parkway to move to the police band, reported the *Inquirer*, they were "happy in jazzing and shimmying . . . in . . . one jostling, swaying mass of sweltering humanity, in which a censor, if there had been one, would have had about as much chance of imposing his ideas as the proverbial snowball." Dancers "toddled and shimmied, dipped and slid to their hearts content."

Someone needed to train police in antidance tactics and prevent "cheek-to-cheek dancing, abdominal contact, [the] shimmy, [and the] toddle." Enter dance master Miss Marguerite Walz, who would instruct fifty-four officers "to keep their eyes peeled for violators of the 'No Shimmy' rule" while the police band played on. During their first outing, just "a few couples drew the attention of the censors, but policemen would step forward and touch one of the offenders on the shoulder and that was the end of it."

Or so they hoped. The very next year, the "hip-dip" "wiggled its way into local terpsichorean circles," complained Miss Walz. During a visit to South Philadelphia High School, she noticed that, as well as other "new and very undesirable dances," including the "flapper flop," the "debutante slouch," and the "windmill stride." Dance censorship, it turned out, would be a never-ending game of whack-a-mole.

Sources: "Shimmy's Death Blow," *Variety*, December 13, 1918; "Philadelphia Sneezes at Shimmy Dance," *Inquirer*, January 18, 1919, 3; "Police Dance Censor Taboos Street Shimmy," *Inquirer*, May 7, 1919, 3; "Dancing Masters Join Clergy to Purify Dance," *Inquirer*, June 13, 1919, 16; "Another Creator of the Shimmy," *Inquirer*, October 19, 1919, 8; "'Sedate Dancing Only' Lansdowne Club Edict," *Inquirer*, January 15, 1921, 19; "15,000 Crowd at First Dance on Parkway," *Inquirer*, July 8, 1921, 3; "18,000 at City Dance Miss Walz, Censor, Finds Few Violations of 'No Shimmy' Rule," *Inquirer*, July 29, 1921, 3; John R. McMahon, "Unspeakable Jazz Must Go!," *Ladies' Home Journal*, December 1921; "New Dances Banned: South Phila. High Girls Promise to Eschew Latest Steps," *Inquirer*, March 29, 1922, 16; "'Hip Dip' Appears Here at City's Public Dance," *Inquirer*, July 14, 1922, 3; Rebecca A. Bryant, "Shaking Things Up: Popularizing the Shimmy in America," *American Music* 20, no. 2 (Summer 2002): 168–187.

Figure 10.6. Bellevue Theatre, 2210 North Front Street, March 14, 1916

In 1913, "seventy vaudeville and motion picture theatres were under construction," wrote Irvin Glazer, and "virtually all of them were open by the fall," providing Philadelphia with about 350 venues theatres, excluding downtown "legitimate theatres." Each and every one screened silent films.

Options were everywhere. In addition to the Victoria at 913 Market (open since in 1909), the Ruby Theatre opened its doors at 618 Market, the Arcadia at 1529 Chestnut, and the Palace Theatre at 1214 Market. The massive new 1,400-seat Stanton had opened at Sixteenth and Market, not far from the Regent, a block to the west. But moviegoers didn't have to come to town; they could stay in their own neighborhoods and enjoy films at the Tioga near Seventeenth and Venango, the Apollo at Fifty-Second and Girard, or many others theatres—and even more were on the way. By 1915, as one film trade publication recorded, in Kensington, film fans could also visit the newly opened 830-seat Bellevue Theatre. Front and Susquehanna had become a happening place.

Beyond the Bellevue's "marble and mahogany" ticket booth and lobby lined with stone tiles, potted palms, and wall-to-wall movie posters, the theater accommodated patrons from noon to an hour before midnight. They filed past brass railings and opal fixtures and strolled down crimson-carpeted aisles to upholstered seats where they could hear the echo organ and a five-piece orchestra. Visitors would take in the latest films, which were advertised in circulars, in the daily papers, and on billboards and posters mounted on wagons.

With a boom in venues and production burgeoning, the screen was now the place to see and be seen. The "celebrated and pulchritudinous" Kitty Gordon held back from film as long as she could, but as 1915 came to a close, Gordon gave in to "the green glare of the lights of a motion picture studio." "I felt positively tremulous as I made my first scene," confessed Gordon. "But that feeling soon wore off and by the time the camera man was ready to 'grind' I was perfectly cool again. I am quite in love with this wonderful new art that furnishes one with surprises no matter which way one turns."

In the role of the beautiful, charming, and conniving Lena Despard, in an updated version of F. C. Philips's *As in a Looking Glass*, Gordon managed to make "an especially striking and attention-compelling photo drama." The bar had been set high by stars on the stage. Sarah Bernhardt had owned the role for a time in Paris, admitting to a reporter that the "frank and easy style" of the story "touched" her "dramatic fibre." Philadelphia ticket holders had packed the Walnut to witness Lillie Langtry as the "soulless adventuress" Despard, who was displayed in one after another glamorous gown, just as Lillian Cleves had been at the Girard Avenue Theatre.

In her debut, Gordon delivered. "Quite frequently," observed critic Lynde Denig, she turned "her back to the camera and it generally happened that her gown was pronouncedly—need it be added—becomingly décolleté." The director "surely bore in mind the probable spirit of the public, how eagerly it would await a convincing display of Miss Gordon's much advertised back," and, Denig noted, "how little the story mattered by comparison." If the script "lacked inspirational qualities," the production "was fortunate in having a star capable of carrying so much responsibility on undraped shoulders." Denig gave a thumbs-up: "nobody is going to be disappointed in Miss Gordon's beauty from whatever angle it is viewed."

Motography's reporter agreed, adding a bit of pre-Hollywood snark on Gordon's gowns, which "began late and ended early." As it turned out, the anticipated "brilliance" of her "'polished shoulders' . . . had caused widespread halation . . . on the film." Makeup had to "dull the gleam of that famous back and those celebrated shoulders with whole shaker-fulls of powder" before the camera could refocus "its undazzled eye on the dulled surface."

Audiences were dazzled by all they saw, which culminated in an updated suicide scene, "a final thrill" of the Thelma and Louise variety, when Gordon and her vehicle "hurled over a precipice."

Projectors at the Bellevue kept rolling on into the 1930s, and at some point, the place was reincarnated as a car parts shop. Today, the much-compromised, largely anonymous building barely survives.

Sources: "Mrs. Langtry at the Walnut," *Inquirer,* January 23, 1888; "Mrs. Langtry's Second Week," *Inquirer,* January 24, 1888; "Bellevue Theatre Opens
in Philadelphia," *Accessory News* 10, no. 25 (October 1914–January 1915):
112; "At the Theatres Last Night: The Girard Avenue," *Inquirer,* October 27,
1891; "Kitty Gordon Is Filmed," *Inquirer,* December 26, 1915; Lynde Denig,
"'As in a Looking Glass': Kitty Gordon Is Introduced to World Film Audience in Melodrama of Intrigue and Love," *The Moving Picture World,*
vol. 27 (New York: World Photographic, 1916); "Notes from All Over,"
Motography 15, no. 1 (1916): 48; Irvin R. Glazer, *Philadelphia Theatres, A–Z:
A Comprehensive, Descriptive Record of 813 Theatres Constructed since 1724*
(Westport: Greenwood Press, 1986).

Figure 10.7. Ludlow Street, looking west from Twentieth, June 26, 1924

In 1915, when Hollywood released *The Sea Hawk*, the silent film directed by Frank Lloyd based on an adventure novel by Raphael Sabatini, "Mae Tinee" had been on the beat for nearly a decade. This long-standing, all-purpose byline was used by *Chicago Daily Tribune* reporters assigned to review movies on slow news days.

"'The Sea Hawk' is more than just a motion picture!," Tinee declared in a review of July 1, 1924. "It is the dream of the tired business man; it is the fiery secret ambition of romantic youth. It carries the wistful passion that, carefully concealed, lives in most of us—to be gorgeous, spectacular, abused, talked about with baited breath—a creature dominating a world of winds and waters and clothes that never, never came from the shops of 'what men wear.' (Or women, either.)" It was a "love story" of "a noble brother; weakling half-brother; pirate ships, duels, intrigue" presented "in kaleidoscopic fashion to the sway of music that warms the blood."

"You may work at a regular job for a living," added Mae Tinee, "but once inside this little theater you get aboard a Spanish galleon or a Moorish vessel or an English ship. Your mission, for a brief time, becomes either pirating or revenge. Jagged cliffs, Moorish castles, and the fair countryside of old England furnish you with picturesque background."

Americans loved the expensive extravaganza, which included a cast of thousands led by Milton Sills, Enid Bennett, and Wallace Beery. They loved *The Sea Hawk*'s four full-sized ships created just for this production. And audiences especially loved that no expense, no sentiment—nothing whatsoever—was spared.

The Sea Hawk "sailed right into the heart of Los Angeles! And anchored there!" bragged a July 3 advertisement in the *Los Angeles Daily Times* after the Hollywood premiere. "Thousands! Thousands! Thousands!" reveled "in the glamour of the settings!" and were "swept away by the immensity!"

"The grand old swashbuckling days are with us once again," wrote Edwin Schallert. "'The Sea Hawk' visions them with rip roaring spirit of adventure. The picture is one of the ablest achievements in this history of the screen and in the current season it shines forth as a magnificent flare among a host of flickers. The premiere . . . the first big gala . . . this season . . . took place at [Los Angeles's] Criterion Theater," a classic movie palace on Grand Avenue, which had opened in 1917 as the Kinema Theater. The "Criterion Audience Gives Enthusiastic Approval" for the cast of thousands, declared yet another critic, who called the lavish twelve reeler "brilliant."

Frank Lloyd was well on his way to directing scores of films, including *Les Misérables* (1917), *Oliver Twist* (1922), *Mutiny on the Bounty* (1935), and *The Last Command* (1955). In *The Sea Hawk*, Lloyd fully embraced Sabatini's spirit in ships, scale, and sentiment.

The film had staying power. Five weeks after the premiere, a *Los Angeles Times* reported that "action thrills and adventure on the high seas continue to please large audiences at the Criterion" under the headline: "'Sea Hawk' Packs 'Em In."

Philadelphians had been reading copies of the best-selling *Sea Hawk* since 1915, when the Washington Square publisher J. P. Lippincott introduced the first American edition. Philadelphia moviegoers who had been looking forward to the film adaptation kept it in theaters after it finally arrived the summer of 1924. As late as the following spring, screenings of *The Sea Hawk* would continue at the Great Northern Theater on North Broad Street.

———

Sources: Mae Tinee, "Love, Thrills, Adventure in 'Sea Hawk': It's Your Young Dream Come True," *Chicago Daily Tribune*, July 1, 1924; "It Sailed Right into the Heart of Los Angeles! And Anchored There!," advertisement, *Los Angeles Daily Times*, July 3, 1924; Edwin Schallert, "'Sea Hawk Enthralls': Frank Lloyd Achieves His Biggest Success, Premier at Criterion Is Brilliant Event," *Los Angeles Daily Times*, July 3, 1924; "Premiere of 'Sea Hawk' Is Brilliant: Criterion Audience Gives Enthusiastic Approval," *Los Angeles Times*, July 6, 1924; "'Sea Hawk' Packs 'Em In," *Los Angeles Times*, July 27, 1924; T. M. C., "Thinks 'The Sea Hawk' Is Superb: T. M. C. Believes This Film Spectacle Brings Frank Lloyd, Its Director, in Class with Cruze and Ingram," *Baltimore Sun*, September 14, 1924; "Adventure, Atmosphere in Big Film: 'The Sea Hawk,' Opening at Metropolitan," *Washington Post*, Oct. 19, 1924.

Figure 11.1. Liberty statue, South Penn Square, April 16, 1918

CHAPTER 11

Art, Public Art, and Landmarks

LIBERTY UNVEILED

Little "blue-eyed, pink-cheeked" Nona Martin, a five-year-old from Chestnut Hill, stood motionless, "awed by the numberless masses that stretched away before her vision down Broad Street, as far as the eye could see." By her side on the platform was her grandfather, William G. McAdoo, the "tall, gaunt, commanding" treasury secretary. Behind them loomed the giant statue, draped in white.

The parade had started as the clocks struck noon. Twelve hundred schoolgirls "dressed as Goddesses of Liberty," escorted by the police band, marched northward from Broad and Jackson Streets. Each one held in her uplifted hands a torch of Liberty and a flag of France, England, Belgium, Italy, Canada, Japan, Poland, or the United States. Behind the "procession of the goddesses" marched five thousand marines and sailors. The pageant was great, the crowd greater, and the music spectacular.

Bands played "Over There." Then Clarence Whitehill, baritone of the Metropolitan Opera Company, stepped forward. "A hush fell over the multitude. His voice rang out with the first words of the hallowed 'Battle Hymn of the Republic.'" As Whitehill's voice echoed over the silent crowd, "it was as though an electric current had been sent through the solid masses of humanity."

According to plan, at the conclusion of the singing, at the moment the words "Sweet land of liberty . . . wafted to the crisp Spring air from many thousands of throats," McAdoo would pull the cord, allowing "the veil to fall from the Statue of Liberty." He then would announce the start of the Third Liberty Loan Campaign to finance the war. But McAdoo had another idea. As "the last strains of patriotic song still were echoing down Broad street, over the heads of thousands upon thousands of men, women and children, between the walled land made by skyscraper office buildings," he handed the cord to his granddaughter. The crowd fell silent in anticipation. The time had come to unveil Philadelphia's Statue of Liberty, a 29-foot replica of Frédéric Auguste Bartholdi's 151-foot monument in New York Harbor.

This Liberty lookalike, the work of sculptor Max Voight, was mounted on a twenty-two-foot base designed by architect John T. Windrim. Voight had been an arrival from Germany among the "huddled masses yearning to breathe free;" his handpicked team of sculptors included immigrants from Italy, France, and Russia. Their work on the statue had been followed in the newspapers and documented in newsreels. Towering fifty-one feet above Broad Street, Liberty's flaming torch would light up Philadelphia's nights and serve as a beacon, a symbolic site, and a sales booth for Liberty bonds.

As the crowd stood in silence that April afternoon, Nona Martin "seemed for a moment lost as to her exact part of the affair. Her famous grandfather leaned over, spoke a word or two, and the child responded. She gave a sudden, vigorous tug at the rope, while the draperies opened and fell, and Liberty—the personification of that for which America and most of the civilized world [was] waging—stood revealed."

Then "as the white sheeting fluttered to the base of the statue," the band played "America" and "100,000 men, women and children joined in lifting the air as though in message to the Nation" that Philadelphians would soon do their share in raising $136 million more to fund a bloody world war "in civilization's and humanity's cause."

———

Sources: "Copy of Famous Liberty Statue Rising in Phila.," *Inquirer*, February 10, 1918; "M'Adoo to Open Loan Drive Here; to Unveil Statue," *Inquirer*, March 31, 1918; "Huge Crowd Electrified with Patriotic Fervor at Statue's Unveiling," *Inquirer*, April 7, 1918.

Figure 11.2. William Penn statue, City Hall, ca. 1886

Even though the statue of William Penn would be bolted in place more than five hundred feet above the sidewalk and seen only in profile by most Philadelphians, it really mattered that the statue's details made a good and lasting impression. After all, at thirty-six feet eight inches, the statue at

City Hall would stand as the tallest figure on a building anywhere in the nation, nearly seventeen feet taller than the Statue of Freedom on the U.S. Capitol.

"Notwithstanding its great height," argued sculptor Alexander Milne Calder in 1886 as he sculpted the figure, Penn "will be quite plainly visible from the street, therefore every care has to be taken with regard to the features and every other detail." What Calder had in mind was a statue facing South Broad Street, its confident facial expression bathed in sunlight. When the sculptor's plans were scrapped by a new architect who turned Penn's face away from the sun to gaze northeast to Penn Treaty Park, the scorned Calder quipped that his greatest work had been "condemned to eternal silhouette."

In fact, *Calder* had many reasons for turning Penn's back on the past, especially the place where he and the Native Americans *may* have signed a treaty. In his modernized redo of Penn, Calder wanted to pull away from the old image (and the myth it rode in on) and create something entirely new: "What we want is William Penn as he is known to Philadelphians, not a theoretical one or a fine English gentleman." Even as he worked, Calder admitted he felt conflicted, adding "I have not absolutely settled upon the final figure."

Ever since 1872, when John McArthur, City Hall's original architect, had proposed to replace the first idea, an allegorical figure of Justice, with the statue of a real person, there had been no shortage of opinions about how this giant Penn might be made to look. This image would dominate the city's skyline immediately and, presumably, forever. What it might suggest about Philadelphia, Philadelphians, and Philadelphia history mattered then, and Calder knew it would continue to matter long after.

Calder hadn't gotten any real pushback on the hundreds of statues he had created for City Hall closer to the ground—figures people could actually see but didn't care all that much about. After working thirteen years on the massive City Hall project, when Calder finally got to the tower groupings and the largest sculpture of all, he planned on going for a "manly beauty," something different than the rotund, jowled, patriarchal founder painted by Benjamin West in the eighteenth century or the jolly Penn reinforced ad infinitum by Edward Hicks's paintings in the nineteenth.

Historians really had nothing to go on since there were no contemporary portraits of Penn to serve as a guide, but they still insisted on accuracy and authenticity, arguing at length about the clothing and the style of his hat. City fathers, who had seen the entire project take far longer and become far more expensive and controversial than anyone had ever imagined, just wanted the building and sculpture done—with no further embarrassments.

And what could possibly have been embarrassing in 1886? A roly-poly founder figure defining the city's skyline, perhaps. Or a statue reminiscent of a corrupt Gilded Age politician (similar to Thomas Nast's caricatures of Boss Tweed). This was the same year Philadelphia politician Boies Penrose, a.k.a. "Big Grizzly," a man of massive appetite (he was known to have a dozen eggs for breakfast and an entire turkey for lunch) and girth (he reached 350 pounds) won his seat in the state senate. What could be embarrassing atop the white-marble wedding cake of City Hall? Perhaps a figure recalling the heaviest American president to date—Grover Cleveland—who was wed at the White House the previous June.

So it did matter—a lot—what this new Penn looked like. And as he worked through his series of maquettes, Calder would come to give his Penn a complete makeover of figure and face. He'd lose the gut and the double chin, adding a dimple. He'd introduce fancy ruffles, buckles, and curls. Most of all, Calder made a figure that could stand joke-free. He gave the city something no one thought possible: a Quaker Zeus.

————

Sources: Thomas H. Keels, "Contractor Bosses (1880s to 1930s)," *Encyclopedia of Greater Philadelphia* (Camden: Rutgers, 2016); "Model for the Statue of William Penn," in *Philadelphia: Three Centuries of American Art,* ed. Darrell Sewell (Philadelphia: Philadelphia Museum of Art, 1976), 432–433; Nicholas B. Wainwright, *Sculpture of a City: Philadelphia's Treasures in Bronze and Stone* (Philadelphia: Fairmount Park Art Association, 1974).

Smack dab in the center of Philadelphia is a building with scads of sculpture and one persistent mystery. Philadelphia City Hall is encrusted with no less than 250 marble figures, heads, allegories, and attributes by Alexander Milne Calder and his creative team. It has been called "the most ambitious sculptural decoration of any public building in the United States." Yet historians have always been somewhat perplexed. City Hall is without "a coherent plan for the iconography." All that money, all that marble—and no comprehensive interpretation? How frustrating.

People have long suspected that there are clues that might help explain the cacophony of sculpture on the building's exterior and tower. There's a theme of world geography not too unlike London's Albert Memorial, which Calder cut his teeth on before coming to Philadelphia. But then, oddly, when it comes to City Hall's courtyard, there are no figures at all, nothing to interpret. All visitors see are smooth white marble surfaces. In City Hall's courtyard, the world's largest and most complex sculptural program comes to a dead stop.

How could this be? Why did these prolific Philadelphians—architect John McArthur, sculptor Calder, and building Commissioner Samuel Perkins—opt for utter silence in City Hall's courtyard? Or maybe we've been asking the wrong questions, placing emphasis on the wrong sculptural syllable. Maybe it's more about what *isn't* there than what is.

McArthur, Calder, and Perkins didn't run out of ideas when they came to City Hall's courtyard. Instead, what they embraced in the heart of the building—in the heart of the city—was the opportunity to express a startlingly modern idea: a sculptural program turned inside out.

We the people complete the sculptural program of City Hall. The courtyard is a massive, interactive, do-it-yourself civic sculpture, maybe the only one of its kind. By being there, citizens literally bring City Hall to life. The sculptural program isn't about sculpture, historicism, or representations of any kind—it's about the living, breathing here and now.

City Hall comes alive in the same way a city does, the same way a Quaker Meeting does; it's powered by the people.

Still not convinced? Stand in the center of the courtyard and look up. There, 510 feet above the sidewalk, more than 330 years in the past, symbolically stands the founder himself. Visitors can't see him beyond the beak of one of the giant eagles, but his presence is unmistakable. Then look around; there's the very center of the city his dreams led to, but it's not Penn's city anymore—it's the people's. The building is a timeline starting in the 1680s and ending in the present day.

Standing in the center, searching for confirmation, we see the four portals, the four points of the compass, and the city beyond. To the north, beneath the tower, is a place criticized in 1876 as a "chamber of horrors," with the carved heads of animals from the four corners of the earth: bull, bear, tiger, and elephant. They focus our attention inward toward four robust, perfectly polished red granite columns. Atop them are human figures from around the world. They are our stand-ins, arms locked and straining as they bear the burden of the tower.

But these stone figures are only symbolic. Standing there, witnessing and understanding, anyone and everyone present participates in the meaning of the place and joins the continuum of Philadelphia. It's all, as Walt Whitman once famously put it, "a majestic and lovely show—silent, weird, beautiful."

———

Sources: Penny Balkin Bach, *Public Art in Philadelphia* (Philadelphia: Temple University Press, 1992); Michael J. Lewis, "'Silent, Weird, Beautiful': Philadelphia City Hall," *Nineteenth Century* 11, no. 1 and 2 (1992): 13–21; Nicholas B. Wainwright, *Sculpture of a City: Philadelphia's Treasures in Bronze and Stone* (Philadelphia: Fairmount Park Art Association, 1974).

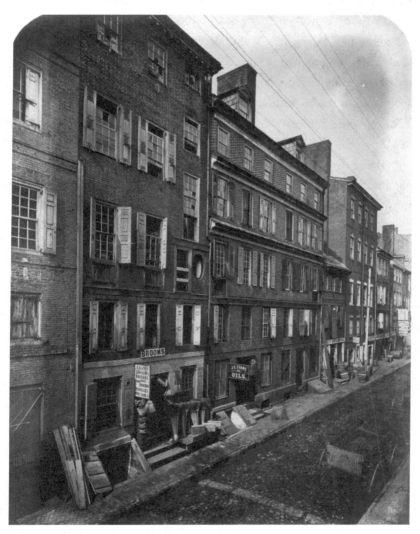

Figure 11.3. "Nos. 44 & 46 N. Water St., 1868," photographed by John Moran (Library Company of Philadelphia)

Despite John Moran's best efforts, Mary Panzer tells us, his "photographs were never considered art. His audience believed that art was historical and made by hand, whereas photography was scientific and made by machines. In 1903, the year Moran died, Alfred Stieglitz won the battle to establish photography as a fine art, but by that time, Moran's work was long forgotten, shelved as topography by the same audience who believed Moby Dick was a book about whales."

Moran's brief obituary in the *New York Times* confirmed his role as "one of the pioneer photographers of this country," but instead of crediting him with being among the first art photographers, it described his role as the chief photographer of a 1871 federal survey, who took "the first pictures of the original route of the Panama Canal." It mentioned his participation to observe the transit of Venus across the face of the sun, and it discussed his abandonment of photography and turn to landscape painting.

In 1865, while Alfred Steiglitz was in still in diapers, Moran connected the idea of photography and art. In February of that year, he addressed the Philadelphia Photographic Society on "The Relation of Photography to the Fine Arts," declaring that photography "speaks the same language, and addresses the same sentiments." Moran noted the need for the photographer's "perceiving mind to note and feel the relative degrees of importance in the various aspects which nature presents." Without that, "nothing worthy of the name of pictures can be produced."

Moran's landscapes made in and around Philadelphia in the early 1860s earned him the reputation as "a young Nature artist." In fact, he would allow aesthetic choices to influence everything he photographed. During the Civil War, Moran's views of the Mower General Hospital were more than a record, they were richly expressive. By the end of the decade, images he and his brother Thomas, a painter, made in the Wissahickon Valley helped inspire the city to add it to the expanding Fairmount Park.

In the late 1860s, Moran put his ideas to work on the streets of historic Philadelphia. He searched for scenes that reframed the past not merely as illustrations for anecdotes but as a visual aesthetic. At a time of great growth, industrialization, and diminishing history, Moran relished the textures and sensibilities of the city's oldest streets and alleys. Between 1867 and 1870, he and his six-by-nine-inch wet-plate camera and wooden tripod were fixtures on the city streets. Again and again, Moran blocked out the modern and focused in on the past, offering it renewed life in the medium. The results were compelling. Moran mounted seventy-eight of his prints in an album titled *A Collection of Photographic Views in Philadelphia and Its Vicinity* and sold it to the Library Company of Philadelphia. Their accession book confirms the purchase from "John Moran, artist."

In all, Moran probably made as many as one hundred views of the city in the late 1860s before moving on. He would soon be drawn to expedition photography for the federal government, creating and documenting at the same time. Back in Philadelphia, Moran's ideas about art had been tested and his confidence was even more firm. In June and October of 1875, Moran shared with his colleagues at the Photographic Society his "Thoughts on Art, Nature and Photography" and his "Reflections on Art."

The photographer has "the power to see the beautiful," declared Moran, but "good work cannot be produced unless the workman has the instincts, feelings and education akin to those of the artist." The best photographs are "quickened to life by their own spirit and intelligence . . . speaking the universal language of art." As "a realistic art," photography "is a translator . . . and we, the translators, ought to look to it that we take noble themes, not false and artificial subjects." Moran claimed that "art in all its forms is the form of thought, and the photographic work that rises to this plane, is the expression of the photographer."

So how is Moran's "discovery" of expression in photography accounted for today? One measure, of course, is the art marketplace. In 2010, Christie's auction house sold a Moran photograph of the Bank of Pennsylvania. Never mind that the cataloger misidentified the scene as construction (it's the demolition of the building in 1867). The $32,500 price that was realized broke the record for Moran.

How does this compare with the auction records for, say, Alfred Stieglitz? At Christie's sales a few years ago, six Stieglitz prints fetched more than $200,000 each. The priciest of these was a view from the back window of the 291 gallery (the very place where Stieglitz successfully promoted photography as art forty years after Moran's first declaration of the same idea). That Stieglitz print brought $363,750, more than ten times what Moran's did, but hardly a record. "Top Stieglitz photographs have sold for more than $1 million," shrugged the *Wall Street Journal*. It looks like it'll be a while longer before the books of photographic history get balanced properly.

———

Sources: Ellen Gamerman, "A Big Test for Vintage Photos," *Wall Street Journal*, July 31, 2014; John Moran, "The Relation of Photography to the Fine Arts," *Philadelphia Photographer* 2 (March 1865): 33–35; John Moran, "Reflections on Art," *Philadelphia Photographer* 12 (October 1875): 294–295; John Moran, "Thoughts on Art Nature and Photography," *Philadelphia Photographer* 12 (June 1875): 179–181; Mary Panzer, "John Moran," in *Legacy in Light: Photographic Treasures from Philadelphia Area Public Collections*, ed. Kenneth Finkel (Philadelphia: Philadelphia Museum of Art, 1990): 24–25; Bernard F. Reilly, "The Early Work of John Moran, Landscape Photographer," *American Art Journal* 11, no. 1 (January 1979): 65–75; "John Moran Dead: Was One of the Pioneer Photographers of the Country and Did Much Government Work," *New York Times*, February 20, 1903.

Figure 11.4. "Gallery C" in Memorial Hall, American department, Centennial Photographic Co., 1876 (Library Company of Philadelphia)

Construction delays scuttled the original plan to open the centennial in April 1876, in time for the one-hundredth anniversary of the battles at Lexington and Concord. It was just as well; the nation's first world's fair wasn't really focused on the past as much as the American present and, even more, its future.

The bell at Independence Hall signaled the opening of the centennial on May 10, 1876. Four miles away, more than 186,000 people gathered for a heady celebration in a temporary Centennial City in West Fairmount Park. In all, more than 9.8 million visitors would arrive over the next several months to witness evidence of the growth of America from idea to flourishing nation.

At its symbolic and ceremonial center, centennial planners built a place where America would be represented by the nation's artists. Inside, surrounded by an array of other galleries filled with art from around the world, was America's "Grand Salon," or "Gallery C," the place for the nation's artists to see and be seen. Here would be the best of the best in American art, works expressive of what this nation had become, or as Kimberly Orcutt put it, "the first officially sanctioned, full-scale reckoning of the nation's art."

The organizers had hoped to present "a unified 'American school'"— not an easy goal to achieve. By the 1870s, America's artists were more divided than united. New York landscapists conflicted with European-trained cosmopolitans from Philadelphia and Boston. And Philadelphia artist John Sartain, appointed chief of the Art Advisory Committee eight months before opening day, created a top-heavy bureaucracy with a Committee on Selection and a Committee on Arrangement. The ever-political Sartain, Orcutt writes, "was careful not to place himself on the Committee on Selection," but after the committee reviewed more than one thousand works of art in early April—rejecting some interesting newcomers like the young and little-known Thomas Eakins and others who had trained abroad—Sartain carried out a series of end runs around his committees, soliciting works he thought merited display, particularly from artists who were longtime friends and allies, including Albert Bierstadt and Thomas Moran.

In all, Sartain and his committee assembled far more than could possibly fit in Gallery C. Americans would be hung in the long, narrow connecting gallery at Memorial Hall as well as in a handful of small square rooms in the one-story wooden annex built directly behind Memorial Hall to accommodate overflow.

Installed, Gallery C spoke about the contested state of American art rather than anything like a coherent American school. In its center stood two sculptures by P. F. Connelly (*Ophelia* and *Death and Honor*) and another by Howard Roberts (*Le Premier Pose*, now at the Philadelphia Museum of Art). Visitors witnessed John Vanderlyn's *Ariadne Asleep on the Island of Naxos* (now at the Pennsylvania Academy of the Fine Arts) and Albert Bierstadt's *Entrance into Monterey: The Settlement of California, Bay of Monterey, 1777* (now in the U.S. House of Representatives building). They saw Eastman Johnson's *Catching the Bee, 1872* and Winslow Homer's *Snap the Whip*. They took in Peter Rothermel's gigantic (16′ × 32′) blood-less *Battle of Gettysburg* and Thomas Eakins's *Portrait of Dr. Rand* (now at the Crystal Bridges Museum in Bentonville, Arkansas). Of course, they didn't see Eakins's bloody *Portrait of Dr. Samuel Gross*, which the Selection Committee famously passed on. That refusée made an appearance in the far-flung Army Medical Department Exhibition. Eakins's *Gross Clinic*, according to Sylvan Schendler, had been dumped for a cow painting titled *The Return of the Herd* by Peter Moran, Thomas and John Moran's younger brother. (In a recent twist, a version of the Peter Moran sold for the sum of $38,025, minuscule compared to the $68 million sale price for *The Gross Clinic* in 2006.)

In 1914, nearly four decades after taking his best shot to redefine American art, the mature Eakins reflected on the dilemma that had shaped his entire career: "If America is to produce great painters and if young artists wish to assume a place in the history of the art of their country, their first desire should be to remain in America to peer deeper into the heart of American life, rather than spend their time abroad obtaining a superficial view of the art of the Old World." When the thirty-one-year-old Eakins painted *The Gross Clinic* in 1875, American artists were nowhere near ready to speak in anything like a clear, creative voice representative of an American school. Decades later, the dust still hadn't settled. If anything, the international influences on American art were kicked up even more in 1913 by the Armory Show and collector Albert Barnes, who focused intensely on what made good art rather than what made good *American* art.

The search for a pure, distinctive, and exclusively American art may well be what stymied success at the centennial's Gallery C. When art intersects with nationalism, things get complicated, if not compromised.

———

Sources: Kimberly Orcutt, "H. H. Moore's *Almeh* and the Politics of the Centennial Exhibition," *American Art* 21, no. 1 (Spring 2007): 50–73; U.S. Centennial Commission. *International Exhibition, 1876: Official Catalogue; Art Gallery, Annexes, and Out-Door Works of Art: Department IV—Art,* 10th and rev. ed. (Philadelphia: Centennial Catalogue Company, 1876); Russell F. Weigley, *Philadelphia: A 300 Year History* (New York: W. W. Norton, 1982), 465.

Figure 11.5. "The Protest of the Germans of Germantown against Slavery on February 18, 1688," Western facade of the Pastorius Monument, Vernon Park. Albert Jaegers, sculptor. Photographed by Kenneth Finkel.

German Americans found 1933 to be a very tricky year. An elaborate 250th-anniversary celebration of Philadelphia's Germantown settlement would converge at the Pastorius monument. And just as Philadelphians with German ties had done every October since the 1880s, they would celebrate German Day with marches, speeches, and song. But for the fifteen thousand paying respects in 1933, the future loomed as large as the past: Adolf Hitler had come to power.

For *this* German Day, Chancellor Hitler and President Hindenburg sent congratulations via telegram. Ambassador Hans Luther had been invited to speak. But when Luther learned, at the last minute, that the swastika flag wouldn't be raised—a decision the German Society of Pennsylvania apologized for as lacking in "decency and tact"—he canceled his appearance.

Exuberant, extravagant displays by German Americans in Philadelphia had long generated large crowds and overwhelming pride. They also raised hackles. In 1891, an *Inquirer* editorial urged German Day participants to "keep the celebration an American one, as it ought to be kept." It urged resisting "the tendency to make this celebration a German celebration."

But it wasn't resisted.

Just as the Peter Muhlenberg statue dedicated in 1910 at City Hall evolved as an example of contested public art, the monument to Daniel Francis Pastorius in Vernon Park would become a flash point—even before it existed. In 1908, at the 225th anniversary of Germantown's settlement, twenty thousand people marched to the site and joined another thirty thousand already gathered to hear eight hundred "united voices" of Philadelphia German American singing societies and speeches in both English and German. The crowd witnessed the unveiling of a cornerstone for the newly commissioned monument. But the unveiling of the finished monument would be delayed twelve years. First, the commission was taken from sculptor J. Otto Schweizer and handed over to Albert Jaegers. Then one of Jaegers's sculpted panels cracked in transit. Finally, the dedication was put off until after the First World War. "A wise move," agreed an editorial.

In 1920, when the public finally got to see the Pastorius monument, critics had a field day. "Miss Civilization," its regal central figure, resembled traditional Germania and not familiar allegories of "American Independence and Progress." The Germantown Historical Society advocated its removal, calling it "crude, gross and meaningless as art or history." Controversy continued during World War II, when the Pastorius monument was boxed in to remove it from public view.

Meanwhile, Germany borrowed back and rebranded the Pastorius name for "Operation Pastorius," a plan to sabotage strategic American industrial sites, including at least one in Philadelphia. In its appropriation and obfuscation of seventeenth-century Pastorius, the twentieth century effectively forgot the historical figure's actual contribution. The real Pastorius—lawyer, poet, and leader—was one of the most intelligent, talented, and compassionate settlers in the New World—qualities Jaegers attempted to convey in one of the monument's four panels.

In 1683, Pastorius and others followed the Quakers to Pennsylvania and even joined the Society of Friends, fully intending to create a colony where basic human rights were understood and respected. What they found was very different: a society that accepted—and an economy based on—slavery. In 1688, more than 175 years before the Thirteenth Amendment, Pastorius and three other enlightened Germantowners composed a thorough and carefully reasoned protest against slavery and presented it to the Quaker leadership.

This monument, which had been censored, delayed, and removed from the public eye, becomes more potent when we become aware of the whole story.

––––––

Sources: Katharine Gerbner, "'We Are against the Traffik of Men-Body': The Germantown Quaker Protest of 1688 and the Origins of American Abolitionism," *Pennsylvania History* 74, no. 2 (Spring 2007): 149–172;

Nicholas B. Wainwright, *Sculpture of a City: Philadelphia's Treasures in Bronze and Stone* (Philadelphia: Fairmount Park Art Association, 1974); "The Celebration of German Day," *Inquirer*, October 11, 1891; "Bronze Tablet Will Honor Memory of German Pioneers in America to Be Set into Corner-Stone," *Inquirer*, September 23, 1908; "50,000 See Unveiling at Vernon Park," *Inquirer*, October 7, 1908; "Pastorius Statue Design Accepted," *Inquirer*, June 8, 1913; "The Germantown Monument," *Inquirer*, April, 27, 1917; "Monument Repaired," *Inquirer*, June 30, 1920; "To Speed Acceptance of Pastorius Statue," *Inquirer*, September 26, 1920.

Figure 11.6. Claes Oldenburg's *Clothespin*, Fifteenth and Market Streets, 1979

At first, the idea of a fifty-one-foot paintbrush in front of an art school and museum seemed unoriginal, little more than a logo for the Pennsylvania Academy of the Fine Arts. Had Claes Oldenburg, after more than thirty-five years, given up on nuance for his fourth major work in Philadelphia?

People familiar with this work expected Oldenburg to continue as the outrageous outsider. They wanted the *old* Oldenburg, the one whose work released "all these stored up ideas," as he described to the *Wall Street Journal* in 2011—the sculptor who once proposed replacing the Washington Monument with a giant pair of upended scissors. *That* artist had imagined a giant toilet float for the Thames in London and a working windshield wiper threatening the Chicago waterfront.

In Philadelphia, that artist reportedly proposed a giant screw monument for Fifteenth and Market Streets. Oldenburg had imagined and sketched a giant screw monument for São Paulo, Brazil, in 1972. But fabricating and installing it? Not happening. In the mid-1970s, when the sculptor turned from the studio to the streets, would he put Rizzo-era Philadelphia to the test with a forty-five-foot-tall screw across from City Hall tower? Not on your life.

Though the full story about Oldenburg's first Philly proposal is unknown, we do know he had a less offensive idea in the wings. In 1976, Philadelphia dedicated the *Clothespin*, the first of several major, tamer Oldenburg works in the city. The other three were *Split Button*, *Giant Three-Way Plug*, and *Paint Torch*. Their installations span much of Oldenburg's career.

In the early 1960s, in his New York studio, Oldenburg pushed the envelope plenty. His pop art manifesto staked out new artistic territory: "I am for an art that is political-erotical-mystical, that does something other than sit on its ass in a museum." Would Oldenburg be willing and able to push the envelope outside the studio and on the streets in Philadelphia? The result across from City Hall and at the Academy of the Fine Arts seems something less than the "political-erotical-mystical" art that he promised.

But looks can be deceiving. As it turns out, *Paint Torch* floats above its site and gently commands Broad Street with scale, color, and texture. It deploys a Pixar-like quality reminiscent of a helium parade balloon. Its form renders precious—in the best sense of the word—details of the Academy's Furness façade as well as those of City Hall a block to the south.

By comparison, *Clothespin* is upright and uptight. Its rough Cor-Ten steel surface does no favors for the promise to be playful, although the stainless steel spring does invite imagination. (Does it show the arms of two figures in an embrace? Does it depict "76," the year of installation? Or is it merely a sculpted spring?)

Today, as in 1976, Oldenburg likes to play with our reading of these details. Looking at the top of *Paint Torch*, we see the "wet," orange-loaded brush pushing against something. But there's no canvas above Broad Street—only the real world. Maybe it's not a giant brushstroke after all. Maybe it's a tongue sticking out.

Could this be a lesson for art students inside the academy to creatively mock their art professors, as Oldenburg did? Or could it be that he was finally getting back at Philadelphia for putting the kibosh on his giant screw? Or maybe it is only meant to be an innocent dab of orange paint.

Oldenburg *has* made something here that is, after all, "political-erotical-mystical." The sculptor *didn't* sell out. What he did, it seems, was perfect the subtle, sometimes necessary art of tweaking one's host.

———

Sources: Claes Oldenburg, "I Am for an Art: Claes Oldenburg on His 1961 'Ode to Possibilities,'" *Sightlines,* Walker Art Center, https://walkerart .org/magazine/claes-oldenburg-i-am-for-an-art-1961; Victoria Donohoe, "Here Comes 4-Story Clothespin," *Inquirer,* November 3, 1974; Marciarose [Shestack], "Here's a Line of a Clothespin," *Inquirer,* June 18, 1976; "Hanging Tough: After 25 Years, We've Come to Love the Clothespin," *Philadelphia Daily News,* November, 29, 2001; Kelly Crow, "A Pop Sculptor on Thinking

Big," *Wall Street Journal*, August 20, 2011; Tom De Kay, "Claes Oldenburg's Paintbrush Erected in Philadelphia," *New York Times*, August 23, 2011.

WHO WILL PUT THE BALL IN MOTION?

In their very first season, the Pythians proved themselves on the ballfields of Philadelphia, Camden, West Chester, and Harrisburg. Later the same year—1867—when the National Association of Base Ball Players met in Philadelphia, the Pythians applied for membership and soon heard the unanimous decision: "Any club which may be composed of one or more colored persons" could *not* join. This African American team led by Octavius Catto would be excluded from organized baseball.

The decision didn't sit well with baseball organizer, journalist, and reformer Thomas Fitzgerald. At the start of the 1869 season, Fitzgerald proposed going "against the rules" and called for "a game between one of our white clubs and the Pythians." "Who will put the ball in motion?" he challenged.

Working out the details took most of the season, but the Pythians and the Olympics arranged to play, and Fitzgerald agreed to serve as umpire on September 3, 1869, at Jefferson Street Ball Park. "Perhaps the first base ball game of the kind was played yesterday afternoon at Twenty-fifth and Jefferson streets," reported the *Inquirer*. The Pythians "acquitted themselves in a very creditable manner, especially their outfielders, who made several very fine catches." The crowd was "one of the largest that has been on those grounds for years."

"A Novel Game in Philadelphia—A Negro Club in the Field," read a page-one headline in the *New York Times*. "The novelty of the affair drew an immense crowd of people, it being the first game played between a white and a colored club." Word of this "novelty" spread as far as Utah.

The game between the Pythians and the Olympics was, it turned out, curiously off kilter. The Pythian strategy was to not challenge *any* calls. The Olympics, on the other hand, challenged calls at every turn. By the third inning, when the Olympics scored fourteen, including two home runs, the pattern was set. According to the *Inquirer*, the Pythians then suffered "their first whitewash, their men going out in rapid succession." They held up better in the fourth inning, when the Pythians scored one more run than the Olympics. And "to the astonishment of all," according to the *Inquirer*, "the whites were treated to a blank" in the seventh inning. But the Pythians were only able to add four runs during their next turn at bat. And they went scoreless in the eighth. In the final inning, the Pythians made "a desperate effort . . . to reduce the disparity" but only came up with two more runs than the Olympics did.

The Olympics defeated the Pythians that historic game, 44–23.

A few weeks later, Fitzgerald's all-white team from the *City Item*, his newspaper, played the Pythians at another field on Columbia Avenue (now Cecil B. Moore) near Seventeenth. That game, the Pythians won, 27–17.

The *New York Clipper* appreciated Philadelphia's racial breakthrough: "The prejudices of race are rapidly disappearing. . . . we chronicled a game between the Pythian (colored) and Olympics (white) clubs, of Philadelphia. This affair was a great success, financially and otherwise." The *Clipper* noted the second game with the *City Item* and a third between white and black teams in Washington, DC, and put out a challenge: "The Unique Club, of Williamsburgh, composed of colored gentlemen, is anxious to get on a match with the Pythians. What say the Quakerdelphians?"

In its earliest years, the field where the Pythians and the Olympics met could be described as fitting into the angle of two country roads: Turners Lane and Mineral (or Market) Street. By the 1870s, these roads had disappeared, giving way to Philadelphia's ever-expanding grid. We may not be able to know the exact original location of home plate, but one thing is for sure: the Jefferson Street Grounds—or Athletic Field (as it became known for the team that made its home there), which was renamed the Athletic Recreation Center in the early twentieth century—has been a baseball venue since May 1864—more than 150 years. Is there a field with a more venerable vintage?

On April 22 and 24, 1876, the Philadelphia Athletics and the Boston
Red Caps played two games on the same field (Boston won the first, 6–5,
and Philadelphia won the second, 20–3). The former was the first game
the National League played in Philadelphia, and thanks to rainy weather
elsewhere, the first National League game played *anywhere* in the United
States. Is there a place with more historic associations for baseball?

Walking the field today, we ask why this place is so understated. Actually, it was partially remedied in September 2017 with the dedication of
a historical marker. Still, there's no public art, no mural, no monument.
Why not make *more* of this place? It's time to again challenge ourselves
with the big questions: "What say the Quakerdelphians?" and "Who will
put the ball in motion?"

———

Sources: Daniel R. Biddle and Murray Dubin, *Tasting Freedom: Octavius
Catto and the Battle for Equality in Civil War America* (Philadelphia: Temple University Press, 2010); Jerrold Casway, "Octavius Catto and the Pythi-
ans of Philadelphia," *Pennsylvania Legacies* 7, no. 1 (May 2007): 5–9; Jerrold
Casway, "The Jefferson Street Ball Parks (1864–91)," in *From Swampoodle
to South Philly: Baseball in Philadelphia and the Delaware Valley* (Society
for American Baseball Research, 2013); "Base Ball: Olympic vs. Pythian,"
Inquirer, September 4, 1869; "A Novel Game in Philadelphia," *New York
Times*, September 5, 1869; "White vs. Colored Clubs," *New York Clipper*,
September 25, 1869; "The Boston-Athletic Game," *Inquirer*, April 24, 1876;
"Athletics vs. Boston: The Latter Badly Whipped," *Inquirer*, April 25,
1876; Julie Shaw, "Honoring a Philly Field Where Baseball Brought Races
Together," *Inquirer*, September 30, 2017.

Acknowledgments

In 2011, Deb Boyer, Azavea's remarkable project manager, asked if I'd write a letter to support *Philly*History.org's nomination for an award by the American Association of State and Local History. The blog won kudos, and a few months later, I wondered if I might join the team as a guest contributor. (No stranger to blogging about Philadelphia, I had published at two previous venues: WHYY's first foray into the medium, *The Sixth Square* [2006–2008], and *Brownstoner Philadelphia* [2010].) My first entry at *Philly*History was on August 11, 2011.

This book would not be possible without the help of many generous and talented folks along the way. I'd like to acknowledge several people on the always-supportive team at Azavea: Deb Boyer, Robert Cheetham, Rachel Cheetham-Richard, Matthew Berylant, Scott Hearn, and Karissa Justice. Former commissioner Joan Decker at the Philadelphia Department of Records was an early and enthusiastic supporter. Thanks to Commissioner James Leonard, Jill Rawnsley, and Elizabeth Downey. Research help came ably and generously from the staff at the Special Collections Research Collection at Temple University's Paley Library, especially (but not limited to) Margery Sly, John Pettit, and Brenda Galloway-Wright. Diane Turner and staff at the Charles Blockson Collection offered essential guidance. At the Library Company of Philadelphia Print Department, helpful aid came from Nicole Joniec, Sarah Weatherwax, and Ann McShane. Many others deserve thanks, especially (but not limited to) Penny Bach, Rich Banie-wicz, Bill Bolger, Sam Briger, George Bryant, Jim Duffin, Charles Hardy, Betsy Manning, Elizabeth Milroy, and Dan Traister. Many thanks to Micah Kleit, Elisabeth Maselli, and the team at Rutgers Press.

Last but not least, I thank my wife, Margaret O. Kirk, and our sons, Kirk, Ben, and Mack. Each and every day they help and provide inspira-tion. This book is dedicated to them.

Index

Page numbers in *italics* refer to figures.

About the Author

KENNETH FINKEL is a history professor at Temple University. Finkel began his career in Philadelphia studies as curator of prints and photographs at the Library Company of Philadelphia, followed by stints at the William Penn Foundation and WHYY. He and his wife have raised three sons in the same Philadelphia neighborhood where Finkel grew up. This is his ninth book on Philadelphia.